M000314033

Searching for ORDER IN the COMPLEXITY of Evolving Worlds

THE PUBLISHER ACKNOWLEDGES

The SFI Press would not exist without the support of William H. Miller and the Miller Omega Program.

[EX MACHINA]

Coevolving Machines
& the Origins of
the Social Universe

JOHN H. MILLER

THE SANTA FE INSTITUTE PRESS

1399 Hyde Park Road
Santa Fe, New Mexico 87501

Ex Machina:
Coevolving Machines and the Origins of the Social Universe
ISBN (HARDCOVER): 978-1-947864-44-3
Library of Congress Control Number: 2022942595

The SFI Press would not exist without the support
of the Miller Omega Program.

IF YOU HAVE BUILT CASTLES IN THE AIR, your work
need not be lost; that is where they should be.

Now put the foundations under them.

HENRY DAVID THOREAU
Walden (1854)

TABLE OF CONTENTS

For full-sized, color versions of the figures in this book,
please refer to the Github repository:
HTTPS://GITHUB.COM/SANTAFEINSTITUTE/EXMACHINA

LIST OF FIGURES

LIST OF TABLES

ACKNOWLEDGMENTS

Louis Pasteur tells us that chance favors the prepared mind. Of course, preparing your mind in the right way is also due to chance. For me, chance arose in a number of forms.

As an undergraduate at the University of Colorado I was exposed to the ideas of Kenneth Boulding, who thought about the necessity of melding economics and ecology[1] to understand social systems. I was also born when computers were largely inaccessible but as I finished graduate school they started to become commonplace, and so I was able to develop useful skills from both worlds. Given this background, it is not too surprising that as an undergraduate I began to wonder how one could use a computer to study adaptive social behavior.

By chance I went to the University of Michigan's Department of Economics for graduate school. There, I was fortunate to work with some remarkable and open-minded theorists: Ted Bergstrom, Carl Simon, and Hal Varian. They let me explore my unconventional interests, while also keeping me well-grounded in current practice. Bergstrom and I began to work on a computerized tournament of a noisy Prisoner's Dilemma, and that resulted in discussions with Bob Axelrod. Axelrod mentioned the work of John Holland, a broad-thinking computer scientist who, in 1975, wrote a seminal book about using evolution-based algorithms to solve hard problems. Holland's ideas provided a useful path for realizing

---

[1] They share the same Greek root, *eco* or *oikos*, capturing the basic unit of society in Greek city-states, namely the house or household.

the nascent ideas I had had as an undergraduate for exploring adaptive social systems.

Throw in a few more chance encounters: Ariel Rubinstein giving a talk at Michigan on using the formal theory of automata to study strategies in games, Brian Arthur contacting one of my advisors in a search for the first postdoctoral fellow at the newly formed Santa Fe Institute (SFI), and finding a job (based on a talk tied to a three-page proto-paper) in the Department of Social and Decision Sciences at Carnegie Mellon University (CMU), a place that fully embraces Herb Simon's approach to science.

Chance also brought me together with a wonderful group of scholars who have participated in various conversations and collaborations connected with the ideas explored here. In particular, I would like to thank Tanmoy Bhattacharya (Los Alamos National Laboratory/SFI), Carter Butts (University of California, Irvine), Simon DeDeo (CMU/SFI), Laura Fortunato (University of Oxford/SFI), Chris Kempes (SFI), Scott Moser (University of Texas at Austin), Scott Page (University of Michigan/SFI), David Rode, Cosma Shalizi (CMU/SFI), Ariana Strandburg-Peshkin (Max Planck Institute), and Huanren Zhang (University of Southern Denmark). Some of the research presented in this book directly benefited from contributions by Luis Alejandro Lee (Mercado Libre), who joined me as a postdoctoral fellow for a year, and Jarrek Holmes, a CMU undergraduate.

A few colleagues provided more extensive comments on an earlier draft of the manuscript, and without undue implication in this enterprise, I'm especially grateful to Willemien Kets (Utrecht University/SFI), David Krakauer (SFI), and Kevin Zollman (CMU).

The final form of this book was the result of a wonderful collaboration with an amazing group of people. Laurence Gonzales and Eleanor Bolton provided valuable editorial comments. Mj Willbanks from Wise Pine Design was able to take a crude set of technically demanding sketches and turn them into coherent, carefully designed illustrations. Finally, I was extremely fortunate to be able to work with SFI Press. As is evident from the various pages of this book, SFI Press has revitalized the art of book design for presenting twenty-first-century science. To achieve this end, the Press has assembled an incredible group of creative, thoughtful, smart, and accomplished individuals: Laura Egley Taylor, Sienna Latham, Katherine Mast, Bronwynn Woodsworth, Jake Hebbert, and Shafaq Zia.

The various interactions described above are one of the great benefits of social behavior, and through such odd combinations of chance, I found favor. ❧

PROLOGUE

Science consists of testable and partially tested fantasies about the real world.

KENNETH E. BOULDING

Ecodynamics (1978a)

Is social life inevitable?

Suppose we could engage in Stephen Jay Gould's (1989, p. 48) experiment of "replaying life's tape," rewind the tape of the Earth's deep history back to the beginning, and rerun the world anew. Will social behavior arise again? Will it be similar to what we have now? Alternatively, suppose we happen upon alien life (versus it happening upon us). Will it be social? In the pages that follow we attempt to answer such questions.

Even asking such questions raises some interesting issues. One issue is how to define social behavior. While agent interactions seem important, what else is required? Another issue, perhaps biased by the rich social worlds we tend to inhabit, is whether the answer to the question of social behavior being inevitable is too obvious. However, we don't see social life everywhere, and even if we did, we would still want to know the conditions that allow it to emerge so easily.

To explore the emergence of social behavior we develop a new scientific apparatus, embodied in a computer, that allows worlds of simple computational machines to interact and coevolve with one another.[2] By carefully observing the output of this new apparatus we can identify, analyze, and experiment on those critical events that might reveal the key elements that allow social behavior to emerge. Such an approach will not only give us insights into the potential origins of social behavior, but also improve our understanding of more mature social systems as the elements that drive the origins of a system tend to persist long into the future.

Following Boulding's notion of science in the epigraph, we can use this approach to engage in new, and hopefully insightful, fantasies about social worlds.

As Cox and Forshaw (2010, p. *xi*) noted: "In science, there are no universal truths, just views of the world that have yet to be shown to be false." The yin and yang of science requires, to borrow Paul Saffo's phrase, "strong opinions, weakly held."[3] To make progress we need to have strong opinions to provide the momentum necessary to undertake new inquiries. Yet, the engine of science also requires that such opinions remain weakly held, so that when contradictory evidence arises we can let go of our old theories and explore new, and perhaps more fruitful, directions.

A field like economics often maintains the fantasy that systems are driven to a unique equilibrium by collections of agents with the desire and ability to optimize their behavior. There is nothing wrong with maintaining such fantasies and, indeed, they have allowed economists to make great progress in understanding social systems under conditions of scarcity.

Unfortunately, in economics (and most other academic fields) such opinions are often strongly held. Real social

---

[2] The software used in this research, as well as full-sized, full-color images, is available at: https://github.com/SantaFeInstitute/ExMachina
[3] https://www.saffo.com/02008/07/26/strong-opinions-weakly-held/.

behavior is likely rife with multiple equilibria, making the task of predicting *the* behavior of a social system difficult. Also, studies from behavioral and experimental economics have raised questions about both the motives of economic agents and their abilities to optimize behavior. The strongly held paradigm of economics has tended to dismiss such issues, for example, Friedman (1953) argued that agents act "as if" they are optimizing, and thus a baseball outfielder is able to run to the appropriate spot on the field to catch a pop fly without having to explicitly calculate Newton's laws. Yet, research has shown that outfielders are not implicit Newtonians running in a straight line to the required location (McBeath, Shaffer, and Kaiser 1995). Rather, they follow an arc-shaped path consistent with a simple visual-field-based heuristic—different paths may lead to the same end, but the journey may be more important than the destination.

Such critiques are not unique to economics as they are easy to generate for any academic field and serve as fodder for endless inter- and intra-field debates.

Social science is fundamentally hard. In physics, understanding the behavior of colliding particles comes down to knowing a few (typically) easily observable properties of each particle or being able to average over a large ensemble of such particles. Social science also has particles, and while these particles are subject to some observable, fundamental forces, they are also driven by more elusive elements such as strategic thinking and expectations. Predicting the path of a billiard ball is far easier than predicting the path of the social interactions surrounding that same game of pool.

Ultimately, if we want to pursue interesting problems in the world such as that concerning the origins of social behavior, new approaches, sensibly melded with the old ones, are needed.

Over the past few decades there has been a confluence of ideas and techniques that make this new exploration of the emergence of social behavior possible. The elements of this approach come from across the sciences. The theory of games provides a useful framework for investigating systems of interacting agents with the ability to thoughtfully anticipate, and respond to, the actions of others. It also provides a useful historical record, derived from over a half-century of publications, that reveals the types of social behaviors that have most enchanted the social sciences. The formal theory of computer science—starting with the contributions of Turing (1937) and others—provides some foundational ideas about how to model and understand simple information-processing machines. Computer science also demonstrates how Darwin's (1859) ideas on the origins of the species can be explored *in silico* to deepen our understanding of adaptive systems (Holland 1962, 1975). Finally, dramatic improvements over the last few decades in the speed and storage capacities of computers allow us to explore more fully the origins of social life using models of adaptive information-processing agents.

The Latin phrase *deus ex machina* (literally "god from the machine") comes from a convention in ancient Greek drama where a machine (often a crane, in Greek, a *mechane*) is used to bring "gods" to the stage to solve an apparently insoluble difficulty that arises in a storyline. The use of such unlikely machinations (yes, the same root) to bring order to chaos has, not surprisingly, been held in low regard by drama critics. Of course, fantasies, including scientific ones, often invoke their own forms of *deus*. Nonetheless, *deus ex machina* may contain an important hint about how to approach, and answer, the question of the emergence of social life. While we want to avoid invoking godly powers to solve the storyline of social life, perhaps the origins of social life are *ex machina*. That is, simple interacting machines subject to fundamental evolutionary forces may, in perhaps the most poetic and profound words in science, create a social system where "from so simple a beginning, endless forms most beautiful and most wonderful have been, and are being, evolved" (Darwin 1859).

Berry *et al.* (2011) published a paper titled "Can Apparent Superluminal Neutrino Speeds be Explained as a Quantum Weak Measurement?" with an amusingly succinct abstract: "Probably not." In a similar spirit, to the question of whether once life arose was social life inevitable, we suggest that the answer is "probably yes." More exactly, in worlds governed by basic evolutionary forces there are large sets of environmental conditions that are conducive to the emergence of social life among interacting agents that have the ability to sense and respond to one another using simple computations. ✯

I

INTRODUCTION

The main fallacy in this kind of thinking is that the reductionist hypothesis does not by any means imply a "constructionist" one: The ability to reduce everything to simple fundamental laws does not imply the ability to start from those laws and reconstruct the universe.

PHILIP W. ANDERSON
More is Different (1972)

From the earliest millennia-old creation myths to twenty-first-century modern science we have tried to understand our place in the universe. Where did we come from? Are we unique or ubiquitous? Whether one relies on the biblical account in *Genesis* or Miller and Urey's (1959) connected flasks filled with chemical soups, questions about our origins occupy our minds.

Of course, we can study life, social or not, without knowing its origins, but doing so leaves a key and potentially quite insightful gap in our understanding of the world. One of the driving forces of science is to replace gaps that are occupied by placeholders such as "then a miracle happened" with sound explanations. Here, we will be seeking to understand the origins not of life itself, but of the social life that, at least on this planet, followed.

The study of origins is a study of essentials—what is the set of, perhaps minimal, conditions needed to bootstrap the world? That is, can we create a constructive proof of existence? And, if we can, do such origins have an infinitesimal chance of arising or are they almost inevitable?

Essentials also have a way of reappearing throughout time. For example, traces of primitive metabolic pathways are shared across most of Earth's organisms. So, along with gaining insights into our origins, such explorations may also help us understand how the social world as we know it today works.

The origins of social behavior are studied across many fields. Fields like archaeology and anthropology focus on (mostly human) societies from the past. Within these fields, efforts are made to identify the earliest evidence of certain types of social behavior. For example, the earliest evidence to date of *Homo* trade comes from around 320,000 years ago in Africa's Rift Valley (Brooks *et al.* 2018). Of course, data about early societies is difficult to acquire, and what is gathered may be more tied to what survives the ages than to what originated in them—whether social or biological, origins may not fossilize all that well. Researchers in other social science fields, such as economics, political science, psychology, and sociology, are also interested in the origins of (typically higher-order) social behavior. Axelrod's (1984) work on the evolution of cooperation (a theme we will take up in Chapter 9) used a computer tournament to study a set of expert-generated strategies for playing the Prisoner's Dilemma game to gain insights into how systems can develop cooperation. The quest in this book is similar to that of Axelrod's, though our goal is to develop a more general theory of social origins across a wider range of behaviors using only primitive agents.

Social behavior has also been a key topic in biology. Much of this work has focused on social groups, such as, nonhuman primates and eusocial insects (see, for example, Wilson 2000). Biologists have also considered the "evolution of sociality" (see, for example, Alexander 1974). The work that follows in this book complements these prior efforts by providing a new method for analyzing and understanding the emergence of social life.

Early forms of life on Earth may have been involved in primitive social behavior. For example, the early exchange of resources[1] may have been captured in stromatolites—fossilized microbial mats that provide some of the first physical evidence of life on Earth. Moreover, symbiotic relationships between bacteria and prokaryotes (Sagan 1967) allowed the emergence of the eukaryotes, which in turn provided the basis for the rise of multicellular organisms that take advantage of finely honed networks of communication, trade, policing, and so on, worthy of the most advance human society.[2] Given the potential benefits from social behavior, it may have been a powerful means by which to survive, and thrive, in the world. Thus, the origins of social behavior on Earth may run deep (for a more detailed discussion, see Appendix A).

~ 5 ~

A major impediment to understanding the origins of social behavior is that standard scientific techniques, which focus on reducing systems to their simplest components, are often ill-suited for gaining insights into systems composed of interacting agents. Social systems are composed of interacting, thoughtful (but perhaps not brilliant) agents. It is in the nature of these thoughtful interactions that social worlds are constructed, often taking on aggregate behaviors that are seemingly disconnected from the direct actions and intentions of any individual agent in the system. In a prescient essay on complex systems, Weaver (1958, p. 58) recognized the difficulty of exploring such systems: "A watch spring can be taken out of a watch and its properties usefully studied apart from its normal setting. But if a heart be taken out of a live animal, then there

---

[1] Social science ideas, such as trade theory in economics, can be applied to these types of systems (see, for example, Tasoff, Mee, and Wang 2015; Kallus, Miller, and Libby 2017).
[2] As discussed in Appendix B, the process of symbiogenesis may have broader implications for the social sciences.

is a great limitation on the range of useful studies which can be made."

As noted by Anderson (1972) (see the epigraph), using the reductionist paradigm of isolating and dissecting a system to understand the whole, may not allow us to reconstruct, and ultimately understand, the social worlds that such agents induce and inhabit. If we wish to "reconstruct the social universe" we need a scientific approach that goes beyond the usual reductionist paradigm. This approach must embrace not only reductionist simplification, but also the constructionist complexity that arises when simple agents interact.

The scientific basis of what follows relies on a model derived using a computational substrate that allows us to explore social worlds composed of simple, interacting model organisms. These model organisms are based on fundamental notions of information processing drawn from computer science. Each organism has the ability to process, and act on, information generated by the other organisms with which it interacts. To drive the system we use an artificial analog of evolution. Evolution is a fundamental force of nature and, as such, it is a reasonable choice for driving the origins we wish to understand.

Thus, to understand the origins of social behavior, we will create a computational model of interacting agents capable of processing, and acting on, the information generated by other agents, with the behavior of each agent honed by basic evolutionary forces.

The above approach circumvents the usual barriers to making scientific progress on complex phenomena. It is innately constructive, so we can study both the simple elements of the system *and* the implications of their interactions. It is easily observable, allowing us to generate the data needed to develop new and productive theories. If something unusual happens in the system, we can rewind the tape and rerun the world with whatever new probes might be useful for understanding what happened, and through this process we can develop and refine our theoretical understanding of the system's behavior. We also can experiment on this system. Much like the use of fruit flies, *Drosophila melanogaster*, in biology, our computational organisms, perhaps *Drosophila cognosco*,[3] can be subjected to whatever experimental conditions we can dream up—a social lab on a chip.

~7~

While the computational substrate of this method is relatively recent, the principles driving its design are as old as science itself. Ultimately, to understand the world we need to be able to observe and experiment on it, and our computational model provides a new means by which to achieve these ends. The history of science is punctuated by improvements in old tools, such as Galileo's telescope and van Leeuwenhoek's microscope, leading to new ways to view and understand the world. The computational model we develop here also expands old tools in new ways to give us a new view of social life (Miller and Page 2007). The overall method we develop is quite general and can be used to explore the evolution of information processing in many contexts. Here, we will use it as a time machine to explore the origins of social behavior.

1.1   Defining Social Behavior

Before embarking on our study of social origins, we need to have a working definition of social behavior. Existing definitions all agree that social behavior requires interaction, but beyond that they often diverge across many other dimensions, for example, whether social behavior can cross species.

---

[3] *Drosophila* is a Latinization of the Greek roots *droso* (moisture or dew) and *philos* (loving), while *cognosco* is the Latin verb that gives us cognition. With sincere apologies to Latin scholars everywhere, this proposed "species" roughly means "wetware loving."

Our working definition of social behavior embraces three elements. Like previous definitions, we require that agents must interact with one another to be social. Of course, agents interact with all kinds of entities in their world, so interaction *per se* is not enough.

Beyond interaction, we impose the additional requirement that each interacting entity has agency. Agency implies that the entities involved in social behavior have choices to make. The sociologist Max Weber (1978, p. 22) used agency as his criterion for human social behavior:

> *Not every type of contact of human beings has a social character; this is rather confined to cases where the actor's behavior is meaningfully oriented to that of others. For example, a mere collision of two cyclists may be compared to a natural event. On the other hand, their attempt to avoid hitting each other, or whatever insults, blows, or friendly discussion might follow the collision, would constitute "social action."*

Without the potential for agency and choice, interactions become more natural than social.

Finally, we draw on the etymology of the word social. Social has two Latin roots, *socius* meaning friend and *socialis* meaning allied, both of which are associated with the opportunity for mutual benefit.

Thus, for social behavior we will require three key elements:

(i) (I)nteracting entities with

(ii) (A)gency to make choices that have the potential for

(iii) (M)utual benefit.

This IAM definition of social behavior provides a reasonable basis from which to proceed. It easily encompasses a wide variety of agents and allows social interactions across species, both a relief to dog owners everywhere and a sensible addition given the history of life on this planet. Indeed, it may not even require life per se, as it doesn't eliminate computer-based systems (such as self-driving cars) or systems of interacting molecules driven by chemical reactions (such as metabolisms) from having the possibility of social behavior. The IAM definition is sufficient for us to move forward, though we acknowledge the potential for a more substantial investigation and debate on this topic.

1.2 Discovering Social Origins

In the following chapters we explore the origins of social behavior across many domains. The domains we consider were chosen based on the definition of social behavior discussed above and by identifying the archetypal behaviors that have been the foci of the social sciences. For example, the field of economics is often focused on exchange or commerce. The other social themes that frequently arise in the literature (see Chapter 2) include conflict, coordination, and cooperation.

Finally, we want to explore the role of communication in social systems, since interaction implies the passing of information among agents. At its most primitive level, communication occurs when an agent receives the immediate consequences of the actions taken by other agents. However, communication becomes more abstract when such actions and consequences get repurposed as symbolic proxies, allowing the transmission of more subtle messages with their exact meanings tied to emergent social conventions.

Thus, the broad types of social behaviors that we will investigate include archetypes of the Four C's: conflict, coordination, cooperation, and commerce (exchange). Moreover, we will also consider the potential role of communication in mediating such interactions.

Of course, social behaviors tend to intermingle freely with one another, so even in a simple model of commerce elements of coordination (agents must come to the market with a double coincidence of wants), cooperation (agents must uphold the trade agreement), conflict (dividing the gains to trade may be zero sum), and communication (about the terms of trade) arise. The various models we consider will emphasize different aspects of the Four C's, with the ultimate goal of providing a coherent view of social origins more generally.

To explore social origins, we will create a primitive substrate, based in an artificial world, from which we can observe the evolution of thoughtful agents. Driving this system is a simplified notion of evolution—a primitive and plausible force that is likely available in systems where social behavior might arise. This does not exclude other paths that can lead to social behavior, for example, thoughtful optimization, but given that we are interested in origins, we will embrace the simple to understand the complex. Similarly, we use a basic notion of thoughtful agents as the fundamental entities in the systems we explore. Such agents are modeled by primitive computing machines. As before, while more elaborate notions of cognitive agents exist, our interest here is in a minimal model of thoughtful agents.

The agents we will explore have an easily controlled notion of their ability to process information—a thoughtfulness dial if you will. At one extreme, agents respond to the world by taking a single, unchanging action. As we increase an agent's ability to compute, it can begin to sense and respond to its environment by processing more information in more ways, allowing its choices to incorporate increasingly subtle and sophisticated manipulations of, and reactions to, the information flowing in from its environment.

The methodology above produces a useful engine of discovery, allowing us to explore the behavior of an open-ended adaptive system composed of thoughtful agents across a rich set of potentially social environments. By reinterpreting the meaning of the various inputs to, and outputs of, the agents, we can repurpose the methodology to consider novel scenarios while maintaining a consistent model and set of tools to analyze and understand the resulting behavior. This approach provides a unified framework not only for understanding the origins of particular types of social behavior, but social origins more generally.

We will focus on three fundamental elements that are potentially tied to the origins of social behavior. The first is the degree to which agents interact with one another. The second is the ability of an agent to sense and respond to its world—in essence, its ability to compute. Finally, we consider the underlying features (payoffs) of the environment.

Ultimately, we find that the emergence of social behavior is intimately connected to these three elements: (I)nteraction, (C)omputation, and (E)nvironment (ICE). Across broad swathes of social behavior, it takes only small changes in ICE for social behavior to emerge—similar to the dramatic phase transition we see when ice turns to water as the temperature rises slightly above freezing.

We also find that the emergence of social behavior is often characterized by an ostensibly stable regime of asocial behavior being rapidly transformed into a similarly stable regime of social behavior. Such revolutions are driven by a random series of seemingly small, innocuous changes that eventually conspire to put the system into a state where a single random spark can generate a sequence of niche construction events that rapidly and completely transform the system's behavior. When such unexpected revolutions by evolution—(r)evolutions?— intervene in a hopeless asocial world and produce a bountiful social one, we find the essence of *deus ex machina*. ❦

PART I:
THE APPROACH

THE APPROACH

We have to look for power sources here, and distribution networks we were never taught, routes of power our teachers never imagined, or were encouraged to avoid . . . [sic] we have to find meters whose scales are unknown in the world, draw our own schematics, getting feedback, making connections, reducing error, trying to learn the real function . . . [sic]

THOMAS PYNCHON
Gravity's Rainbow (1973 [2012])

To understand the origins of social behavior, we develop a methodology that brings together some key ideas from various scientific fields. This methodology uses game theory as the framework for defining agent interactions in settings with social potential, automata theory to create bounded, computationally able agents, and the theory of evolution embedded inside of a genetic algorithm to allow the agents to adapt. The resulting Coevolving Automata Model (CAM) provides the substrate from which to explore and, ultimately, better understand the origins of social behavior.

Game theory was developed for the analysis of interacting, thoughtful agents and, not surprisingly, it has become a fundamental tool for exploring social behavior. Game theory provides a useful way to identify and frame the social scenarios that we will explore. Unfortunately, game theory has yet to develop a general and robust set of solution schemata to predict system-wide behavior. The CAM addresses this issue by introducing a way to create and analyze games composed of computationally bounded, interacting, adaptive agents. This provides an interesting extension to game theory, as well as an environment consistent with the potential emergence of social behavior.

We also use game theory to identify the key domains and examples of social behavior. Over the past half-century a vast literature has emerged from game theory that is focused on interesting cases of social behavior. For example, thousands of studies have been conducted on games of cooperation (such as the Prisoner's Dilemma) and coordination (such as the Battle of the Sexes). Using this literature we will acquire the needed touchstones of social behavior.

At the heart of the CAM are simple computational machines, derived from abstract theories of automata tied to mathematics and computer science. Automata are the atoms of computation underlying general theories of computing and they capture a class of behavior rich in applications and possibilities (Hopcroft, Motwani, and Ullman 2006). Of particular interest here is that automata provide a simple notion of thoughtful choice-making agents able to interact with, and respond to, other such agents. Another advantage of basing agents on automata is that of being able to appropriate existing mathematical results to further our understanding of agent and system-wide behavior.

Finally, rather than analyzing a static set of automata the CAM allows each machine to learn and adapt over time. This adaptation is driven by the theory of evolution, encapsulated *in silico* using a genetic algorithm. Genetic algorithms are a powerful technique for machine learning. By taking an open-ended set of possibilities—here the possible computations of an automata—and through the application of simple evolutionary operations such as selection biased by performance and random modification, it is possible to identify and refine potential solutions to difficult, and often otherwise intractable, problems. Evolution is a fundamental force of nature and thus it is an appropriate way to drive our system given our interest in the origins of social behavior.

The next few chapters are devoted to these key components of the CAM. ❦

2

SOCIAL GAMES

The use of computers seems thus not merely convenient,
but absolutely essential for such experiments which
involve following the games or contests through a very
great number of moves or stages. I believe that the
experience gained as a result of following the behavior
of such processes will have a fundamental influence
on whatever may ultimately generalize or perhaps
even replace in mathematics our present exclusive
immersion in the formal axiomatic method.

STANISLAW ULAM
Adventures of a Mathematician (1991)

Game theory is a transcendent framework created to explore
systems of interacting, thoughtful agents. It has proven to
be useful across many fields, including biology, economics,
and political science, providing a convenient way to frame
social behavior. It has generated solution concepts for how
agents might behave in such situations. Unfortunately, it
has been much harder to solve games than to define them.
The initial successes of game theory focused on solutions
consistent with hyperrational agents identifying and pursuing
static equilibrium, but the founders of game theory recognized
that this was just an initial foray into a vast wilderness. Of
course, one can easily get distracted during such forays, seeking
a mythical *El Dorado* while ignoring the true richness of the
real world. More recently, game theorists have had a renewed

interest in understanding the behavior that arises in games played by adaptive agents.

Game theory provides a general framework for understanding strategic interaction among agents. At its core is the careful delineation of the agents, their possible actions and strategies, the information they have access to, and the payoffs that accrue to the agents given their mutual actions. Using this framework, game theory then considers possible ways for agents to solve the game, that is, what action should an agent take given the available information. As will be discussed in section 2.2, formulating such solutions has been an important, and often frustratingly difficult, part of game theory.

2.1 Researching Social Behaviors

The framework of game theory provides a flexible way to explore a wide range of thoughtful interactions. While any possible social interaction could be captured as a game, in practice most research has concentrated on a few types of interactions. Table 2.1 provides a rough accounting of past research. Note that most of the categories at the top of the list contain broad swathes of behavior, while most of the games lower down are various embodiments of these higher-level categories.

Insofar as this past research focuses on important areas of social behavior, the table reveals the preferences of a broadly defined research community. For example, there is a large emphasis on general topics surrounding cooperation, coordination, and conflict (the latter of which is key to the popular games of Chicken and Hawk Dove, its equivalent). With the exception of Ultimatum, a game designed to explore the limits of self-interest, the other top five games contain various elements of cooperation, coordination, and conflict. For example, Prisoner's Dilemma concerns cooperation,

GAME	RESEARCH ITEMS
Cooperation	1,900,000
Coordination	855,000
Public Goods	202,000
Signaling	132,000
Chicken	121,000
Ultimatum	44,800
Prisoner's Dilemma	34,700
Battle of the Sexes	9,670
Stag Hunt	6,460
Centipede	6,160
Hawk Dove	4,660
Matching Pennies	3,510
Blotto	1,900
Rock, Paper, Scissors	383
Keynesian Beauty Contest	275

Table 2.1. Count of research papers and books by keywords using Google Scholar (on February 20, 2018). Game names were searched using the name of the game in quotes and "Game" and "Theory" as keywords. Searches using alternative configurations of the keywords yielded different counts, but the order tended to be the same. Note that the categories in the upper panel capture more general concepts while those below are specific games, thus there is an overlap, for example, the Prisoner's Dilemma is also a game about cooperation, and so on. It appears that the game theory gods have an inordinate fondness for chicken.[1]

Battle of the Sexes focuses on coordination and conflict, and Stag Hunt contains elements of both cooperation and coordination.

Moreover, a key reason that the research community focuses on some of the games that appear in the table, such as Chicken, Prisoner's Dilemma, Battle of the Sexes, and Stag Hunt, is that these games were designed to have innate incentives that work against productive social behavior. Thus,

---

[1] Gould (1993) provides a comprehensive discussion of the better known quote about beetles attributed to J. B. S. Haldane.

they capture scenarios that make the emergence of social behavior challenging.

The preferences of researchers revealed above provide a useful guide for the studies that follow. These preferences suggest that, in general, the social domains of cooperation, coordination, and conflict are important. Furthermore, they identify some specific games that are useful incarnations of these higher-level domains. Given that the popularity of these games is largely tied to the challenges they present for the emergence of social behavior, they provide the perfect fodder for some of the explorations we will conduct in Part II.

2.2   Solving Games

While game theory has provided a valuable way to frame issues of social behavior, unfortunately, it has been difficult to leverage this framework into an easily implemented and generally useful prescriptive or descriptive notion of agent behavior. Proposed strategic solutions to games have ranged from assuming rational behavior on the part of the agents to systems that are driven by basic evolutionary forces or learning. Below, we discuss these various approaches and how they relate to the purely adaptive approach used in the Coevolving Automata Model.

2.2.1   RATIONAL AGENTS

One branch of game theory uses a formalized prescription for how rational agents should play a game. Nash's (1950a, 1950b, 1951) seminal contributions to this approach focused on finding a static equilibrium wherein every player simultaneously takes a self-consistent action, in the sense that no player has an incentive to deviate from its chosen action assuming the actions of the other agents remain unchanged. Nash identified a relatively general set of conditions under which a game would embody at least one such equilibrium (sometimes in mixed strategies that probabilistically choose among possible actions).

While the basic logic of Nash's equilibrium, once attained, makes sense, in practice it raises a number of issues. First, it places high requirements on an agent's ability to deduce the equilibrium and on the degree of common knowledge needed in the game. Second, there may not be an obvious dynamic process that could drive the agents to such equilibria. Third, games often have multiple Nash equilibria, which complicates the task of deciding which one will be chosen. Multiple equilibria arise even in simple games, for example, in a game of coordination where two players wish to coordinate on one of two possible meeting venues, there are two pure Nash equilibria and one mixed one. Sometimes, outside considerations may make an equilibrium more focal, such as when both players in a coordination game strongly prefer one of the two meeting venues. Fourth, various anomalies arise in Nash equilibria, such as when "irrational" behavior on the part of an agent allows that agent to receive a higher payoff.[2]

~ 25 ~

---

[2]Such cases were anticipated by von Neumann and Morgenstern (1944, p. 32):

> ... the rules of rational behavior must provide definitely for the possibility of irrational conduct on the part of others. In other words: Imagine that we have discovered a set of rules for all participants to be termed as "optimal" or "rational" each of which is indeed optimal provided that the other participants conform. Then the question remains as to what will happen if some of the participants do not conform. If that should turn out to be advantageous for them and, quite particularly, disadvantageous to the conformists then the above "solution" would seem very questionable. We are in no position to give a positive discussion of these things as yet but we want to make it clear that under such conditions the "solution," or at least its motivation, must be considered as imperfect and

Given that the origins of social behavior may be tied to the degree of agent interaction, one issue of particular interest is what happens when a game is played for multiple rounds. Such repeated games have unusual implications for game theory. The definitions of most games only rely on an ordering of the potential payoffs. While such orderings are sufficient to clarify an agent's incentives when the game is played for a single round, they are insufficient when payoffs are accumulated over multiple rounds, since agents might enter into productive patterns of actions over time that are unavailable in the single-round game. While this result is widely known, it often gets ignored. For example, there are many studies of repeated games that use a single set of cardinal payoffs drawn from the much broader space of potential payoffs. As will be demonstrated in Part II, different sets of payoff parameters from the same game can lead to dramatically different agent behavior.

A related issue with repeated games is the proliferation of Nash equilibria. This easily derived "Folk theorem" relies on the ability of agents to punish their opponents in a repeated game by taking unfavorable future actions if a prespecified set of actions is not followed. Such strategies result in a Nash equilibrium for the prespecified set of actions.

One response to the various issues that arose with the notion of Nash equilibria was to seek more refined equilibrium

---

incomplete. In whatever way we formulate the guiding principles and the objective justification of "rational behavior," provisos will have to be made for every possible conduct of "the others." Only in this way can a satisfactory and exhaustive theory be developed. But if the superiority of "rational behavior" over any other kind is to be established, then its description must include rules of conduct for all conceivable situations including those where "the others" behaved irrationally, in the sense of the standards which the theory will set for them.

concepts. This resulted in a vast "refinements" literature, with a zooful of new equilibrium notions ranging from the divine to the perfect. While these refinements proved useful under particular circumstances, a more universal solution to rational play remains elusive despite many attempts over the last seventy-five years by some thoughtful and clever minds.

Another trend that challenged the rational-solution approach was the advent of experimental techniques for exploring human behavior in games that started to take hold around 1990. As experimental results began to accumulate, it became increasingly clear that equilibrium predictions driven by rational agents often failed to describe human behavior in even simple, carefully controlled conditions. Such mounting evidence must ultimately result in the abandonment of old theories and the creation of new ones. While this process has been slow in the social sciences, even decades of clever theoretical accomplishments that fail to predict the world must eventually succumb to Kenneth Boulding's (1978b) first law: "anything that exists is possible."

2.2.2 EVOLVING GAME THEORY

Even if there was a clear way to identify the rational solution to a game—and, so far, there isn't—the analysis of social origins diverges from a rationalist paradigm in at least two major ways. First, in the beginning, agents were likely limited in their ability to gather and process information. There is, of course, the question of how limited is too limited, a question that will be of interest in the analyses to come. Nonetheless, if social behavior can arise with simple agents, presumably it can do so with more sophisticated ones. Second, origins involve moving from a world where something doesn't exist to one where it does, so the story we seek is inherently dynamic. Thus, the existence of, say, a Nash equilibrium for a system that is stable once it is achieved is meaningless if we cannot show how it could have emerged. Our focus in the work presented in this book will be on finding a reasonable set of sufficient conditions that can generate the phenomenon of interest (Epstein 2006)— we want to grow it, to show it.

The notion that a reasonable theory of games requires a coherent dynamic story arose early in the history of formal game theory. In *Theory of Games and Economic Behavior* (1944, pp. 44–5), von Neumann and Morgenstern noted:

> *The next subject to be mentioned concerns the static or dynamic nature of the theory. We repeat most emphatically that our theory is thoroughly static. A dynamic theory would unquestionably be more complete and therefore preferable. But there is ample evidence from other branches of science that it is futile to try to build one as long as the static side is not thoroughly understood. On the other hand, the reader may object to some definitely dynamic arguments which were made during the course of our discussions. This applies particularly to all considerations concerning the interplay of various imputations under the influence of "domination." We think that this is perfectly legitimate. A static theory deals with equilibria. The essential characteristic of an equilibrium is that it has no tendency to change, i.e. that it is not conductive to dynamic developments. An analysis of this feature is, of course, inconceivable without the use of certain rudimentary dynamic concepts. The important point is that they are rudimentary. In other words: For the real dynamics*

which investigates precise motions usually far away from equilibria, a much deeper knowledge of these dynamic phenomena is required.

A dynamic theory—when one is found—will probably describe the changes in terms of simpler concepts: of a single imputation—valid at the moment under consideration—or something similar. This indicates that the formal structure of this part of the theory— the relationship between statics and dynamics—may be generically different from that of classical physical theories... Thus the conventional view of a solution as a uniquely defined number or aggregate of numbers was seen to be too narrow for our purposes, in spite of its success in other fields. The emphasis on mathematical methods seems to be shifted more towards combinatorics and set theory—and away from the algorithm of differential equations which dominate mathematical physics.

John Nash, in his Ph.D. thesis[3] (1950b), recognized the potential for a more dynamic theory, one even predicated on simple agents (p. 21):

We shall now take up the "mass-action" interpretation of equilibrium points. In this interpretation solutions have no great significance. It is unnecessary to assume that participants have full knowledge of the total structure of the game, or the ability and inclination to go through any complex reasoning processes. But the participants are supposed to accumulate em-

---

[3] The thesis was twenty-six pages long, not counting front matter and the acknowledgments. It had only two citations, one to Nash's *PNAS* (1950a) paper and one to von Neumann and Morgenstern (1944).

pirical information on the relative advantages of the various pure strategies at their disposal.

To be more detailed, we assume that there is a population (in the sense of statistics) of participants for each position of the game. Let us also assume that the "average playing" of the game involves n participants selected at random from the n populations, and that there is a stable average frequency with which each pure strategy is employed by the "average member" of the appropriate population.

The empirical-population approach mentioned by Nash in his thesis was largely forgotten until it was independently resurrected by biologists. While some of the ideas for "evolutionary" game theory were around in the 1960s, publications emerged in the 1970s (see, for example, Maynard Smith and Price 1973; Maynard Smith 1974, 1982) that developed the notion of an evolutionarily stable strategy (ESS). The ESS—while still a static equilibrium concept (see Huttegger and Zollman 2013)—adds a locally dynamic, biologically inspired twist to the refinements literature to justify the equilibrium. It begins by assuming that the strategy of each player in a game is represented by a large population of agents, each preprogrammed to execute the identical strategy out of some well-defined set of possible strategies. It then imposes an evolutionary dynamic on the system whereby populations are continually tested by small invasions of mutant strategies (drawn from the previously defined set of possible strategies). An ESS occurs when natural selection allows the existing equilibrium population to stave off invasion by any initially rare, mutant strategy.

More formally, let $\pi(i, m)$ give the payoff to strategy i when it faces strategy m. In the original formulation, incumbent strategy i is an ESS if, for all $m \neq i$, either:

1. $\pi(i, i) > \pi(m, i)$ or
2. $\pi(i, i) = \pi(m, i)$ and $\pi(i, m) > \pi(m, m)$.

Both conditions guarantee that the expected payoff to the incumbent is greater than the expected payoff to the mutant, implying that natural selection favors the incumbent. More specifically, let the proportion of mutants in the population be given by μ, then (in expectation) for the incumbent to outcompete the mutant we need:

$$(1 - \mu)\pi(i, i) + \mu\pi(i, m) > (1 - \mu)\pi(m, i) + \mu\pi(m, m). \quad (2.1)$$

Recall that the incumbent population is assumed to be large. As μ goes to 0, the first ESS condition is sufficient to guarantee equation 2.1. The second ESS condition allows for the possibility that the mutant does as well as the incumbent, in which case there might be the potential for natural selection to allow the mutant population to grow by neutral drift. However, when $\pi(i, i) = \pi(m, i)$, equation 2.1 still holds if the second ESS condition is true.

Note that a Nash equilibrium requires that $\pi(i, i) \geq \pi(m, i)$ for all m. Such an equilibrium is a *strict* Nash equilibrium when $\pi(i, i) > \pi(m, i)$ for all $m \neq i$. Thus, the first ESS condition implies a (strict) Nash equilibrium. However, the second ESS condition adds a refinement to the (non-strict) Nash equilibrium (since $\pi(i, m) > \pi(m, m)$ must also hold) in those cases where the alternative strategies do as well, implying that while all ESS are Nash equilibria, not all Nash equilibria are ESS.

The ESS provides a locally dynamic justification for a system being able to maintain an essentially static equilibrium.

It provides a useful refinement of Nash equilibrium both by its minimal assumptions about agent rationality and its inclusion of a locally dynamic story that ensures stability. Of course, it still focuses on relatively simplistic preconditions and dynamics, and some subsequent refinements of ESS have attempted to address such issues. Moreover, it begs the questions of how the allowable set of strategies was chosen and how the system acquired its homogenous, incumbent population.

An alternative biological approach to games has focused on models of population dynamics that draw from the study of dynamical systems. For example, in replicator dynamics (Taylor and Jonker 1978) populations of different strategic types interact with one another and are subject to evolutionary forces modeled by having the growth or decline of any particular type of strategy tied to that strategy's fitness (payoff) relative to the mean fitness of the population. While this dynamic has a similar flavor to ESS, and various relationships between the two ideas have been identified, replicator dynamics provide a richer picture of the dynamic system as a whole. For example, the resulting phase diagrams and analysis of attractors arising from replicator dynamics show how mixes of strategies can flow over time. Other models, like that of Moran (1958), provide alternative views of evolutionary dynamics using different assumptions. For example, Moran processes focus on finite populations that experience pulses of mutations, while replicator dynamics assume extremely large populations undergoing continuous change. Further details of these biological approaches are discussed in Appendix C.

2.2.3 LEARNING IN GAMES

The learning in games literature offers another view of how dynamics can lead to strategic choice. This literature has two major motivations. The first is whether dynamic learning processes can cause the system to converge to, say, a Nash equilibrium. The second, a response to the various anomalies that have arisen in the ever-growing set of results from laboratory experiments, is whether such anomalies can be explained via some form of learning.

~33~

A good representative of the first motivation is the notion of fictitious play. Fictitious play was an early attempt to develop a dynamic mechanism that might lead to a Nash equilibrium (Brown 1951). In fictitious play, players form a belief about what their opponent will do based on observations of that opponent's past play (and an assumed initial distribution), and then they myopically pick the best strategic response to those observations under the (likely faulty) assumption that the opponent is implementing a stationary (though possibly mixed) strategy. Agents must have some sophistication to employ fictitious play, as they need to track the observed play of the opponent and be able to calculate the best response to those observations. One interesting aspect of fictitious play is that an agent's strategic calculations ignore the payoffs facing the opponent. Much of the research in this paradigm has focused on the conditions under which fictitious play converges to various notions of equilibrium, and a variety of results and anomalies have been discovered—Fudenberg and Levine (1998) offer a modern treatment.

Another focus of the learning literature has been on adaptive learning. This literature arose as an attempt to better explain the deviant, vis-à-vis existing theory, human behavior observed in laboratory experiments. One branch of adaptive learning (Andreoni and Miller 1995) connects to the previously discussed biological approach. Key ideas from this branch of adaptive learning are discussed and implemented in the chapters that follow.

The other branch of adaptive learning draws inspiration from various psychological theories. For example, the reinforcement learning approach of Roth and Erev (1995) and Erev and Roth (1998) use Bush and Mosteller's (1955) work on positive and negative stimuli. Reinforcement learning models allow agents to derive propensities for various actions given that action's past performance. These propensities then form a probability distribution from which the player draws its next action in the game. Each time an action is executed, its propensity is updated using a reinforcement function tied to that action's current propensity and payoff. This basic learning scheme can be modified in different ways. For example, Camerer and Ho (1999) also alter the weighted propensities of actions that were *not* chosen based on their potential payoff and some discount rates, allowing their model to capture both reinforcement learning and fictitious play as special cases.

2.3 Conclusions

Game theory was created to explore systems of interacting, thoughtful agents. Thus, it provides both a convenient way to frame our quest to understand the origins of social behavior and a useful touchstone by which to identify key social phenomena. The general framework of game theory— interacting players, choosing actions, generating information, and receiving payoffs—provides a minimal set of elements required to set the stage for social behavior.

Since it was developed, game theory has been applied to a vast array of social behaviors. Particular social phenomenon and games, such as cooperation in the Prisoner's Dilemma, coordination in the Battle of the Sexes, and conflict in the game of Chicken, have received concentrated attention. These research preferences provide a key set of social phenomena worthy of exploration, drunks searching for their keys under the lamppost notwithstanding.

While the general framework of game theory has proven valuable across numerous fields, it has yet to yield a reasonable theory of what strategic behavior will arise in a given game. Early theories concentrated on static-equilibrium solutions that were consistent with rational behavior. Even as these approaches were being developed, their creators recognized the importance of more dynamic explanations for how such equilibria are achieved and maintained. Nonetheless, forays into finding rational equilibrium solutions dominated the field for decades and led to a vast campaign to refine the existing concepts in hope of finding a useful distillate. Unfortunately, no such spirits arose.

More recently, game theory has revived its focus on strategic dynamics and adaptation. The initial push for such an approach came from evolutionary biologists harnessing ideas from game theory to better understand how animals interact with one another when, say, there is the potential for conflict. The flow of observations of human behavior in laboratory games has also promoted the development of learning theories tied to ideas from psychology.

Game theory has entered a new period of investigation, disciplined by observation and driven by a desire to create theories rooted in the dynamic behavior of adaptive agents.

The approach we will pursue here follows this imperative to consider dynamic models of adaptive agents. Given our focus on the origins of social behavior, we rely not on some notion of rational agents or cognitive learning, but rather agent adaptation driven by the basic forces of evolution. While evolution can certainly result in cognition, and can even give cognitive beings the ability to think about hyperrational beings,[4] we will focus on primitive agents subject to evolution. The rest of our methodology involves ideas drawn from mathematics and computation, along with some algorithmic analogs of biological evolution from computer science. The result is an unusual mix of both old and new techniques that will help us to understand social origins. In this, we take solace from von Neumann and Morgenstern (1944, p. 6):

> *The importance of the social phenomena, the wealth and multiplicity of their manifestations, and the complexity of their structure, are at least equal to those in physics. It is therefore to be expected—or feared—that mathematical discoveries of a stature comparable to that of calculus will be needed in order to produce decisive success in this field. (Incidentally, it is in this spirit that our present efforts must be discounted.) A fortiori it is unlikely that a mere repetition of the tricks which served us so well in physics will do for the social phenomena too. The probability is very slim indeed, since it will be shown that we encounter in our discussions some mathematical problems which are quite different from those which occur in physical science.*

---

[4]In the 2001 movie *Heist*, Gene Hackman's character Joe Moore noted:
D.A. Freccia: [If] you're not that smart, how'd you figure it out?
Joe Moore: I tried to imagine a fella smarter than myself. Then I tried to think, "what would he do?"

These observations should be remembered in connection with the current overemphasis on the use of calculus, differential equations, etc., as the main tools of mathematical economics. 🖘

3

FINITE AUTOMATA

So I've got a god in the room here. I know a lot about gods and I have found what god this is by the way it behaves. This is the God of the Old Testament: a lot of rules and no mercy. And if he catches you picking up sticks on Saturday you're finished.

JOSEPH CAMPBELL
The Hero's Journey (1990)

Along with using game theory to formulate challenging, fundamental social scenarios, our approach requires two additional elements: a useful way to embody thoughtful agents and a means by which to adapt such agents to their environment. The solution to the first of these elements, discussed below, is the use of simple computer programs or machines modeled by finite automata. The solution to the second, discussed in the next chapter, is the application of a genetic algorithm that uses the principles that drive natural evolutionary processes to adapt these automata.

To model thoughtful agent behavior we use simple computer programs known as finite automata. Automata provide a mathematical model of systems that operate in a world where streams of discrete inputs generate streams of discrete outputs, and thus they represent a fundamental class of behavior that is rich in both applications and possibilities (Hopcroft, Motwani, and Ullman 2006). Automata play a central role in the theory of computation as they are a subset of universal Turing machines, which can be used to model any computation.[1]

Depending on the size of the automaton, its behavior can range from simply ignoring inputs and always producing the same output to something akin to sophisticated decision-making involving the elaborate processing of a stream of inputs. This wide range of behaviors is large enough to explore the origins of social behavior.

The interesting question, especially for the origins of social behavior, is how much computational ability does it take before systems can become social? Fortunately, we can explore this question directly by adding states to the automata to increase their computational abilities.

There are many ways to represent finite automata, all with various isomorphisms, and we will represent our automata as Moore machines. Formally, Moore machines consist of a set of states, S, one of which is designated as the initial or starting state. Each state $s \in S$ is associated with an output that is produced each time the machine enters that state. Let $\lambda: S \to A$ define this association, where A is the set of possible outputs (or actions). Each state also has a corresponding transition function, $\delta: S \times A^{\sim} \to S$, which determines the next state that the machine will enter when it receives a particular input (drawn from the set $A^{\sim}$).

A more intuitive description of a Moore machine is given by its transition diagram (see fig. 3.1). This machine embodies some simple behavior. It begins in the left-most state and outputs a 0. If the input it receives is a 0, it follows the labeled transition arc and remains in the starting state and, again, outputs a 0. Alternatively, if the input is a 1, the machine transitions to its second state and

---

[1]Of course, some functions are not "computable" and cannot be solved using algorithms.

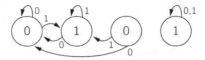

Figure 3.1. A diagram of a Moore machine. This four-state Moore machine has binary ($\{0, 1\}$) inputs and outputs. The circles represent the states of the machine. The label inside of each state gives the machine's output upon entering that state. The arcs, labeled for each possible input, give the transition state contingent on the associated input. We assume that the machine always starts in the left-most state and that the states are numbered sequentially from left to right starting from 0. This machine begins in the left-most state and outputs a 0. If the input is a 0, it remains in this left-most state and again outputs a 0. If, however, the input is a 1, it transitions to the next state and outputs a 1. Once in this second state, an input of 0 will cause a transition back to the starting state where the machine will output a 0, while an input of 1 will keep it in the second state and produce an output of 1. Note that the third and fourth states, while still part of the machine, are *inaccessible* since, given the starting state, there is no possible set of inputs that will cause the machine to transition to either of these two states. The right-most state is also a *terminal* or *absorbing* state—if the machine enters this state it stays there forever, regardless of input.

outputs a 1. Once it is in the second state, if the input is a 0 it transitions back to the first state and outputs a 0. However, if the input is a 1 it remains in the second state and outputs a 1. States that can be visited given the machine's starting state and some possible set of inputs are *accessible*, while those that can never be visited are *inaccessible*. In the figure, the first two states are accessible while the last two are inaccessible. If the machine ever enters the state on the far right it stays there forever, as all of its transitions return back to this state—such states are known as *terminal* or *absorbing* states.

The behavior of the machine given in figure 3.1 is, in this case, easy to characterize. It begins by outputting a 0 and then mimics the behavior of its input stream by always outputting the last input received. Thus, if the input stream is $\{1, 0, 1, 1\}$

then the machine will output $\{0, 1, 0, 1, 1\}$. While the utility of such mimicking behavior might seem dubious, this machine can implement the famously effective Tit-For-Tat strategy used in the Prisoner's Dilemma (with 0 implying cooperation and 1 designating defection).

Finite automata can perform a variety of computations. For example, the first two states of the automaton shown in figure 3.1 are able to condition (branch) behavior based on the input. Automata also have the ability to remember the past by capturing it in a state (note that the first two states in the previous automaton track the most recent input). As we increase the number of states in a machine, its potential information-processing abilities also increase. With more states, machines can, for example, do more elaborate branching, remember longer sequences of past inputs, count the number of times a particular input has been seen, determine the parity of a given input, and so on. Larger automata can also implement pseudo-random numbers, and thus can introduce a form of randomness into their outputs.[2] Larger machines can do everything smaller machines can do, and more. In general, the larger the machine the more potential it has to do more complex computations that may involve higher-level constructs, such as counting.

While the number of states in a machine is tied to its computational abilities, measuring the size of a machine is more complicated than one might first assume. The *nominal* size of a machine is the total number of states available to the machine. As discussed above, a nominal state is *accessible* if, given the machine's starting state, there is some possible set of inputs that causes the machine to enter that state. If we are in an accessible state, then all of the transition arcs emanating from that state must

---

[2] Though, in practice, it may be easier to provide some external randomization device or implement nondeterministic automata for such behaviors.

also point to accessible states (since receiving the input associated with an arc moves the machine to that state). Thus, by following the transitions from the starting state (which, by definition, is accessible) to the transition states, and then following the transitions from those states and so on, we can identify all of the accessible states. While the machine in figure 3.1 has four *nominal* states, only two are accessible.[3] Since inaccessible states are never visited, they never influence the machine's output and thus have no immediate impact on the machine's computations. Inaccessible states (as discussed later) can, however, play an important role in the evolution of an automaton and thus become relevant over evolutionary time scales.

Two machines perform the same computation if they produce the same output stream when facing an identical input stream. While the number of accessible states provides an upper bound on a machine's computational ability, accessible states may be redundant, in the sense that they induce behavior that is captured elsewhere in the machine. For example, consider a machine with one hundred accessible states, all of which output 0. Such a machine behaves identically to a single-state machine that outputs 0. Of course, most such isomorphisms are far more subtle. Take the machine in figure 3.1 and add a fifth state that outputs a 0 and transitions to the first state on a 0 and the second state on a 1. Now, alter either the first or second state so that its transition on 0 points to this newly added state. Such a machine behaves identically to the original machine, since the added state just replicates the behavior of the first state. One could keep adding such redundant states to create a very complicated web of transitions and accessible states, without ever altering the original computation.

---

[3] Transition arcs from inaccessible to accessible states are irrelevant here.

One theorem from the study of automata (see, for example, Hopcroft, Motwani, and Ullman 2006) shows that for any machine performing some computation, there exists an isomorphic minimized-state machine that performs the identical computation.[4] That is, given a machine, one can derive a minimized machine that uses the fewest possible states to produce the same output stream as the original machine does for any possible input stream. Sometimes, the original machine is such that it cannot be compressed further. At other times, a machine might embody a large amount of "slack" whereby its nominal or accessible size is much larger than its minimized size. While the amount of slack in a machine doesn't influence its computation, it may play an interesting role in determining the machine's potential for evolvability.

Even the minimized size of a machine may, at times, be misleading. For example, consider a machine with 1,001 states, where the first state always transitions to the second state (regardless of the input), the second always transitions to the third, and so on down the line, with the last state transitioning back to the first state. Let all of the states output a 0 except for the last state, which outputs a 1. Thus, regardless of the input stream, this machine outputs one thousand 0s followed by a single 1, and then repeats this pattern. This machine is minimized, as there is no way to use fewer states and still be able to count the thousand 0 outputs needed to perform the computation.[5] However, note that a single-state machine that always outputs a 0 generates *almost* the identical behavior (with

---

[4]The theorem also suggests an algorithm for finding minimized machines (see, for example, Harrison 1965).

[5]The ability to perform computations, in this case counting outputs, is tied to how we represent the machines. Other representations, such as giving machines access to "counters," would result in a different sized machine, though we would still need to account for the computation embodied in the counter itself.

the exception of not throwing in a 1 every 1,001 outputs). Thus, we have two minimized machines, one with 1,001 states and the other with 1 state, yet their behaviors are very similar.

Another issue that can arise when assessing how a machine's states affect its computations, is that the actual states that get visited depend on the input stream—just because a state is accessible, doesn't mean that it will be accessed. If the machine in figure 3.1 has inputs of only 0, it never leaves its starting state. Of course, accessible states that are never visited during a particular input stream may still be important, as it is often the behavior that *could* happen that shapes the behavior that *does* happen. For example, part of the power of Tit For Tat in the Prisoner's Dilemma is that if the opponent ever defects, then Tit For Tat will defect until the opponent resumes cooperation. Similarly, the number of times a machine visits a particular state during a computation may be skewed. For example, a two-state machine that begins by outputting a 0 and then unconditionally transitions to a terminal state that outputs a 1 thereafter, visits its first state only once.

Ideally, there would be a simple, all-encompassing measure of the complexity of a machine. The number of states is often used as such a measure though, as noted above, there are different ways to measure even this quantity, such as nominal, accessible, and minimized states,[6] as well as various anomalies tied to such measures. Nonetheless, a single, easily derived quantity with some validity in terms of measuring machine complexity is the minimized number of states—that is, the fewest states needed to implement a given computation.

A plausible working hypothesis about the emergence of social behavior is that it will be tied to the computational abilities of the

~ 45 ~

---

[6]For a given machine, the number of nominal states $\geq$ accessible states $\geq$ minimized states.

agents. If so, we may observe computational thresholds that, once achieved, allow a particular type of social behavior to arise.

At the extreme, the output stream of a single-state machine is independent of its inputs and thus such machines are incapable of truly interacting with other agents in the short term.[7] Moving from one- to two-state machines embodies a remarkable computational leap.

Once a machine has two states, it can begin to sense and respond to its environment, and this capability may elevate its potential for meaningful social behavior. Even here, given the primitive worlds we wish to investigate, our agents are allowed to sense and respond only to the inputs received by an opponent (in the case of repeated play in a game, the opponent's previous action), so this channel is still quite limited. Nonetheless, a strategy like Tit For Tat can be implemented by a two-state machine, so there is some evidence, at least in a model of cooperation using the Prisoner's Dilemma, that an important strategy able to promote cooperation can be captured by a two-state machine. Of course, maintaining a behavior may have different requirements than allowing it to emerge in the first place, so we may discover social scenarios where the number of states needed for emergence differs from the number needed for maintenance.[8]

The ability to add quanta of computation to the automata by altering the number of nominal states allows us to explicitly explore the above ideas in the modeling that follows.

~ 46 ~

---

[7] Of course, on evolutionary time scales, even one-state machines can be tuned to the behavior of others.

[8] Indeed, as we will see later, this does happen.

3.1 The Space of Automata

Automata allow us to explore how the introduction of computational quanta admits different forms of behavior. One-state machines can neither sense nor respond to the world that they inhabit, as these machines produce the same output regardless of the input. Moving from one- to two-state machines introduces the possibility of sensing the world and, based on that input, responding to it in different ways.

As a first step we can enumerate the number of possible machines given some number of states. The size of these spaces depends on how many possible inputs and outputs the machines must handle—below we will assume binary inputs and outputs. A state in a machine is defined by its output and transition function. With binary outputs each state has two possible output symbols. With binary inputs the transition function for a state must pick a transition state for each of the two possible inputs, thus with S states each state can have one of S^2 possible transition functions. Therefore, under binary inputs and outputs, there are $2S^2$ possible configurations of actions and transitions for each state. This implies that there are $\left(2S^2\right)^S$ possible machines, assuming that we always start the machine in its first state.[9] This calculation gives the number of unique machine *structures*, but some of these structures may share the same minimized machine and perform redundant computations.

Table 3.1 provides an enumeration of the number of possible machines and computations using binary inputs and outputs for a given number of states. As we increase the number of states there is an explosion in the number of

---

[9]In general, the number of possible automata is given by $\left(AS^I\right)^S$, where A is the number of possible outputs, S is the number of states, and I is the number of inputs. If the machine can start in any of the states, then the number of possible machines increases by a factor of S.

| | POSSIBLE | POSSIBLE |
STATES	AUTOMATA	COMPUTATIONS
1	2	2
2	64	26
3	5,832	1,054
4	1,048,576	57,068
5	312,500,000	?
6	1.4×10^{11}	?
7	8.7×10^{13}	?
8	7.2×10^{16}	?
9	7.7×10^{19}	?
10	1.0×10^{23}	?

Table 3.1. Enumeration of automata with binary inputs and outputs. For a given number of states, the second column gives the number of unique automaton structures given all possible configurations of the outputs and transition functions across the states. The third column gives the number of unique minimized machines across the ensemble of structures. Two structures that share the same minimized machine produce an identical computation (output stream) when facing the same input stream. The number of possible automata is calculated analytically (see text) while the number of possible computations is derived by enumeration (which, here, was limited to machines with fewer than five states).

possible automata given the exponential impact of states on the combinatorics. The third column of the table gives the number of unique computations possible from the ensemble of automata of a given size. For example, with two-state machines, of the sixty-four unique structures, twenty of them share the same minimized machine that always outputs a 0 (and given symmetry, twenty always output a 1). The remaining twenty-four machines produce unique computations in the sense that there exists at least one possible input stream that will produce different output streams between the machines. In the table, the number of possible automata was derived analytically while the number of possible computations was derived by

Figure 3.2. Ensemble of one-state automata with binary inputs and outputs. The machine on the left always outputs a 0 and the one on the right always outputs a 1, regardless of the input.

enumerating across the ensemble of machines, minimizing them, and identifying the isomorphic machines.

~ 49 ~

The number of possible computations shows some interesting patterns as machines add states. With one-state machines, each of the two possible structures yields a unique computation. With two-, three-, and four-state machines, the respective yields of unique computations are 41%, 18%, and 5% of the possible structures. Even though the yields are dropping, the actual number of possible computations is exploding as machines get larger. Recall that larger machines always contain the computations available to smaller-sized machines. For example, consider the two computations available to one-state machines. Of all possible two-, three-, and four-state structures, 62%, 40%, and 28% replicate these one-state computations, respectively, though again the absolute number of such replicants explodes as machines increase in size. Finally, as the number of states increases so does the number of replicant machines. Given any machine, we can always create an equivalent machine by keeping the same starting state and reordering the other states, thus there are at least $(S - 1)!$ replicants for any machine.

To build further intuition on the space of machines consider just one- and two-state machines. One-state machines must send the same output each time, regardless of the input stream. Thus, the behavioral ensemble of such machines is given by the two machines shown in figure 3.2.

Moving from one- to two-state machines produces a jump in computational ability—increasing the number of possible computations from two to twenty-six. Here, the addition of a single state allows the machines to react to an input by branching to a different state and producing a different output.[10] Two-state machines can potentially have a "memory." For example, if the machine in figure 3.1 is in the first state it has either just initialized or has had a 0 as its most recent input, while if it is in the second state the previous input was a 1. As will be shown in later chapters, the quantum leap in computational power moving from one to two states can have a dramatic impact on a system's social behavior.

Figure 3.3 shows the twenty-six unique computations contained within two-state, binary input and output machines. The first two machines replicate the two possible one-state machines. A machine of size m can always be configured to replicate the behavior of a machine of size n, if $m \geq n$. Indeed, when $m > n$, there will always be more than one structure of size m that replicates the behavior of a size-n machine. (At the very least, we can embed the n states directly into the m-state machine, leaving $m - n$ inaccessible states in the larger machine that could be arranged in various ways.)

The possible computations that arise out of the sixty-four possible two-state, binary automata fall into a few classes. Most of these machines (40/64) replicate the computations that we saw in the one-state world. However, twenty-four new computations become available. Some of these new computations (4/64) also ignore the input stream, but given the additional state, produce slightly more elaborate output streams that either Alternate Outputs or use a Non-

~50~

---

[10] If the two states emit the same output, then the machine is isomorphic to a one-state machine.

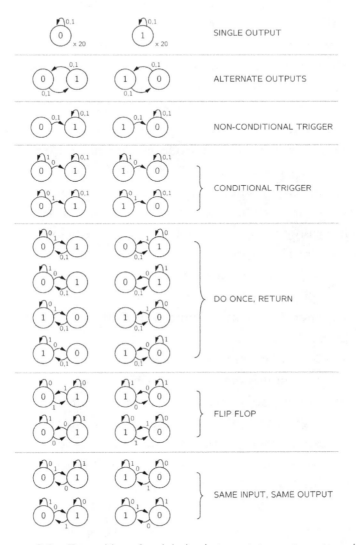

Figure 3.3. Ensemble of minimized two-state automata with binary inputs and outputs. The machines are grouped into sets of equivalence classes that capture similar types of computations. The sixty-four possible two-state machines implement twenty-six unique computations. The two top-most computations each arise in twenty of the sixty-four possible two-state automata. All of the remaining computations occur only once in the ensemble.

Conditional Trigger to have the first output differ from the ones that follow. The remaining (20/64) machines are more interesting, as they all respond to their inputs. Four of these machines have a Conditional Trigger that produces the same output as long as an expected input is received, but any deviation from that input triggers these machines to send the alternate output thereafter. Eight of the machines follow a Do Once, Return rule that produces the same output as long as they receive the expected input, but send the alternative output once if an unexpected input occurs, before reverting back to their initial behavior. (Half of these previous machines begin by producing the alternate output once before starting the described behavior.) The remaining eight machines closely track and respond to the input stream, with half of them tracking the parity of a given input (Flip Flop) and the other half (Same Input, Same Output) more directly linking their output to the most recent input.

A key link between automata and game theory is that we can allow the inputs and outputs of a machine to correspond to actions in a repeated game. A machine can implement a strategy in such a game by letting its output give its choice of action in the current round of the game and its input represent the most recent action taken by the opponent. Remarkably, some of the most discussed strategies in game theory can be embodied by two-state machines. For example, trigger strategies—often used as an extreme means to encourage an opponent to take the non-triggering action—can be captured by the Conditional Trigger class of machines. The behavior of Win Stay, Lose Shift, a strategy that may appear in games of cooperation, is given by a parity-tracking machine from the Flip-Flop class. Finally, Tit For Tat, perhaps the most famous strategy in game theory, is identical to a machine from the Same-Input, Same-Output class. Thus, even with relatively small automata, some major strategic ideas can be realized by these machines.

3.2 Mutating Machines

The studies that follow use artificial evolution to adapt the automata. Evolution uses the selective survival of randomly varying agents to drive productive adaptation. To create such random variation, we will use a mutation operator to make a small, random change to a machine's structure.[11] The smallest change we can make to a machine of fixed size is to either alter a state's output or one of its transition arcs.

The mutation space of a one-state machine is more limited. Since the machine must always transition back to its solitary state, the only possible mutation is to its output. Thus, a one-state binary machine that always outputs a 0 must mutate to a one-state binary machine that always outputs a 1, and vice versa.

Mutations become more interesting once machines have more than one state. For example, in the class of binary two-state machines there are six possible one-step mutations. For each state, a mutation can alter either its output or one of its two transition arcs. For example, figure 3.4 shows the six possible, one-step mutations of a Tit-For-Tat machine. As previously discussed, larger machines can embed the behavior of smaller machines, for example, three of the six Tit-For-Tat mutants are equivalent to one-state machines. In general, the number of possible mutations for an automaton with S states, A outputs, and I inputs is $S(A-1) + SI(S-1)$, where the first term gives the number of possible output mutations and the second term gives the number of possible transition mutations.

---

[11]In biological systems, random variations are introduced in many ways, ranging from small local changes to the genome known as mutations to larger-scale rearrangements facilitated by genetic operators such as crossover that recombine large contiguous sequences of the genomes.

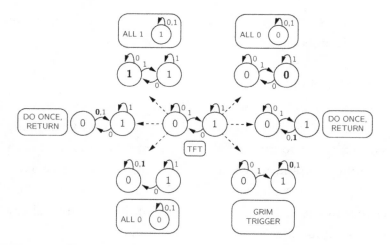

Figure 3.4. One-step mutations of a two-state Tit-For-Tat machine. There are six possible one-step mutations (shown in bold) of the original machine, each of which either alters an output or a transition. After minimizing the resulting machines, three of them have one-state equivalents.

In the model that follows, mutation drives the creation of new behaviors, thus the network of possible mutations provides insight into how novelty arises in this system. In figure 3.4, we showed the six possible machines that arise from Tit For Tat from a one-step mutation. If we then mutate one of these six one-step mutants, we can generate the space of machines that are two mutation steps away from Tit For Tat. One of these two-step mutations revives the original Tit For Tat by reversing the mutation that created the initial one-step mutation. As we continue to mutate the mutants, we generate a network where each node is a possible machine and each edge represents a one-step mutation connecting the corresponding machines. (Appendix D and Appendix E provide detailed information about one- and two-state machines, including their associated mutation spaces.)

We can take a mutation network and describe it in terms of computational links rather than structural ones. In figure 3.4, we saw that Tit For Tat had three mutations that led to machines that minimize to one state. Since mutations can flow in either direction, this implies that there are three machines in the ensemble of sixty-four with one-state-like behavior that can, via a single mutation, turn into Tit For Tat.

Inaccessible states play an interesting role in mutation. Since inaccessible states are ignored by the machine they have no direct impact on its behavior. A state is inaccessible because none of the accessible states can transition to it, thus any mutation to an *inaccessible* state has no impact on the machine's behavior—such mutations are completely neutral in this regard. However, inaccessible states may become important when a mutation to an accessible state makes it transition to a previously inaccessible portion of the machine. For example, in figure 3.1 a mutation in the first state that alters the transition when seeing a 1 from the second to the third state causes the machine to take on a new behavior. Namely, it now takes two consecutive inputs of 1 before the machine mimics the input (with any input of 0 resetting this behavior). Or, if the aforementioned mutation points to the last state, the machine now outputs a 0 as long as the input is a 0, but if a 1 ever arises the machine outputs a 1 regardless of future inputs. Once an inaccessible state becomes accessible, all of its transition states also become accessible, and a transformative cascade can occur.

Thus, in machines with inaccessible states, the impact of a single mutation can vary from no observable change to the machine's behavior—the same stream of inputs induces the same stream of outputs—to a radical change in how the machine responds to inputs.

If a machine's nominal and minimized sizes are identical, then a single mutation will always alter that machine's computation.[12] Alternatively stated, a necessary (but not sufficient) condition for computationally neutral one-step mutations is that the original machine has some slack where its minimized size is less than its nominal size.

The space of possible mutations will be fodder for our evolutionary engine. Each possible machine structure is ensnared within a web, linked to all of the machines that differ from it by a single structural change in either an output or a transition. Evolution will continually test the machines against their environment. Sometimes, newly tested machines fare poorly in the world and the system retreats back to a previous node. At other times, the mutants do well, become established, and begin to throw off their own set of mutations to be tested in future generations.

Mutations can also be neutral, changing the machine's underlying structure but not its behavior. Occasionally, sequences of neutral mutations can accumulate, resulting in a machine that behaves identically to its founding parent, but with a radically different set of possible mutations. Next, we show how such neutral mutations can become important portals to the discovery of novel and productive behaviors.

3.2.1 NEUTRAL MUTATIONS

A neutral mutation is a change to the underlying structure of an entity that does not impact its fitness. In biology, an organism's genotype (the underlying information that generates its physical structure) may change, even though its phenotype (the manifestation of that structure that interacts

---

[12]Since machines are unique up to a canonical ordering of the states, a single mutation is insufficient to alter that ordering.

with the world and determines the organism's ability to survive and reproduce) does not. Such changes are known as neutral mutations.[13]

Neutral mutations allow the population frequencies of the underlying structures to drift due to chance events during reproduction. Kimura (1968, p. 626) recognized the importance of such drift, noting, "To emphasize the founder principle but deny the importance of random genetic drift due to finite population number is, in my opinion, rather similar to assuming a great flood to explain the formation of deep valleys but rejecting a gradual but long lasting process of erosion by water as insufficient to produce such a result." Since drift is tied to random sampling, it is accelerated in smaller populations. For example, if selection is governed by a Moran process (see Appendix C) there is a $1/P$ chance, where P is the population size, of a neutral mutant taking over the entire population.

We consider two types of neutral mutations: *structural* and *environmental*. Structural neutral mutations occur when there is a change to a machine's structure that does not alter its minimized machine. Since the minimized machine captures the automaton's computation, two automata that share the same minimized machine will produce the same output stream when facing the same input stream, and thus receive the same payoff. Even machines that are not structurally neutral may behave identically to one another when exposed to a *particular* set of inputs. We define such machines as environmentally neutral. For example, a one-state machine that always outputs 0 behaves the same as, say, a Tit-For-Tat machine, as long as both machines always receive 0s as inputs. Of course, under a different set of inputs, the behaviors of these two machines will deviate (if a 1

---

[13]Wagner (2015) provides an accessible discussion of this topic in biological systems.

occurs, Tit For Tat responds with a 1 rather than a 0). Thus, two machines are structurally neutral if they always mimic one another's output stream when exposed to the same input stream, and they are environmentally neutral if, conditional on a particular input stream, they produce the same output stream. All structurally neutral machines are environmentally neutral, but the converse does not hold—that is, structural neutrality is a sufficient, but not necessary, condition for environmental neutrality.

The presence of neutral mutations can alter evolutionary dynamics. Occasionally, a sequence of neutral mutations allows the system to traverse a large swath of the mutation network and puts the system into a state where a single, non-neutral mutation results in a dramatic behavioral change that was not possible before the neutral mutations began to accumulate. Figure 3.5 illustrates such a transformation as a series of neutral one-step mutations transforms a machine that always outputs a 1 into a Tit-For-Tat machine—a caterpillar turning into a butterfly.[14] Such transformations may play a critical role in the emergence of social behavior by allowing, say, a nasty and brutish world of defection to be transformed into a world of cautious cooperation.

Environmentally neutral mutations can also transform a system. In the systems that follow, random drift induced by environmentally neutral mutations can drive radical social transformations (see sec. 6.3). For a real-world example, consider a situation in which the loyalty of citizens to the government is continually tested. If all of the citizens are loyal then newly emerging disloyal citizens will be quickly subdued by the loyalists. However, suppose an environmentally neutral citizen arises who

---

[14]The figure traces just one of the many possible neutral walks that achieves this end.

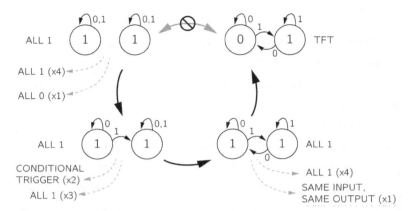

Figure 3.5. A neutral mutation path leading to a radical change in behavior for two-state machines. The system begins with a two-state machine (top, left) that always outputs a 1 regardless of input. Through a sequence of neutral, one-step mutations that proceed in a counter-clockwise direction, the underlying machine is transformed to the point where one additional mutation alters it from always outputting a 1 to implementing Tit For Tat (top, right). Note that prior to the final step, there are no one-step mutations that result in Tit For Tat. (Dashed arcs identify the results of the other five mutations for each machine.)

is loyal to the government if others are, but will join the opposition if it exists. If the numbers of such citizens drifts to become a significant proportion of the population, then the stage is set where the arrival of a single disloyal citizen can catalyze the emergence of a large and transformative opposition party.

3.3   Meta-Machines

To explore social behavior we need interaction. Our automata will interact with one another by having the output of one machine become the input to the other, and vice versa. The behavior embodied by two (or more) interacting machines can be captured by a meta-machine, which is, itself, an automaton. Each state in this meta-machine represents a possible combination of the states of the underlying automata. If we, say, want to form the meta-machine implied by the interactions between a two- and three-state machine, the meta-machine will require six states, each of which corresponds to a unique pair of states from the two underlying machines. The meta-machine's starting state is given by the state that corresponds to the starting states of the constituent machines. Each state in the meta-machine outputs the corresponding outputs from the states of the underlying machines. Furthermore, since these outputs become the inputs to the underlying machines, the next state that the meta-machine enters is known. Thus, each state of the meta-machine has a single transition arc.

Figure 3.6 shows the derivation of a meta-machine. In the figure, when the two machines at the top interact they begin in states A and a, respectively, and both output a 0. These outputs cause the first machine to remain in state A and the second machine to transition to state b, moving the meta-machine to the new pair of associated states. Next, the machine on the left outputs another 0 while the machine on the right outputs a 1. Given these outputs, the machine on the left transitions to state B while the machine on the right cycles back to state a. The results of such interactions are given in the table in the center of the figure. The meta-machine that describes this system's behavior is given by the automaton at the bottom. Note that at the third time step the meta-machine transitions from state Ba to Ab, a previously visited state-pair, and thus the meta-machine falls into a fixed cycle of formerly traversed states.

These meta-machines will always fall into a fixed cycle. Since each meta-machine has a finite number of states (given by all of the possible combinations of the finite states in the constitute machines) and each such state is governed by a deterministic transition to the next state, the meta-machine must eventually return to a previously encountered state after a finite number of

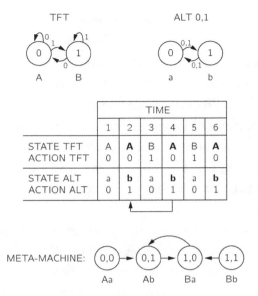

Figure 3.6. Two interacting automata forming a meta-machine. When the machines at the top of the diagram interact, the resulting sequence of outputs and states is given by the table in the middle. The interacting machines form the finite-state meta-machine shown at the bottom. Each state of the meta-machine is composed of unique pairings of the states from the constitute machines, and has a single, fixed transition. The meta-machine will always end up in a deterministic cycle, since with a finite number of states and deterministic transitions it must eventually revisit a previously visited state—this occurs here at time step 4 when the constitute machines transition back to *Ab*.

transitions. Once this happens, the meta-machine enters a fixed cycle that governs the remaining interactions of the underlying machines.

Like Kekulé's dream, these meta-machines behave like a snake reaching back and biting itself (but, unlike Kekulé's ouroboros, these snakes may bite mid body). The meta-machine begins at the snake's tail and travels toward its head, all the while producing a stream of joint outputs from the underlying machines. Once it reaches the head it moves back to its body and again advances toward the head, resulting in a fixed and endless cycle of joint outputs. These cycles either start immediately or have a long preamble depending on how far down its body the snake bites.

The states that appear along the snake that define the meta-machine's path represent the states of the constitute machines that are visited during their interaction. Thus, inaccessible states of the constitute machines never appear on this path. Moreover, since the interacting automata determine each other's inputs, it is possible that some accessible states of the constituent machines are never visited during a given interaction.

If we know the underlying ensemble of constituent machines, we can derive the set of all possible meta-machines that can arise. For example, given the two unique one-state, binary machines, there are four possible pairings, each of which results in a one-state meta-machine that immediately cycles. For example, if two machines that always output a 0 meet, the resulting output stream will be {0,0 0,0 0,0 . . .}. To simplify notation we use $\langle 0,0 \rangle$ to indicate such a cycle (with the symbols separated by a comma, giving the respective outputs of the constitute machines). Thus, the possible output streams of the four possible pairings of one-state binary machines are: $\langle 0,0 \rangle$, $\langle 0,1 \rangle$, $\langle 1,0 \rangle$, and $\langle 1,1 \rangle$ (see Appendix D).

Moving from one- to two-state binary machines creates a much richer class of behavior. As previously noted, there are sixty-four unique automaton structures in this class implying 4,096 potential pairings.[15] These pairings produce 196 unique output streams. These streams include, for example, $\langle 0,0 \rangle$ where the two machines immediately enter a cycle of length one, $\langle 1,1 \ 0,0 \ 1,0 \rangle$ where the machines immediately cycle producing the sequence of outputs {1,1 0,0 1,0} before cycling

---

[15] Of these 64 structures, 26 unique computations are available, implying 676 potential pairings.

back to begin anew at 1,1, and more elaborate behaviors such
as 1,1 0,1 ⟨0,0 1,0⟩ where there is an initial preamble of {1,1
0,1}, at which point the machines cycle through {0,0 1,0} for
the remainder of their interactions. Appendix E provides a
catalog of the possible output streams generated by the dyadic
interactions of two-state, binary machines.

One interpretation of the cycle preambles is that the
machines have an initial "conversation" that leads them to
"decide" on the cycle they wish to execute for the remainder
of their interactions (see Chapter 11).

If we just focus on the cycles of the meta-machines, then the
ensemble of dyadically interacting two-state, binary input and
output machines produces sixty-four possible unique cycles.
Given symmetry, some of these cycles arise from reversing the
designation of the first and second machine. Table 3.2 provides
a summary of the possible cycles that arise from the 4,096
dyadic interactions along with their frequencies. Over 76%
(3,128/4,096) of the possible pairings result in a cycle of length
one, 20% (824/4,096) of length two, 3% (120/4,096) of length
three, and 0.6% (24/4,096) of length four. Thus, if we were
to randomly pair machines out of the structural ensemble,
their interaction will most likely result in a short cycle length.
Because the underlying machines are restricted to two states
each, longer cycles are subject to constraints.[16]

As discussed above, the output stream prior to entering
the cycle may be important. Of the 4,096 possible pairings of
two-state machines, 76% (3,128/4,096) fall into an immediate

---

[16]For example, none of the cycles longer than one can contain the same output
pair more than once in the sequence, since both counting and producing
that pair requires a machine to devote at least two states to the task, which
uses up all of the available states and prevents anything else from being
generated.

CYCLE		CYCLE		CYCLE		CYCLE	
⟨0,0⟩	(782)	⟨0,0 0,1 1,0⟩	(5)	⟨1,0 1,1 0,1⟩	(5)	⟨1,0 1,1 0,1 0,0⟩	(1)
⟨0,1⟩	(782)	⟨0,0 1,0 0,1⟩	(5)	⟨1,1 0,1 1,0⟩	(5)	⟨0,0 0,1 1,1 1,0⟩	(1)
⟨1,1⟩	(782)	⟨0,1 1,1 1,0⟩	(5)	⟨1,1 0,0 1,0⟩	(5)	⟨1,1 0,1 0,0 1,0⟩	(1)
⟨1,0⟩	(782)	⟨0,0 1,1 0,1⟩	(5)	⟨1,0 1,1 0,0⟩	(5)	⟨1,0 1,1 0,0 0,1⟩	(1)
⟨0,1 1,1⟩	(90)	⟨0,1 0,0 1,1⟩	(5)	⟨1,1 0,1 0,0⟩	(5)	⟨0,1 1,1 0,0 1,0⟩	(1)
⟨0,0 0,1⟩	(90)	⟨0,1 0,0 1,0⟩	(5)	⟨1,1 0,0 0,1⟩	(5)	⟨1,1 0,0 0,1 1,0⟩	(1)
⟨0,1 0,0⟩	(90)	⟨0,0 1,1 1,0⟩	(5)	⟨1,0 0,1 0,0⟩	(5)	⟨0,1 1,0 0,0 1,1⟩	(1)
⟨1,0 1,1⟩	(90)	⟨0,0 1,0 1,1⟩	(5)	⟨1,0 0,0 0,1⟩	(5)	⟨1,0 0,1 0,0 1,1⟩	(1)
⟨1,1 1,0⟩	(90)	⟨0,0 0,1 1,1⟩	(5)	⟨0,1 0,0 1,1 1,0⟩	(1)	⟨1,1 1,0 0,1 0,0⟩	(1)
⟨0,0 1,0⟩	(90)	⟨0,1 1,0 1,1⟩	(5)	⟨0,0 0,1 1,0 1,1⟩	(1)	⟨0,0 1,1 1,0 0,1⟩	(1)
⟨1,1 0,1⟩	(90)	⟨0,1 1,1 0,0⟩	(5)	⟨0,0 1,0 1,1 0,1⟩	(1)	⟨1,0 0,0 0,1 1,1⟩	(1)
⟨1,0 0,0⟩	(90)	⟨0,1 1,0 0,0⟩	(5)	⟨0,1 0,0 1,0 1,1⟩	(1)	⟨1,1 1,0 0,0 0,1⟩	(1)
⟨1,0 0,1⟩	(26)	⟨1,0 0,1 1,1⟩	(5)	⟨0,1 1,1 1,0 0,0⟩	(1)	⟨1,0 0,1 1,1 0,0⟩	(1)
⟨0,1 1,0⟩	(26)	⟨1,1 1,0 0,1⟩	(5)	⟨0,0 1,0 0,1 1,1⟩	(1)	⟨1,0 0,0 1,1 0,1⟩	(1)
⟨1,1 0,0⟩	(26)	⟨1,1 1,0 0,0⟩	(5)	⟨0,0 1,1 0,1 1,0⟩	(1)	⟨1,1 0,0 1,0 0,1⟩	(1)
⟨0,0 1,1⟩	(26)	⟨1,0 0,0 1,1⟩	(5)	⟨0,1 1,0 1,1 0,0⟩	(1)	⟨1,1 0,1 1,0 0,0⟩	(1)

Table 3.2. Cycles that arise in dyadic interactions between two-state automata with binary inputs and outputs. There are sixty-four unique two-state binary machine structures, and therefore there are 4,096 possible pairings of such machines. Each of these pairings eventually leads to a cycle, and the table presents the sixty-four possible cycles (ignoring any prior outputs that initiate the cycle). Note that each observation is tied to the order in which the machines are paired— the table allows all possible orderings, counting symmetric cycles separately. The numbers in parentheses indicate the frequency of the given cycle across the 4,096 pairings of the machines in the structural ensemble.

cycle.[17] So, in general, a random pairing of two-state, binary machines tends to produce an output stream that forms an immediate cycle of short length.

3.4   Interactions and Computational Compression

In our studies, machines interact with one another for a given number of repeated rounds. During the first round each

[17]For each cycle in table 3.2, 74% of those with frequency 782, 89% of those with frequency 90, 61% of those with frequency 26, 80% with frequency 5, and none with frequency 1, immediately fall into the indicated cycle.

machine must decide on an initial output. In each subsequent round, a machine's input is given by the other machine's most recent output. This implies that the number of rounds influences the possible computations that a given machine can conduct.

For example, in a one-round interaction only the starting state of a machine is queried. Thus, no matter how many states the machine has, it acts as if it is a one-state machine.

In a two-round interaction, at most the first state and the output from its transition state (but not the transitions from that transition state) are used. Again, this compresses the number of possible computations—with binary inputs and outputs there are only eight possible computations. For example, the two-state machines producing Tit For Tat and Grim Trigger (a machine that outputs a 0 unless it receives a 1, in which case it outputs 1 thereafter) behave identically over a two-round interaction, as they both begin by issuing a 0 and then either issue another 0 (if the initial input was a 0) or a 1 (if the initial input was a 1). If the game had an additional round, these two machines could be differentiated using an input sequence of $\{1, 0\}$, as Tit For Tat would output a 0 as its third output while Grim Trigger would output a 1.

The compression of possible computations due to limited interactions becomes a great equalizer of the possible social behavior in a one-round interaction. In such an interaction, two-state machines with twenty-six possible computations and four-state machines with over fifty-seven thousand can only perform the same two possible computations available to one-state machines. With two-round interactions, only six additional computations become available to machines with more than one state.

In the studies that follow we will find that the amount of interaction between machines has a big influence on the emergence of social behavior. Computational compression caused by limited interactions will help to explain why some systems can never achieve social behavior regardless of the amount of computation available to the agents. Perhaps more remarkable is that, at times, systems will be able to become social using only eight computational archetypes—an eight-fold path to social behavior.

3.5 Conclusions

Automata are choice-making machines. They take inputs that provide information about the world, perform computations, and then respond by sending outputs. Automata are capable information processors and, in theory, if given enough states, they can perform any computation that could be implemented by a general purpose computer. However, even machines with very few states are capable of a surprisingly large number of possible computations, including those that often arise in the analysis of strategic behavior in games.

Finite automata represent a fundamental model of information processing, and thus they provide a useful foundation for creating agents that can both sense, and respond to, their world. Automata have well-defined structures that are easily observed and are amenable to several analytic techniques (such as machine minimization) that can give us insights into their behavior. The computational ability of an automaton is closely tied to its number of states (modulo the level of interaction), and by altering the number of states available to a machine we can quantize an agent's potential choice-making ability and explore how this influences the emergence of social behavior. Moreover, the structure of an automaton is easily manipulated, providing us with a simple mechanism for altering a machine's behavior and making it useful fodder for the evolutionary engine that we will use to drive agent adaptation. All of these features make finite automata a valuable substrate for modeling primitive, thoughtful agents.

By allowing one machine's output to serve as another machine's input, we can take two (or more) automata and have them interact with one another. The resulting interactions can be captured using the convenient shorthand of a meta-machine. A meta-machine is also an automaton, so it is also precisely defined, easily observable, and amenable to analytic techniques. Thus, the complexity of the system is reduced as the interactions of automata at one level are captured by a single meta-automaton at another level.

Complex systems often exhibit such behavior, where out of the chaos of agent interactions at one level emerges a new agent that captures that level's behavior and, potentially, forms the basis for a new series of interactions at a different level. In a twist on archaic cosmology, rather than turtles all the way down, perhaps it is automata all the way up?

The use of primitive computing machines to embody thoughtful agent behavior aligns nicely with our quest to understand the origins of social behavior across systems. For example, in many (most?) biological systems, computation does not require a brain or neurons *per se*. Systems driven by simple molecular binding and signaling, such as those involved in bacterial chemotaxis (see, for example, Wadhams and Armitage 2004), are capable of performing computational tasks.

Even the crudest ability to sense and respond to the world provides a remarkable evolutionary advantage—once evolution happened upon such rudimentary forms of computation, life on Earth was profoundly changed.

Ultimately, to understand the origins of social behavior we need to have a precise way to explore systems of interacting, thoughtful agents. As argued above, finite automata provide a sound basis for creating models of interacting, choice-making agents. Of course, there is a difference between choice-making and thoughtful choice-making, and to introduce such "thought" the machines need a means by which they can be modified and improved over time. There are many ways to do this. For example, we could rely on insights from cognitive science and behavioral economics on decision making or we could use a more rational agent approach, such as Bayesian learning, to modify the machines. However, given our focus on the origins of social behavior, we want the model to be driven by simple, fundamental forces so universal that they would be available to a broad swath of primitive systems. Evolution is such a force. As discussed in the next chapter, we will use a version of Darwin's engine to provide the mechanism needed to breathe social life into existence. ❧

4

GENETIC ALGORITHMS

*There is grandeur in this view of life, with its
several powers, having been originally breathed into
a few forms or into one; and that, whilst this planet
has gone cycling on according to the fixed law of
gravity, from so simple a beginning endless forms
most beautiful and most wonderful have been, and
are being, evolved.*

CHARLES DARWIN
On the Origin of Species (1859)

Agents can learn in many different ways, from sophisticated
rational-choice approaches that rely on Bayesian statistics
to more heuristic-based approaches that use simple rules to
improve behavior. Here, we assume that agents adapt based on
the principles driving evolution in natural systems.

The evolutionary approach has many advantages. The
forces that drive evolution are fundamental and so universal
that assuming their presence to drive the origin stories we
wish to understand seems reasonable. Evolution also requires
a minimal set of assumptions for adaptive learning, and thus
it provides a useful lower bound for such models. Finally,
evolution has proven itself to be adept at solving the problem
of survival in natural environments as is apparent given the
"endless forms most beautiful and most wonderful" (Darwin
1859, p. 490) that surround us.

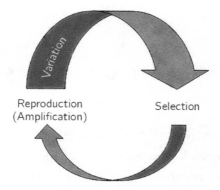

Reproduction
(Amplification)

Selection

Variation

Figure 4.1. The theory of evolution. Evolution relies on a simple cyclic engine: selection biased by performance followed by the reproduction and amplification of these fitter agents with some variation. Each such cycle constitutes a generation.

Natural evolution is a powerful engine of discovery, resulting in life forms ranging from amoebas to zebras, with an occasional platypus thrown in to keep things interesting. At the heart of the theory of evolution is a simple, yet sophisticated algorithm (see fig. 4.1). Organisms—representing potential solutions to the problem of survival—are tested in the environment. Then, the better-performing organisms are amplified in number and subjected to some random variation in their structures via genetic operators like mutation and crossover. The process begins anew, with each subsequent generation of the algorithm cycling through the three phases of testing, selection biased by performance, and amplification with variation.

How can such a simple scheme ever produce good solutions to the problem of surviving in difficult environments?

Even though evolution involves randomness (both during biased selection and in the creation of new variants) this does not imply that it is randomly searching for better organisms. A random search would fail as it is equivalent to an enumerative search over all possibilities, which falters given the sheer number of possible structures (for example, in humans there are roughly $4^{3\times10^9}$ potential genotypes).

Instead, evolution uses randomness to facilitate a directed search. While selection may incorporate randomness, it is biased toward better performing structures. Genetic operators also use randomness to create new structures tied to the old ones, introducing variation on a theme rather than outright chance. The evolutionary engine is driven by the "non-random survival of randomly varying replicators," a phrase widely attributed to Richard Dawkins.

While evolution itself is simple, the resulting search it produces is sophisticated. Evolution is implemented at the level of manipulating organisms within a population. However, these manipulations are executing a surprisingly elegant sampling scheme at a much deeper level. Each individual organism contains many different structural patterns or schemata, with many of these schemata shared across different members of the population. Holland (1975) showed how the high-level manipulation of organisms by biased reproduction and genetic operators results in a sophisticated low-level manipulation of the underlying schemata. The frequency of a given schema (across the entire population) rises if it is associated with better performing organisms.

Each organism, whether it survives or dies, provides an opportunity for the evolutionary system to test and refine a multitude of possible schemata, ultimately leading to the system identifying and synthesizing the higher performing schemata independent of the actual organisms that exist in the population at any given time. Similar to the magic that happens in Markov chain Monte Carlo algorithms (see

Appendix C), a set of simple operations results in the sophisticated manipulation of the overall system in a deep, and otherwise computationally inaccessible, way.

4.1 Artificial Evolution

The effectiveness of natural evolution at discovering novel and productive solutions to the problem of survival inspired a class of algorithms in computer science known as genetic algorithms (Holland 1975). These algorithms have proven to be very effective at solving difficult optimization problems involving nonlinearities, discontinuities, and large search spaces, and we will use such an algorithm as the basis for adapting our automata.

Genetic algorithms begin with a population of potential solutions, each of which is encoded in a machine-manipulable form. A generation begins when these potential solutions are tested on a problem and each receives a measure of fitness or payoff. A new population is then formed by reproducing the current solutions biased by performance. During reproduction, some solutions are modified using analogs to simple genetic operators such as mutation and crossover. A new generation begins when this newly formed population is again tested on the problem and subjected to reproduction and modification. Over the course of generations, the population converges on a set of good solutions to the problem of interest.

Genetic algorithms were developed to solve "hard" problems. A classic computer science problem is trying to optimize the value of a function where you are limited in the number of function evaluations that can be performed. One of the simplest algorithms that can be applied to such problems is hill climbing. Hill climbing begins its search at a randomly chosen status quo point and then proceeds by iterating two simple steps. First, it searches over the immediate neighbors of the status quo and identifies the best one.

Second, if that neighbor is better than the existing status quo, it becomes the new status quo. These two steps are iterated until all of the neighbors are inferior to the status quo, at which point the algorithm halts with the status quo as the solution (guaranteeing at least a local optimum). If the function is continuous with a single peak, hill climbing will eventually identify the global optimum regardless of the initial status quo.

However, most real-world functions have properties that tend to confound not only hill climbing, but also more sophisticated variants that rely on, say, local gradients. For example, nonlinear functions have multiple peaks, and under such conditions hill climbing easily gets trapped on inferior peaks, leading to local but not global optima. To mitigate this problem, hill climbing can be run multiple times using different starting points, in the hope that one of the starting points will be in the basin of attraction of the best peak. Along with nonlinearities, functions often have discontinuities that pose a problem for algorithms that rely on gradient search. Functions are also more difficult to solve when they incorporate stochastic elements that provide variable payoff values for each query of the domain.

Genetic algorithms were designed to work well on the types of hard problems that confound traditional approaches like hill climbing. Rather than using a single status quo point like hill climbing, genetic algorithms maintain a population of potential solutions across the search space. As the genetic algorithm proceeds, it uses the mutual information across the members of its population to formulate new search points. By exploiting this mutual information, genetic algorithms can perform well in environments characterized by nonlinearities, noise, and discontinuities. If such environments were rare, more traditional algorithms that rely on linear (or linearizable) systems would be fine, but nonlinear environments tend to be the norm rather than the exception. Stanislaw Ulam (or perhaps John von Neumann, as the original source is unclear) commented on the relegation of nonlinear systems to a small, esoteric part of mathematics, by equating this to defining the bulk of zoology as the study of non-elephant animals.

Genetic algorithms are a general class of algorithms. Thus, to implement one, choices must be made about how to represent potential solutions, select populations biased by performance, and apply genetic operators.

We want to use a genetic algorithm to drive a general model of complex adaptive systems.[1] Good models, whether they are instantiated in mathematics or computation, should be as simple in construction and as general in application as possible. Thus, the choices we make for the algorithmic options that we will adopt are driven by seeking the simplest elements possible that result in a robust and generally applicable algorithm.

The initial step needed to deploy a genetic algorithm is that of representing the potential solutions. Such representations range from binary encodings of values to more sophisticated encodings of computer programs such as Lisp trees or, here, finite automata. However encoded, good representations tend to share some common characteristics. Namely, they cover the space of potential solutions in a compact way that is both coherent and consistent (see Miller and Page 2007, p. 181).

Good representations must cover a broad class of potential solutions in a compact way. Representations must be rich in possibilities as the solutions that arise often incorporate surprising elements, and thus one should not limit such possibilities unnecessarily. The representation must also be compact to be

---

[1] Most genetic algorithms are used to solve "engineering" problems and thus the emphasis is on tuning the algorithm's parameters to the particular problem at hand, rather than seeking a more generic and robust method capable of solving a wide range of problems.

effective. Compactness requires that the encoding uses a small set of elements that can be recombined to form many potential solutions. Compactness is facilitated by using a set of simple, easily recombined building blocks. For example, consider a Mr. Potato Head toy where one must choose a particular hat, eyes, ears, nose, mouth, arms, and legs, to create a complete figure. Suppose that there are ten different hats, ten different eyes, and so on, implying a total of seventy different pieces. Given ten options for each of the seven choices, how many unique Mr. Potato Heads can be made out of these seventy pieces? Each possible hat choice can combine with each possible eye choice and so on, resulting in a total of $10 \times 10 \times 10 \times 10 \times 10 \times 10 \times 10 = 10^7$ possible Mr. Potato Heads. Thus, seventy pieces lead to ten million possibilities.

Coherence and consistency are also needed for good representations. Coherence implies that any variation of a solution is also a potential solution. Any Mr. Potato Head with a choice of hat, eyes, and so on, creates a recognizable Mr. Potato Head. Of course, that figure may not be to our liking (our aesthetic appreciation can serve as a measure of fitness), but it is still a possible solution. Representations are consistent when neighboring variations are connected to one another. Thus, swapping one hat for another results in a new figure that looks a lot like the previous one. When representations are consistent, small changes result in slightly different solutions. As long as partial solutions give partial answers, having a consistent microstructure to the solution space gives the algorithm a better chance of finding, and fine tuning, better solutions. For example, randomly searching for an integer between 1 and 1,000,000 will, on average, require half a million queries, while being able to ask whether the integer we are seeking is above or below a particular value requires only twenty questions.

Once a representation for the potential solutions has been implemented, the genetic algorithm begins by creating an initial population of randomly generated solutions. The algorithm then starts the first generation by giving each potential solution in the population a measure of fitness derived from testing it on the problem.

In traditional genetic algorithms the fitness measure is given by an exogenous performance measure. For example, in a function-optimization problem, fitness is the value of the function at a particular point in its domain. This fitness is exogenous in the sense that whenever the same solution is proposed, it receives the same performance measure.[2]

A more interesting fitness environment arises when performance is endogenous. In such an environment the fitness of an agent depends on the other agents. For example, in biology the fitness of, say, a gazelle depends on the structure of a cheetah. In evolutionary systems, endogenous fitness leads to coevolution, whereby the evolutionary paths of species become linked—faster cheetahs may result in longer-legged or better-camouflaged gazelles.

Interactions among agents in social systems are inherently coevolutionary. The payoff to an agent of pursuing a particular strategy in a given interaction often depends on the strategies used by the other agents. For example, poker players must adapt their style of play to their opponents—if an opponent is aggressively playing any hand and rarely folding, then pursuing a strategy that relies on bluffing will fail. In general, social systems are ripe with endogenous fitness.

Genetic algorithms have been applied to coevolutionary environments. Miller (1988, 1996) showed that coevolution in the Prisoner's Dilemma discovers strategies similar to the best

---

[2]A slightly more complex exogenous fitness measure might include the addition of some noise, where each evaluation of the function reports its underlying value modified by some random variation.

ones submitted by human experts to Axelrod's (1984) series of tournaments. Hillis (1990) coevolved a set of sorting solutions against a set of sorting problems. He found that the addition of coevolution significantly improved the resulting solutions to the point where they almost bested the top algorithm derived by experts over many decades of research. Andreoni and Miller (1995) explored coevolution in the context of agents acquiring optimal bidding strategies in an auction. They found that systems of adaptive agents coevolving against one another were able to acquire optimal bidding behavior far more effectively than in a non-coevolutionary system where the adaptive bidders faced an exogenous environment composed of near-optimal bidders.

The advantage of coevolution is its ability to provide productive feedback to the agents. In the early stages of coevolution, agents make a lot of errors, resulting in an environment with gentle feedback that encourages even slight improvements in behavior. As the agents improve, so does the coevolutionary environment, allowing the agents to further refine their behaviors.[3]

Once each potential solution in the population has a measure of fitness, a new population is formed by first reproducing solutions biased by performance. There are many ways to implement biased reproduction. For example, in roulette (or lottery) selection each potential solution is given some space on a roulette wheel (or lottery tickets) with the better solutions being given more space (or tickets). The wheel is then spun (or a ticket is drawn) and the winning solution is copied into the new population. Alternatively, in tournament selection two (or more, depending on the parameter) solutions are randomly drawn

---

[3]As an analogy, think about learning how to ride a bike by either using training wheels that are slowly raised over time versus having no assistance of any kind.

(with replacement) from the population and the solution with the higher fitness is copied into the new population. Whatever the selection mechanism, the reproduction procedure is repeated (with replacement) until, typically, the new population is the same size as the old one.

Both of the above reproductive schemes (and many others) bias the selection of the solutions that enter the new population by performance. That is, better performers are more likely to survive into future generations. However, neither scheme guarantees that the best performer will always be reproduced or that the worst performer will be eliminated. For example, there is a chance that tournament selection never picks the best performer during a given generation, eliminating it from the new population, or that it picks the worst performer twice (given replacement) during a step, and includes it. While such behavior may seem problematic, recall that while the algorithm directly reproduces potential solutions, it is indirectly manipulating key patterns or schemata contained within the *entire* population of potential solutions. Thus, the inclusion or exclusion of any particular solution in a given generation is not critical to the functioning of the algorithm.

For the work reported here, we will use tournament selection of size two, that is, we randomly pick two agents (with replacement) and make a copy of the better one (or, if there is a tie, randomly pick one). Tournament selection is a simple way to bias selection by performance. It also has the property that monotonic transformations of the fitness values do not alter its behavior, as tournament selection only relies on the ordering of the payoffs versus their absolute differences.[4]

---

[4]Some parts of social science theory can be derived based solely on ordinal rankings. However, as previously noted, in a repeated game the ordinal comparison of the *accumulated* payoffs may depend on the cardinal values of the single-round payoffs.

Selection biases the new population toward the better-performing solutions in the old population. Since selection is biased by performance and done with replacement, there may be multiple copies of the same solution in the new population. Thus, the new population is an amplification of the previous one, with a tendency to contain multiple copies of the better-performing solutions.

The final step in a genetic algorithm is to introduce some variation into the new population. Typically, each member of the new population has some probability (say, 33%) of receiving some variation. The variation that is introduced into the structures uses analogs of genetic operators found in natural systems. While nature has many such operators, most genetic algorithms rely on mutation and crossover.

Mutation introduces small, random perturbations into a solution without regard for the underlying structure. In the case of Mr. Potato Head, a mutation might randomly pick one of the seven features, and replace it with a randomly chosen piece from the appropriate feature set. Mutations typically make minor alterations to a solution. Unlike most B-movie monsters, where a single mutation creates a giant whatnot that goes on to destroy the city, most mutations are either neutral or detrimental—if you randomly hit a car's engine with a hammer, rarely will the car run better.

Given that mutation is typically detrimental, why is it so common in nature? One answer is that perhaps it is just unavoidable. Nonetheless, even if one could avoid mutation there is a sound basis for its inclusion in a search algorithm. Selection biased by performance, in the absence of any genetic operators, eventually results in a population of homogeneous structures.[5] If all of the structures in a population are identical, the system can no longer explore new configurations and it becomes relegated to exploiting the existing structure. Thus, an important role for mutation is to keep the system from entering such exploitive traps. However, if there is too much mutation the system is unable to maintain promising solutions and it reverts to a random walk across the space of all possibilities, mired in mutational muck. Fortunately, in the experiments performed here and elsewhere, there appear to be large Goldilocks regions of mutation parameters that avoid these two extremes.

Mutation, on rare occasions, results in one of Goldschmidt's (1940) "hopeful monsters." Using the previous car example, occasionally a hammer blow might, say, damage the radiator in such a way that a feasible air-cooled car begins to emerge.

If the space of structural manipulations is relatively small, mutation alone is sufficient to drive productive evolution. Indeed, in the experiments conducted later we only use mutation and the algorithm appears to work well.

Crossover is the other common operator used in genetic algorithms. Crossover introduces variation by swapping larger pieces of the structures. Thus, crossover operates at a higher level than mutation, recombining large coherent parts of the structures versus introducing small random changes. In nature, crossover lines up two structures and randomly selects a common point. It then takes the contiguous part of the first structure before the common point and combines it with the contiguous part of the second structure after that point, and vice versa. Returning back to Mr. Potato Head, crossover might take the hat, eyes, and ears

---

[5]An explicit model of this is given by the Moran process discussed in Appendix C.

of one Mr. Potato Head and combine them with the nose, mouth, arms, and legs of another.

Crossover works by merging potentially productive partial solutions that have been tested by multiple generations of evolution. While the particular location of crossover is random, what is being switched is not. Since the automata used in the experiments that follow are not canonically ordered, crossover is far more disruptive than described above and will not be used.

Genetic algorithms tend to be robust to reasonable variations of the selection mechanism and genetic operators. For example, the notion of selection biased by performance is fairly generic and the algorithm's performance is more tied to having some form of biased selection than the particular implementation of the mechanism itself. Moreover, when genetic algorithms require a particular parametric choice, such as the rate of mutation, there are usually robust sweet spots around such parameters where the algorithm performs well. Of course, extreme choices in the parameters are problematic, but these extremes can be avoided with common sense and simple sensitivity tests.

The algorithmic choices used later are driven by the imperative to keep the model simple and robust. Thus, we will represent potential solutions with a direct and simple encoding of an automaton's structure. We will use tournament selection since it is simple to implement and understand. And, we will use mutation as the only genetic operator, as it was able to generate productive solutions to the set of problems that we investigate and adding crossover did not result in substantially different outcomes.

4.2 Conclusions

Evolution allows populations of potential solutions to "learn" across evolutionary time scales. Selection biased by performance embraces a notion of learning by imitation, where each generation copies either directly or indirectly the better performers from the previous generation. Mutation uses learning by sparks, where a random innovation is tried to see if it results in better performance. Crossover is learning by parts, where large elements of successful solutions are recombined with one another. These learning processes happen at the population level, so while it is difficult to say whether a particular agent is engaged in learning, or even modifying its behavior in some productive way, the population as a whole is doing so, resulting in an arrow of time that moves the system toward better performing agents that have "learned" from the past.[6]

To study the origins of social behavior, we rely on a simple, fundamental force: evolution. Evolutionary forces should be available to systems across vast domains of possible worlds, assuming that the system has the ability to replicate better-performing structures with some variation.[7] The origin story we wish to tell is that of social life versus life itself, so we will assume that the systems we consider have already been, and continue to be, subject to the evolutionary engine. ☙

---

[6]Okasha (2018) provides a detailed discussion of the broader issues of agent thinking in biology.

[7]Fundamental evolutionary forces are recognized in the biblical version of *Genesis*. The first life that emerges is vegetation and there is a notable emphasis on structures replicating with fidelity, and perhaps even variation, namely "yielding seed after its kind," and this notion of "after its kind" continues with the emergence of fish, fowl, and the beasts of the earth. Of course, biased selection is captured by the dictum to "Be fruitful, and multiply."

5

THE COEVOLVING AUTOMATA MODEL (CAM)

A world of automata—of creatures that worked like machines—would hardly be worth creating.

C.S. LEWIS
Mere Christianity (2015)

Here, we combine the ideas from the previous chapters to create a useful methodology for exploring the emergence of complex adaptive social systems. In Chapter 2 we outlined how game theory can provide a framework for studying the interactions of thoughtful agents in environments with the potential for social behavior. In Chapter 3 we showed how automata provide a simple, yet powerful, way to represent thoughtful behavior. And in Chapter 4 we discussed how artificial evolution embodied in a genetic algorithm can be used to create an engine of discovery. It is the combination of these ideas that will allow us to create a model for exploring the emergence of social behavior.

The resulting model is easy to observe, manipulate, and analyze. At times, we will simply observe the millions of interactions among the agents in search of new behaviors that might give us insights into the fundamental forces driving social behavior. At other times, we will take advantage of our ability to manipulate the system and perform computational experiments, altering the environment and agents to improve our understanding of the system in a way that is akin to experimenting on *E. coli* in a petri dish. Throughout the work, when modeling choices arise we will emphasize simple and robust options, given both long-standing scientific imperatives and our desire to establish a useful lower bound on the ability of an adaptive system to create social behavior.

When undertaking computational models, it is important to ground the work by creating touchstones that are easily understood and calibrated. Such opportunities arise in many ways. For example, there are often extreme variants of the model where the system is constrained enough that one can predict its likely behavior, either by intuition or by using analytical methods. Such variants serve as useful "sanity checks." While computational models are often implemented as a way to escape the normal analytic bounds of other scientific methods, applying them to cases that are analytically tractable by normal means provides a way to verify the model, explicate important differences between computational versus conventional assumptions, and increase our confidence in the application of the computational model to realms that cannot be so easily analyzed using conventional means.

The Coevolving Automata Model (CAM) developed here can be applied to any environment composed of thoughtful agents interacting via discrete inputs and outputs. In the analyses in Part II we will emphasize interactions that use the game theory framework discussed in Chapter 2. Game theory has not only developed a structure for exploring interacting, thoughtful agents, but over the last seventy-five years it has identified some quintessential models of social interaction that will provide fodder for our explorations of social origins.

Automata are a useful way to explore strategic interactions in games. They embody a general notion of computation that produces a rich set of possible behaviors that respond to a stream of inputs with a stream of outputs. Automata can interact with one another by cross linking their input and output streams, that is, one automaton's output becomes another automaton's input.

If we interpret inputs and outputs as actions in a game, the interacting automata can model strategic agents playing a repeated game. Initially, agents must choose an action (output) without knowing what their opponent will do, and this is reflected in the output generated by the machine's starting state. These initial actions get fed back as inputs to the players, allowing each machine to react to the previous actions of its opponent. Thus, the interacting automata engage in a repeated game by implementing a strategy that ties each machine's own actions to the observable actions of the opponent.

Automata are also a bespoke mechanism for applying a genetic algorithm. As discussed in Chapter 4, one of the most difficult tasks in designing a genetic algorithm is finding a compact, coherent, and consistent way to represent potential solutions. Automata are compact since they are composed of convenient building blocks (states that have actions and transitions) that easily recombine with one another to create a multitude of possible behaviors. Automata are also coherent, as altering a state's output or transitions always produces another automaton. Finally, automata are consistent, with simple changes to a machine producing a new machine that is often "close" to the old one. In automata, simple changes to a state's action or transitions typically create a new machine with behavior that is similar to that of the original machine, though at times (such as when an altered transition enters a previously inaccessible state) the new machine can produce radically different behavior. Given these features, the use of automata provides a sound way to represent interacting strategic agents in a genetic algorithm.

There are many ways to encode an automaton for the genetic algorithm. Here, we will use a high-level[1] representation where each aspect of the automaton is encoded directly by its value. For example, each state's output will be an integer and its transition function will be composed of an ordered set of integers that indicates the transition state given a particular input. Mutation will consist of randomly selecting a state and either altering its action or one of its transition function entries.

In the CAM, automata will have a predetermined number of nominal states. As discussed in Chapter 3, the number of nominal states sets an upper bound on the number of potential computations that a machine can produce. The actual computation performed by a machine is tied to its accessible states, and even this measure may exceed the minimized number of states needed to perform the computation if there is any redundancy. We leave it to the algorithm to determine the number of accessible states and the degree of redundancy that will be used in the evolving machines.

While at some level inaccessible and redundant states represent "computational waste," evolutionary systems may benefit from such waste. For example, inaccessible states may harbor neutral mutations that can be exploited by evolution, or redundant states might make a machine more robust to mutations and even enhance its evolvability in certain environments.

The automata in the CAM use a simple encoding (see fig. 5.1). States are numbered (using integers) from left to right starting at 0 and the automaton always begins in the left-most state (state 0). Associated with each state is an output and a transition function.

---

[1]While the initial work on genetic algorithms (Holland 1975) suggested that binary encodings are advantageous in terms of the number of potential patterns (schemata) that can be searched, in practice, higher-level representations typically perform well and are easier to implement and analyze.

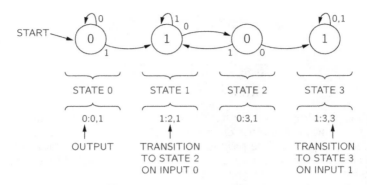

Figure 5.1. A simple encoding for representing an automaton. The automaton is encoded as a string of symbols: 0:0,1 1:2,1 0:3,1 1:3,3. This list is ordered left to right by state, here going from states 0 to 3. Thus, the machine in the figure can use at most four states. Machines always begin in state 0. The associated output of any state is given by the symbol at the start of the encoding for that state (here, either 0 or 1). The encoding then gives the transition function ordered by the possible inputs. Thus, state 2's coding of 0:3,1 indicates that it outputs a 0 when it enters that state, and transitions to state 3 if the input is a 0 or state 1 if the input is a 1.

The output gives the symbol that the machine sends on entering that state and the transitions, one for each possible input symbol, give the next state that the machine will enter given the associated input. This next state can be any possible state of the machine, including the current one. In the context of game theory, we interpret outputs as actions in a game, so the set of possible output and input symbols represents the respective actions taken by the machine and its opponent.

Genetic algorithms search over the set of possible solutions using a measure of "fitness" to guide the search. Fitness is key to the nonrandom selection (of the randomly varying replicators) that drives evolution. In biology, fitness provides a measure of likely reproductive success. In social science, rather than fitness *per se*, some notion of payoff or utility often drives behavior. Game theory uses a payoff matrix that links the mutual actions of the

		COLUMN PLAYER	
		$0(c)$	$1(d)$
ROW	$0(C)$	R, R	S, T
PLAYER	$1(D)$	T, S	P, P

Table 5.1. Payoff matrix for Prisoner's Dilemma. Both the row and column players must choose to either cooperate (output 0) or defect (output 1). The payoffs are given by the ordered pairs in the table separated by commas, with the first value going to the row player and the second going to the column player. In a Prisoner's Dilemma, the symbolic payoffs are known as the Reward (R), Sucker (S), Temptation (T), and Punishment (P). A Prisoner's Dilemma requires that $T > R > P > S$ and $R > (T + S)/2$ (this latter condition prevents alternating plays of cooperation and defection from giving a higher expected payoff than mutual cooperation does). A typical set of cardinal values for a Prisoner's Dilemma is $T = 5$, $R = 3$, $P = 1$, and $S = 0$. Thus, if the row player does $0(C)$ and the column player does $1(d)$, their respective payoffs will be 0 and 5.

players to a set of individual payoffs. Table 5.1 shows the payoff matrix for the Prisoner's Dilemma.

As discussed in Chapter 2, while the generic payoff structure of a game is typically defined by an ordering of the payoff values, when games are played repeatedly the cardinal values of the payoffs become important. In the work that follows, we analyze the behavior of the system as we sweep across different regions of the cardinal values that meet the ordinal criteria for a given game. As will be seen, behavior in a given game often differs depending on the specific payoff values.

Many of the studies that follow use repeated games. In a repeated game, players are matched together and undertake a series of one-shot games with the same opponent over a number of rounds. During each round the players receive their respective payoffs from the joint actions taken in the one-shot game. At the end of each round players know their own action and that of their opponent, and this information gets incorporated into each player's next state (and action) for the next round. Each player's final payoff from the repeated game is given by its accumulated payoffs across all rounds.

We will assume that the only information each player gets about its opponents is what action they took in the previous round of play. This, by design, provides players with a minimum of information. For example, more sophisticated agents might be able to recognize previous opponents and recall how they played the game, and then condition their own play based on this information. Nonetheless, our imperative to consider a primitive model of social origins does not admit this possibility.

5.1 Coevolutionary Learning

Unless otherwise stated, in what follows the genetic algorithm acts on two separate populations of forty automata each.[2] As discussed in Chapter 6, coevolving two separate populations likely increases the difficulty of the system acquiring social behavior. It also allows a broader range of games to be included in the analyses.

Each population is initiated by creating random automata of a fixed number of nominal states with the appropriate set of input and output symbols needed for the given experiment. At the start of every generation each automaton's payoff is set to 0. Then, each automaton from one population interacts pair-wise with every automaton from the other population, all the while accumulating payoffs from each encounter. In such a world the fitness of an automaton is endogenous or coevolutionary, since the payoff received by a machine depends on the machines in the other

---

[2] The choice of population size may be important, as excessively small or large populations can alter the evolutionary dynamics. If the population size is too small, populations may rapidly converge and lose diversity. Large populations may be slow to converge and require large amounts of computational resources. Forty agents in each population appears to be a robust choice that avoids these extremes.

population. Thus, a machine may receive very different payoffs depending on the composition of the other population.

As discussed in Chapter 4, coevolutionary systems can be a productive way for agents to learn how to adapt in novel environments. Such systems begin with a set of agents that are poorly adapted. Thus, when the agents initially interact they do so in a gentle environment that is relatively forgiving of missteps. This provides an opportunity for agents to receive feedback about what broad classes of behaviors might lead to good outcomes. As the agents improve so does the environment, providing a more exacting test of behavior.

Coevolution can refine an agent's behavior to a high level. An analog to coevolutionary dynamics can be found in learning to play tennis. Suppose a novice tries to learn the game from an expert who shows no mercy. In such a world the novice rarely has the opportunity for productive feedback, as either they never get to hit the ball or the ball hits them. Alternatively, consider two novices playing tennis together. During such a game, while many of the hits are errant, there are opportunities for the players to return some slow-moving, high-bouncing balls, and by doing so improve their play. As the skills of the players increase so does the quality of the game, allowing them to further refine their skills. Similarly, coevolution is a natural means by which agents can receive modulated, productive feedback that will facilitate adaptive learning.

5.2 Creating New Populations

Once agents receive their payoffs, the genetic algorithm requires the selection of new populations biased by performance. The CAM uses tournament selection to achieve this end. In tournament selection a fixed number of agents (typically two) are drawn (with replacement) from the population and a copy of the one with the higher fitness is placed in the new population (if they have the same fitness, one is randomly selected). Tournament selection, as well as being simple to implement and understand, has the advantage that it is only the relative (ordinal) fitness of the agents that matters (some popular alternative mechanisms, like roulette selection, rely on cardinal values). Ordinal versus cardinal comparisons can be important, as there are large parts of social theory based on ordinal payoffs, such as modern utility theory, where preferences are specified up to a monotonic transformation. However, in repeated games where payoffs are accumulated over rounds, the cardinality of the payoffs is relevant.

After selecting a new population of machines biased by performance, the next step in the algorithm requires randomly modifying some of the machines using genetic operators. In the CAM, each structure in the new population is (typically[3]) modified with a probability of 33%. Thus, a third of the new population will, on average, undergo genetic operators that might produce a randomly varying replicant.

While there are many possible genetic operators that can be used in a genetic algorithm, the CAM only uses mutation. In the context of our automata, mutation consists of randomly selecting a state of the machine and probabilistically deciding whether to modify that state's action or one of its transitions (these two possibilities are given equal weight in the CAM). If the action is selected for modification, a new action is uniformly randomly drawn from the entire set of possible outputs. If a transition is selected, one of the potential inputs is uniformly randomly selected and then a new transition state for that input is uniformly randomly chosen among all possible states. Given that the random

---

[3] Manipulating the mutation rate can be useful during the analysis of a CAM. For example, setting the mutation rate very low, while slowing the overall rate of evolution, provides a useful way to identify key mutations that initiate particular system-wide transitions.

draws happen across the entire set of either actions or transition states, there is the possibility that the resulting structure remains unchanged. Thus, the effective rate of mutation is below the 33% stated above.

The mutation operator used here performs a single mutation per machine regardless of its size. Given the potential for more inaccessible states in larger machines, such mutations tend to disrupt the behavior of smaller machines far more often than larger ones. One could use a mutation operator that is tied to the number of states. For example, each state could have a constant probability of being mutated. A single mutation per machine is obviously a simpler mechanism, though it does imply that in worlds with more inaccessible states, mutations are more likely to be neutral. Obviously, it is easy to alter this or any of the CAM's assumptions to explore how such changes impact the system's behavior.

Genetic algorithms typically use more than just mutation as a genetic operator. In particular, most incorporate a crossover operator. Crossover creates new structures by recombining large contiguous parts of existing structures. Unlike the randomness introduced by mutation, crossover entwines larger structural "themes" across machines.

We do not use crossover in the CAM for many reasons. First, we follow the imperative to keep the model as simple as possible—introducing another operator like crossover complicates both the underlying story (given the more elaborate mechanism) and the analyses (single mutations are easier to track). More importantly, the automata we are searching over are relatively low-dimensional, requiring only an output and a small set of transitions to be specified per state. Thus, a single mutation has the potential to make a real change within a given machine. Finally, the automata we use are not canonically ordered, other than sharing the same start state, so the sequence of states used in a machine is typically one of many possible permutations. Under such circumstances, crossover is likely to result in a mélange of states that preserves little structure or behavioral themes from either of the parents. (In earlier versions of the model we included crossover and it made little difference.)

5.3 Evolving Productive Automata

The CAM relies on being able to coevolve productive automata using a genetic algorithm. As a proof of principle of this idea, in Appendix F we analyze how a basic variant of the CAM performs in some simple experiments. We find that in these experiments the CAM generates productive automata, thereby giving us increased confidence in our results when we apply the full model to understanding social origins.

The success of these experiments (and, through the years, many other experiments) and the face validity of the machines that evolve in the work that follows, suggest that the overall methodology of coevolving automata using a genetic algorithm is a sound approach for adapting machines to respond productively to a stream of discrete inputs with an appropriate stream of discrete outputs. The previous experiments also provide a demonstration of how larger-sized automata influence the adaptive search and that, at least at the sizes that will be explored here, the system seems well behaved. Finally, we find that the simplified CAM used above is not only robust to coevolution, it actually thrives on it.

5.4 Conclusions

The CAM produces a new scientific instrument that will allow us to explore the origins of social behavior. Automata represent a simple, observable, and manipulable notion of information processing or choice making. Allowing automata to interact with one another by taking actions with payoff consequences ties the system into the framework of game theory. Finally, driving the system using artificial evolution embraces a well-tested, productive, and fundamental force of nature that is easy to posit as being present once life has the potential to become social.

The CAM is a powerful way to explore the emergence of thoughtful behavior in a complex adaptive social system. Given the inherent complexity and dynamic nature of social systems, many of the standard analytic techniques from the social sciences are of limited value, and even simplified dynamic models of evolutionary systems (see Appendix C) are easily confounded. The CAM creates an artificial world that we can easily observe and experiment on to improve our understanding of complex adaptive social systems (Holland and Miller 1991). One advantage of this approach vis-à-vis standard observational techniques is that any time an anomalous or otherwise interesting phenomenon arises, the system can be rerun with additional observational probes and experiments to develop and test new hypotheses about the system's behavior. The ability to intensively observe and experiment on these systems provides a unique window into understanding the model's behavior and, in that process, developing new insights into real-world systems.

Adaptation in the model takes place over evolutionary time scales. While no individual agent thoughtfully reconsiders its choices in an attempt to alter its decision making and improve its performance, the system as a whole does so across the generations. Of course, many organisms do have the ability (derived by evolution!) to think about their thinking and, by doing so, improve their choices over short time scales. While various models of this "more" evolved thinking exist, given our focus on the origins of social behavior and our desire to minimize the assumptions needed in our system, we rely solely on simple evolutionary principles to drive agent adaptation. The various experiments performed in Appendix F provide a proof of concept that evolving automata can solve problems similar to those that social agents might encounter.

In the chapters that follow we apply the CAM and explore the origins of social behavior. Each chapter focuses on a particular aspect of social behavior where the agents in the system can either embrace social behavior or not. The main question we pursue is what drives our system into regimes of recognizable social behavior. Of particular interest is how the potential for social behavior is tied to three fundamental elements: 1) the processing capability of the agents given by the size of the automata, 2) the amount of interaction among the agents given by the repeated rounds of play, and 3) the underlying conditions that define an environment given by the specific payoff parameters. At the outset, the hope is that these three elements will help explain not only the emergence of particular types of social behavior in the model, but also the origins of social behavior more generally. ❦

PART II:
SOCIAL ORIGINS

EMERGING SOCIAL BEHAVIOR

Consider ye the seed from which ye sprang;
Ye were not made to live like unto brutes,
But for pursuit of virtue and of knowledge.

DANTE ALIGHIERI
The Divine Comedy: Inferno Canto XXVI (1867)

What are the fundamental conditions that allow social life to emerge? In Chapter 1 we outlined the Four C's of social behavior: conflict, coordination, cooperation, and commerce, as well as the role of communication in mediating such interactions.

To explore the emergence of social behavior, we will apply the Coevolving Automata Model (CAM) outlined in Part I to a variety of potentially social environments. Most of these environments are drawn from key social science models arising in game theory, and they are constructed so that there are innate incentives that favor asocial outcomes, making the emergence of social behavior challenging.

We apply the CAM to understand how systems of primitive information-processing agents coevolve in such environments. We will find that these systems of automata often display long epochs of stable behavior, punctuated by rapid transitions to new epochs. By carefully observing and analyzing both the epochs and the transitions, we will develop an understanding of the origins of social behavior.[4]

---

[4]Appendix C provides additional discussion about analyzing coevolutionary systems with CAMs and other formal models.

Like all scientific models, implementation choices may matter. When making the various parametric and algorithmic choices needed to implement the CAM, we will default to simple, reasonable, and robust options. Fortunately, in evolutionary models such as the CAM, parameters typically reside in large equivalence classes, implying that non-extreme variations will result in similar behavior. Of course, one advantage of the computational approach is that it is easy to test alternative formulations of the model.[5]

---

[5] There are also automated techniques such as Active Nonlinear Testing (Miller 1998) that can be used to, among other things, stress the model in various ways, identify nonlinear sensitivities, and discover unusual regimes of behavior.

6

A COEVOLVING AUTOMATA MODEL (CAM) FOR SOCIAL ORIGINS

If it was truly a new route over the mountain it's certainly a needed one. For more than three centuries now the old routes common in this hemisphere have been undercut and almost washed out by the natural erosion and change of the shape of the mountain wrought by scientific truth. The early climbers established paths that were on firm ground with an accessibility that appealed to all, but today the Western routes are all but closed because of dogmatic inflexibility in the face of change. . . . But the fact that the old routes have tended, because of language rigidity, to lose their everyday meaning and become almost closed doesn't mean that the mountain is no longer there.

ROBERT M. PIRSIG

Zen and the Art of Motorcycle Maintenance: An Inquiry Into Values (1974)

Throughout the studies in this book we rely on a variant of the Coevolving Automata Model (CAM) developed in Part I. Across these studies we find that the CAM generates systems that fall into epochs of consistent behavior. We also find that there are rapid transitions between these epochs, with neighboring epochs often embracing radically different behaviors. Given that the system is driven by incremental changes due to evolution, such rapid and radical transitions are surprising, and in section 6.3 we illuminate a key motif that explains such transitions.

6.1 The Model

Unless otherwise stated, the CAM used in the subsequent chapters has the following form. During each generation, two populations of forty automata interact with one another. This interaction takes the form of a tournament, wherein each member of one population interacts one-on-one with every member of the other population. Each interaction involves a repeated game of fixed length, with agents in one population acting as the row and agents in the other population acting as the column players.

Social behavior may be facilitated by nontrivial interactions, so the ability to "recognize" whom one is interacting with—either through repeated play or some other observable signal—might matter.[1] While in a more advanced model agents might be able to recognize each opponent and recall the previous history of play, here the only information an agent gets about its opponent is the stream of actions that the opponent takes during the current game. This information stream, while quite limited, is consistent with our emphasis on a minimal set of assumptions to explore social origins. Agents respond to the actions of others when the output (action) of one automaton serves as the input to the other and vice versa.

---

[1] Our assumption of pairwise tournaments of repeated games between populations of agents is, obviously, one of many possible ways to have agents interact. The process of how interactions arise in the first place is of interest to the core question of origins. For example, the emergence of agent mobility or stickiness (either to the substrate or to one another) might facilitate social behavior. Such ideas are amenable to exploration by, say, connecting CAM agents via different network topologies, providing a "geographic" space that agents can traverse, and so on.

During each interaction, the joint outputs (actions) of the automata determine each agent's payoff. These payoffs are accumulated over the rounds in a game and over the games in the tournament, ultimately resulting in a "fitness" measure for each agent that is used during the selection step in the genetic algorithm.

Coevolving two populations should increase the difficulty of developing social behavior. Kin selection may be a useful mechanism for driving social behavior—providing high payoffs to closely related kin is equivalent to helping one's self—and having two separately evolving populations makes this more difficult. Single-population systems are also more favorable to those types of social behavior that require a critical mass of agents. In such systems, if the needed social behavior arises in one of the individuals, that individual may survive and be reproduced, and this might lead to enough of a critical mass that the new behavior takes over the population. However, with two coevolving populations, this path to emergence is more difficult as the social behavior must emerge simultaneously, and be maintained, in both populations. Finally, coevolving two populations allows for models where the agent interactions are asymmetric, for example, agents might occupy very different roles in a system.

At the end of the tournament each population is evolved separately. We use the CAM procedures outlined in Chapter 5. Thus, selection involves randomly drawing two machines (with replacement) from the same population and placing a copy of the machine with the higher accumulated payoff into a new population. This procedure is repeated forty times for each population, ensuring that the new populations are the same size as the old ones. As discussed in Chapter 4, this tournament selection mechanism does not guarantee that the best automaton is always reproduced (there is a chance that it never gets selected in the pairings) or that the worst one is eliminated (the selection mechanism might draw the worst automaton twice), though it does bias the new population toward those machines that received higher accumulated payoffs.

Each newly created automaton has a 33% chance of being modified by a single mutation. When undergoing mutation a randomly selected state of the machine is chosen and it is either assigned a random action or has a randomly chosen transition redirected to a randomly chosen state. Half of the time, mutation alters the action of a state, otherwise a transition is modified. Note that these random changes are done with replacement, so there is a chance that a mutated machine is identical to its parent, thus the actual modification rate is lower than the nominal rate of 33%.[2]

Once the new populations of automata have been reproduced and modified, each machine's payoff is reset to zero, a new generation begins, and the above procedures are iterated.

6.1.1   KEY PARAMETERS

To investigate the emergence of social behavior, we use the CAM to explore the coevolution of agent behavior across various games with social potential. The games will emphasize different fundamental social behaviors and are drawn from the existing literature (see Chapter 2) or derived using basic principles. Most of the games were explicitly designed to make achieving social behavior difficult, as they contain innate incentives that discourage the emergence of productive social outcomes. Indeed,

---

[2]For example, if there are two possible actions and three possible states, the machine remains unchanged 1/2 of the time when an action is mutated and 1/3 of the time when a transition is mutated.

the reason why these games are so prominent in the literature is likely due to this underlying design. Thus, the games we explore provide an appropriate, albeit difficult, environment from which to observe the origins of social behavior.

The analyses focus on three key parameters. As discussed in Chapter 1, social behavior requires interacting, choice-making agents. The first parameter focuses on the ability of an agent to make choices, given by the size of the automaton. As we saw in Chapter 3, as the number of states in an automaton increases so does its ability to process information and make more refined choices. The second parameter captures the notion of interaction, operationalized by the number of rounds being played in each repeated game. As the number of rounds increases the agents can refine their responses to a given opponent. Finally, we parameterize each game's payoff values to explore the underlying environment. As discussed in Chapter 2, the cardinal values of payoffs become important when games are repeated and thus there is the possibility that within a given class of games the emergence of social behavior is tied to specific payoff values. Our working hypothesis is that the origins of social behavior likely depend on all three of these parameters.

In the analyses to come we will explore these key parameters. We will consider machine sizes ranging from one to five states. We will allow repeated interactions of one, four, and ten rounds.[3] And, we will sweep through reasonable sets of payoff parameters, constrained so that the payoffs always maintain the underlying structure that defines the one-shot game.

---

[3] These were chosen *a priori* to represent low, moderate, and high levels of interaction.

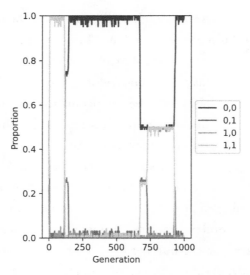

Figure 6.1. The epochal nature of CAMs. A run of a CAM with three-state machines playing a four-round Battle of the Sexes using a low mutation rate. The game is designed so that the agents wish to coordinate on either the $\{0,0\}$ or $\{1,1\}$ outcomes, but the two populations differ on which outcome they prefer. Over the thousand generations of the algorithm the system spends most of its time trapped in epochs characterized by a steady state of actions (the proportion of each action-pair during a given generation is given by the y-axis), punctuated by short transitions that move the system between epochs. Note that in the epoch that starts around generation 750 the outcomes during each generation are roughly split between $\{0,0\}$ and $\{1,1\}$. *Please refer to the Github repository (https://github.com/SantaFeInstitute/ExMachina) for full-sized, full-color versions of all images in this book.*

6.2   Behavioral Epochs

In general, the CAM generates systems that quickly form epochs composed of contiguous generations where the behavior of the interacting machines results in a steady state of actions (see fig. 6.1). Epochs can vary in length and are disrupted by occasional transitions that, often within only a few generations, alter the steady-state behaviors of the machines and move the system into a new epoch.

To identify epochs, we track the frequencies of the joint outputs of the machines during each generation and look for significant deviations in these frequencies from one generation to the next. We consider a deviation significant if there is more than a 10% difference in any of the output frequencies when compared to the mean frequency of the ongoing epoch. Epochs begin whenever five consecutive generations of insignificant deviations occur, with the starting generation of the epoch being set to the first of these five generations. Epochs end whenever five consecutive generations of significant deviations are recorded, with the ending generation set to the onset of the deviations.

We classify epochs by grouping together those that have similar output frequencies. Since epochs are defined by observed behavior rather than the underlying machines, it is possible for the structures of the underlying machines to differ within a given epoch or between two epochs that are classified as the same. For example, a world filled with Tit-For-Tat machines that begin by sending a 0 and then mimicking the last output of the opponent and one filled with machines that always send a 0 result in identical outputs being observed (sets of {0,0} outputs at every interaction), but these worlds have very different evolutionary potentials. Generations not in an epoch are considered transitional, and we find that transition periods tend to be relatively brief. The epochs that arise after a transition may be either the same as, or quite different from, the prior epoch.

For any given set of parameters, we run a *single* 10,000 generation CAM using the aforementioned procedures, and then present a summary of the actions that were observed across all 10,000 generations. The choice of a single run of 10,000 generations was dictated by the notion that the aggregate behavior of many agent-based systems often resembles a Markov chain (Banisch 2016). Thus, a single long-generation experiment should be sufficient for the system to display its characteristic behavior. (In essence, the memory of these systems is captured by the current populations of automata.)

The epochal nature of the system presents some challenges for interpreting the results of a single long-generation experiment. One challenge is that looking at the aggregate actions may obscure important underlying dynamics. For example, suppose we observe a system where, in aggregate, half of the time agents take actions {0,0} and the other half they take {1,1}. Such behavior could arise in various ways, including the system having two types of epochs, one where only {0,0} is played and the other where only {1,1} is played, or the machines could be in a single epoch where the machines alternate between {0,0} and {1,1} after each repeated round. While these two systems are quite different, their aggregate actions are identical.

Another challenge is that instead of the system experiencing a continuous stream of epochs and transitions, it might fall into a single long-lived epoch. If the formation of this epoch takes many generations, for example, it requires a rare set of stochastic events that, once they occur, the system remains locked into the resulting epoch for all subsequent generations, the overall aggregate behavior may not reflect this dynamic.

A more insidious possibility arises if the system locks into one of multiple possible steady states. Under these circumstances, each run of the experiment may break the symmetry in different ways leading to very different observations of the aggregate actions depending on the run. Fortunately, the observed behavior of these latter systems is often easy to recognize, either by looking for symmetries in the game or noticing dramatic differences in outcomes across neighboring sets of payoff parameters.

If the system is characterized by relatively short epochs, then the behavioral differences between one long-generation experiment and multiple short-generation experiments are negligible. Sometimes, there may be systems that require a long preamble of events before a particular epoch emerges and, if so, such behavior is more likely to arise during a long-generation experiment. Systems characterized by multiple lock-in states are more likely to be revealed in multiple experiments.

Finally, experiments designed to illuminate particular features of the system are also conducted. For example, the transitions between epochs are of interest as they can provide the spark needed to transform an asocial system into a social one. Often, these transitions are counterintuitive as they rapidly and radically transform the system's behavior, even though they are driven by small evolutionary changes. The various transitions detailed in the subsequent chapters represent convenience samples, often derived from watching multiple runs and identifying useful examples of a given type of transition. The transitions that are shown are not hard to generate using this method and, while the exact details from one transition to the next may vary, they can be generalized.[4]

When discussing the mechanisms behind a given transition, we occasionally take a "natural" history approach and carefully trace particular sets of strategies. This is both useful, as it provides a specific example of what drives coevolutionary transitions and, occasionally, tedious. We include these discussions as a concrete example—especially in the somewhat alien context of interacting and evolving computing machines—of how such systems transform. It is one thing to know that ecosystems have apex predators, it is another to know the details about the lives of tigers and great white sharks. Nonetheless, the natural history

---

[4]One technique that is particularly useful for understanding transitions is to suppress the mutation rate. This reduces the background noise from mutation and allows the key mutations that drive the transition to be more easily identified. Such experiments are noted in the text when they are used.

discussions tied to transitions can be appreciated even if the details are not—these passages should be read at whatever level of detail is of most use to the reader.

6.3 On Transitions

One general finding from the CAM is that it tends to be dominated by long epochs of consistent behavior punctuated by brief periods of transition that move the system from one epoch to another. Such transitions are a key driver of the system's overall behavior, and therefore understanding how they work is important.

These transitions are perplexing for at least two reasons. First, they cause a seemingly stable system to be rapidly transformed by a series of small coevolutionary changes—revolution by gradual evolution. Epochs that last for hundreds of generations can be disrupted by transitions that last for only a few generations. Second, many of these transitions are quite extreme, such as when an epoch that strongly favors one population gets transformed into an epoch that strongly favors the other. How does evolution "allow" the system to flip between such extremes?

Understanding these transitions has both theoretical and practical importance. On the theoretical side, the origins of social behavior may be tied to such transitions. If so, insights into how transitions occur might give us clues into how social behavior came to be. On the practical side, real social systems often undergo dramatic changes, ranging from revolutions such as the Arab Spring, to radical changes in social norms like the public acceptance of same-sex marriage or marijuana consumption, to the collapse of entire societies (see, for example, Diamond 2005). Understanding the model's transitions may give us insights into the mechanisms behind such real-world social upheavals.

A key advantage of the CAM is that when an extreme transition happens we can rewind the tape and rerun the model, adding whatever additional probes are needed to reveal previously ignored, but ultimately important, factors. This technique was used to develop the theory of extreme transitions that we now present.

Extreme transitions between two epochs with remarkably different behaviors provide interesting insights into both the power and subtlety of coevolving systems.[5] Prior to the transition, the system is composed of two homogeneous populations of simple agents, one of which dominates the other. The two populations are such that there are no other types of agents that could do better than the existing agents given the homogeneous composition of the other population, and thus the system appears to be trapped in its current state.

However, the emergence of an *environmentally* neutral (see sec. 3.2.1) agent in the dominant population can alter the system. This mutant behaves identically to the dominant incumbents in the presence of the subordinate population, and thus through neutral drift it can come to inhabit a nontrivial proportion of the dominant population.

To the outside observer the behavior of the system has not changed, even though the presence of the neutral invader in the dominant population has created a new and, as yet, unexploited niche. The first outward sign of an imminent transition occurs when this newly created niche begins to be exploited by a new mutant in the subordinate population that begins to alter the

---

[5] The notion of evolutionary transitions is encapsulated in more static concepts like Evolutionary Stable Strategies (ESS). For example, ESS consider the invasion of a population of incumbents by a single mutant. The CAM creates a much more complex and dynamic environment, with two coevolving populations, and the potential for multiple waves of change to destabilize the system.

environment facing the dominant population. Prior to the new niche this new mutant was not viable in its own population, but now it can outcompete its incumbent by inducing the previously neutral invader to behave in a more amenable way.

The rise of this new mutant in the subordinate population creates, in turn, another niche that is exploited by the previously environmentally neutral, but now superior, mutant in the dominant population.[6] Thus, in short order the exploitation of these two new, self-reinforcing niches by mutants rapidly transforms both populations, resulting in the system embracing a radically different behavior. Finally, there may be a consolidation phase whereby the two populations settle anew on homogeneous sets of simple agents that capture the behavioral essence of the conquering mutants. This extreme transition motif is shown in figure 6.2.

Table 6.1 provides a more formal account of this extreme transition. Assume, without loss of generality, that population 0 is composed of $P_\alpha = P$ dominant machines, α, and population 1 contains $P_\beta = P$ subordinate machines, β, where P_i is the number of machines of type i and P is the total population size in each population. Let $\Pi_{i,j}$ give the payoff to a machine of type i when playing a machine of type j. Prior to the transition, given dominance, we have $\Pi_{\alpha,\beta} > \Pi_{\beta,\alpha}$.[7] Furthermore, given the stable nature of these populations, we know that there are no other machines that could do better than the incumbent machines, that is, $\Pi_{\alpha,\beta} \geq \Pi_{\sim\alpha,\beta}$ and $\Pi_{\beta,\alpha} \geq$

---

[6]Since the environmentally neutral agent's fitness becomes higher than its incumbent's fitness in the presence of the new mutant from the subordinate population, even if the new mutant arises too early and is nonviable it still enhances the drift of the environmentally neutral agent.

[7]Since each population evolves based on only its own payoffs, cross-population payoff comparisons do not impact the coevolutionary dynamics. They are highlighted here to make the eventual transition in fortunes across the two populations more obvious.

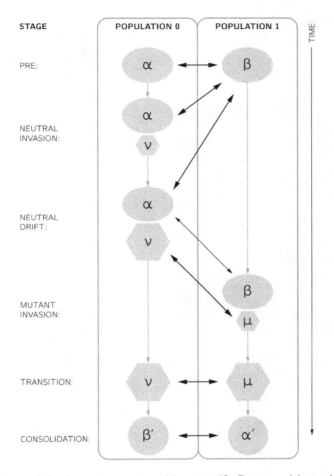

Figure 6.2. An extreme transition motif. Pre-transition, the two populations have stabilized in an epoch where neither population can be directly invaded by mutants. Next, an *environmentally* neutral (relative to the current composition of population 1) mutant, ν, arises in population 0. If the proportion of this mutant in population 0 increases enough through neutral drift it can open up a new and unexploited niche for population 1, setting the stage for a rapid transition. This occurs when a previously untenable mutant, μ, emerges in population 1. This mutant, by sending different inputs, exploits ν's non-neutral *structural* behavior and displaces β in population 1. As μ grows it, in turn, creates a new niche for ν, allowing ν to grow and displace α. As the new epoch begins, the previously subordinate population is now dominant and there may be further consolidations of the machines into simpler forms that embrace the newly acquired behaviors.

PHASE	POPULATION 0	CONDITIONS	POPULATION 1
Pre-Transition	α (dominant) $(P_\alpha = P)$	$\Pi_{\alpha,\beta} > \Pi_{\beta,\alpha}$ $\Pi_{\alpha,\beta} \geq \Pi_{\sim\alpha,\beta}$ and $\Pi_{\beta,\alpha} \geq \Pi_{\sim\beta,\alpha}$	β (subordinate) $(P_\beta = P)$
Emergence of a Neutral Machine	α ν (neutral) $(P_\alpha = P - 1, P_\nu = 1)$	$\Pi_{\alpha,\beta} = \Pi_{\nu,\beta} > \Pi_{\beta,\alpha} = \Pi_{\beta,\nu}$	β $(P_\beta = P)$
Neutral Drift	$(P_\alpha = P - \delta, P_\nu = \delta)$		$(P_\beta = P)$
Emergence of a Mutant Invader	α ν $(P_\alpha = P - \delta, P_\nu = \delta)$	$\Pi_{\nu,\mu} > \Pi_{\alpha,\mu}$ $\frac{P_\alpha \Pi_{\mu,\alpha} + P_\nu \Pi_{\mu,\nu}}{P} > \Pi_{\beta,\alpha} = \Pi_{\beta,\nu}$	β μ (invader) $(P_\beta = P - 1, P_\mu = 1)$
Invasion	ν $(P_\nu = P)$		μ $(P_\mu = P)$
Consolidation	β' (subordinate) $(P_{\beta'} = P)$	$\Pi_{\beta',\alpha'} < \Pi_{\alpha',\beta'}$ $\Pi_{\beta',\alpha'} \geq \Pi_{\sim\beta',\alpha'}$ and $\Pi_{\alpha',\beta'} \geq \Pi_{\sim\alpha',\beta'}$	α' (dominant) $(P_{\alpha'} = P)$

Table 6.1. A transition where the dominant and subordinate populations switch roles. Prior to the transition, population 0 is composed of only αs, which receive a higher payoff than the βs composing population 1, and neither population can be directly invaded by an alternative strategy (designated by $\sim$). An environmentally neutral (given the current composition of population 1) mutant, ν, in population 0 eventually becomes a nontrivial proportion of that population via neutral drift. This sets the stage for population 1 to be invaded by a mutant, μ, that outcompetes β by inducing ν to behave in a non-neutral way. This results in both populations being taken over by their respective mutants. Finally, the populations are consolidated resulting in population 0 now being composed of subordinate machines, β', to the dominant α' machines in population 1.

$\Pi_{\sim\beta,\alpha}$, where $\sim X$ implies all machines other than X. Thus, prior to the transition the system is in a stable configuration with one population outperforming the other.

The start of a transition is marked by the invasion of the dominant population by an environmentally neutral mutant, ν. This mutant encounters only β and thus behaves identically to α, implying $\Pi_{\alpha,\beta} = \Pi_{\nu,\beta} > \Pi_{\beta,\alpha} = \Pi_{\beta,\nu}$. Since α and ν receive the same payoffs, there is a chance that during reproduction the population size of ν increases to δ (indeed, without any further mutations, there is a $1/P$ chance that ν takes over the entire population). Up to this point, other than the growth of ν, the behavior resulting from the two interacting populations is identical to that observed prior to the emergence of ν. Thus, while the underlying system has been fundamentally changed, its outward behavior is unchanged. However, if enough neutral drift is realized, the stage is set for the system's behavior to change.

The observable transition is catalyzed by the emergence of a mutant invader, μ, in population 1. Prior to ν, the β-machines were stronger than (or at least as good as) μ, given the earlier requirement that $\Pi_{\beta,\alpha} \geq \Pi_{\sim\beta,\alpha}$. But the increased presence of ν has changed the evolutionary landscape by opening up a new niche. For μ to grow, $\frac{P_\alpha \Pi_{\mu,\alpha} + P_\nu \Pi_{\mu,\nu}}{P} > \Pi_{\beta,\alpha} = \Pi_{\beta,\nu}$, where the first term gives μ's payoff when facing population 0. We also need ν to survive, requiring $\Pi_{\nu,\mu} > \Pi_{\alpha,\mu}$.

Given these conditions, both ν and μ outcompete their respective incumbent machines, with ν driving α out of population 0 and μ driving β out of population 1. Finally, given the extreme nature of the transition we are modeling, we assume that $\Pi_{\nu,\mu} < \Pi_{\mu,\nu}$, that is, the system is now in a state where the machines in population 1 outperform those in population 0. Less severe transitions can be captured by relaxing some of the prior assumptions.

The final phase of the transition is a consolidation of the machine types in each population. In this phase, new mutants arise in each population that embody the behaviors of the mutants that took over both populations, but in a simplified form. These simplified machines are evolutionarily advantageous as they can avoid unintended consequences due to errant mutations or unexpected behaviors on the part of their opponents.

6.3.1 AN EXAMPLE OF AN EXTREME TRANSITION

An extreme transition of the type discussed above can occur in the repeated Battle of the Sexes. In this game there are two coordinated equilibria each favored by a different population, and both preferred over not coordinating. For example, suppose that agents in population 0 prefer the {0,0} equilibrium while those in population 1 prefer {1,1}, and either of these outcomes are preferred by both types of agents over not coordinating at either {1,0} or {0,1}. Let the payoffs to an agent be 5 at its preferred outcome, 2 at the less preferred, and 0 if there is mis-coordination.

Suppose the system is at the {0,0} equilibrium with, say, both populations being composed of machines that always take action 0 regardless of what the opponent does. In such a world, population 0 dominates population 1 in terms of payoff.

How can evolution, driven by small steps, move this system into the alternative {1,1} equilibrium where population 1 gets its preferred outcome?

In a world where every agent always takes action 0, any agent that deviates and takes action 1 does poorly since it will mis-coordinate and receive nothing. Suppose, however, that in population 0 a mutant arises that implements a trigger strategy that takes action 0 as long as the opponent takes action 0, but takes action 1 for the remainder of the game if the opponent ever deviates from 0. This Trigger mutant is environmentally neutral, as it only encounters machines that play 0 and thus it also coordinates on {0,0}. Given that Trigger receives the same payoff as its incumbents, there is a chance that during reproduction it becomes replicated and increases its representation in the population.

Now, suppose that a mutant Always 1 arises in population 1. When facing only Always 0 machines in population 0, this mutant does poorly since it never coordinates, while its incumbent, Always 0, does coordinate, albeit at the inferior coordination point. However, the existence of Trigger in population 0 alters the evolutionary landscape for population 1. If the number of Triggers in population 0 reaches a critical threshold—the size of which depends on the game's payoffs and the number of repeated rounds—the system becomes poised for a change. An Always 0 in population 1 coordinates at the {0,0} equilibrium when playing either Always 0 or Trigger in population 0, giving it a payoff of $(P-t)r\pi + tr\pi = Pr\pi$, where π is the single-round payoff of the less-preferred equilibrium, r is the number of rounds in the game, P is the population size, and t is the number of Trigger machines in population 0. A mutant Always 1 in population 1 receives a payoff of $(P - t)r0 + t(r - 1)\Pi$, where Π is the payoff of the preferred equilibrium (with $\Pi > \pi$). Thus, a mutant Always 1 will outcompete an incumbent Always 0 in population 1 when $t(r - 1)\Pi > Pr\pi$ or, in terms of the proportion of population 0 invaded by Trigger, $\frac{t}{P} > \frac{r\pi}{(r-1)\Pi}$ for $r > 1$. For example, in a four-round Battle of the Sexes where the preferred equilibrium pays 5 and the less-preferred one pays 2, if slightly over 53% $\left(\frac{4 \cdot 2}{(4-1)5}\right)$ of population 0 is invaded by Trigger, an Always 1 mutant in population 1 can outcompete an incumbent Always 0 and begin to take over population 1. As the number of Always 1 mutants grows in population 1, the system begins to shift from $\langle 0,0 \rangle$ to either not coordinating ($\langle 0,1 \rangle$) or partially coordinating (at 0,1 $\langle 1,1 \rangle$).[8]

---

[8] Recall from Chapter 3 that $\langle i,j \rangle$ indicates a cycle of joint actions $\{i,j\}$. Thus, for example, 0,1 $\langle 1,1 \rangle$ indicates a sequence of play of $\{0,1\}$ $\{1,1\}$ $\{1,1\}$ . . . .

The presence of Always 1 in population 1 also conveys a selective advantage to Trigger in population 0. Since Trigger was environmentally neutral, it does as well as Always 0 does when facing another Always 0. However, it receives a higher payoff than Always 0 does when confronting Always 1 (since Always 0 never coordinates in such a situation, while Trigger at least coordinates at the inferior equilibrium after the first round). Thus, Trigger receives a higher payoff than Always 0 does when playing against a population composed of a mix of Always 0 and Always 1, allowing Trigger to outcompete Always 0 and take over population 0.

Thus, the two mutants take over their respective populations driven by two powerful positive feedback loops, where the growth of one encourages the growth of the other. This implies that the overall behavior of the system moves from $\langle 0,0 \rangle$ to $0,1$ $\langle 1,1 \rangle$, flipping the system from population 0's to population 1's preferred coordination point (with the exception of the first round of mis-coordination). The final stage of this transition occurs when population 0 consolidates from Trigger to Always 1, since this latter machine compared to Trigger is both simpler and receives a higher payoff by perfectly coordinating with population 1 across all rounds of the game.

6.3.2 (R)EVOLUTION IN THE AIR

The above discussions illustrate how extreme transitions can rapidly move a system from a state favoring one population to a state favoring the other population using only incremental changes.[9] The notion that an environmentally neutral mutation can arise, drift, and create a cascade of self-reinforcing niches that allows the system to quickly transition,

---

[9]We do observe other types of transitions as well, for example, ones that move the system to a state that is better for both populations.

provides a powerful example of how gradual change can cause rapid and radical revision.

The extreme transitions explored here also follow an ancient motif: Thetis holding Achilles by the heel to dip him in the River Styx to make him invulnerable, introduces an inadvertent weakness into the system. In the CAM, the emergence of an environmentally neutral mutant in the *dominant* population introduces a seemingly innocuous change into the evolutionary dynamics. If, by chance, neutral drift allows this mutant to reproduce enough, a new niche is created for a previously untenable strategy in the subordinate population. This new niche is revealed to an outside observer when the emergence of a mutant in the subordinate population catalyzes the next phase of the transition by sending a surprising input that alters the environment facing the dominant population. This new input induces the previously neutral mutants to respond with new computations that have not been honed by evolution, allowing the mutant in the subordinate population to outcompete its incumbents and, in so doing, create a niche that allows the previously neutral mutants to outcompete their incumbents as well.

These new, self-reinforcing niches cause the system to rapidly transition into a very different regime of agent behavior and fortune. Such transitions require a carefully aligned set of events: an environmentally neutral mutation of the proper type must first arise and then propagate enough via neutral drift to create a viable niche that can be invaded by a mutant in the other population. Depending on the type of transition involved, the likelihood of such events transpiring may be low enough that epochs persist for long periods of time. Moreover, during a given epoch, the preconditions for a transition may wax and wane multiple times, before an actual transition is realized.

6.4 What Follows

Each of the remaining chapters in Part II focus on a particular type of social behavior. The main research question in these chapters is whether interacting agents can evolve strategies that allow mutually beneficial behavior to arise and persist. If so, the hallmarks of social behavior defined in Chapter 1 will have been achieved. To allow us to generalize across different classes of social behavior, we apply the identical CAM across many different, potentially social, scenarios.

One focus of our analyses is on how the number of states available to an automaton influences the emergence of social behavior. As machines are given more states they can condition their behavior on the actions of their opponents in more complex ways (see Chapter 3). With more states, machines can make their behavior contingent on longer periods of past interactions, more sophisticated counting procedures, and more elaborate input patterns, among many other possibilities. Escaping cognitive constraints by increasing the number of states may, however, be difficult as larger machines may also increase the difficulty of learning or even produce brittle and elaborate Rube Goldberg–like contraptions (though our experiments in Appendix F suggest that the CAM is able to productively evolve machines across the range of sizes we will investigate).

Another focus of the analyses will be on how interaction influences the emergence of social behavior. By manipulating the number of repeated rounds during a given encounter, we can alter the degree to which agents interact with one another. As the number of repeated rounds increases, new possibilities arise for refining one-on-one interactions, and such refinements may be important for the emergence of social behavior.

Finally, within a given class of games we will focus on scenarios that, *a priori*, should make the emergence of social behavior difficult to achieve. Even within a given repeated game, the environment facing the agents may depend on specific payoff values. Therefore, we will also explore each game's payoff space to gain an understanding of the sensitivity of the system to various realizations of an environment.

The general question we want to understand is what conditions promote the emergence of social behavior. By definition, social behavior requires thoughtful agents interacting in an environment with the possibility, though perhaps not the immediate incentives, for mutual gain. Using the CAM we will develop an understanding of how such systems move from asocial to social. That is, what specific elements of the environment, combined with what degrees of agent computational ability and interaction, spark the emergence of productive social behavior. It is this view of social life that we explore in the following chapters. ❧

7

CONFLICT

Who trusted God was love indeed
And love Creation's final law—
Tho' Nature, red in tooth and claw
With ravine, shriek'd against his creed—

ALFRED LORD TENNYSON
In Memoriam A.H.H. (1851)

Conflict is an interesting social behavior as it captures a common interaction among agents and its thoughtful resolution has the potential to result in mutual benefit. Of course, given the potential costs of conflict, agents would like to avoid such interactions altogether. Nonetheless, when resources are scarce, conflicts arise and must be resolved.

The classic model of conflict is captured by the game of Chicken. The traditional description of Chicken has two drivers barreling toward one another down a single-lane road, each with a choice to either swerve off the road or go straight. If they both go straight, the cars crash and both drivers die (a.k.a., they receive a really low payoff). If they both swerve, they survive to live another day, each with some loss of prestige. The intrigue of the game comes from what happens when one driver swerves and the other goes straight. The driver that swerved is a chicken, which is worse than if they both had swerved, but obviously better than death, while the driver that went straight has proven their nerve and becomes a hero, receiving the highest possible payoff. Table 7.1 provides the payoff matrix for Chicken.

COLUMN

PLAYER

		0 (swerve)	1 (straight)
ROW	0 (swerve)	S, S	C, H
PLAYER	1 (straight)	H, C	D, D

Table 7.1. Payoff matrix for Chicken. Each player must decide whether to swerve or go straight. The payoffs require $H > S > C > D$, representing the payoffs for being a hero, a mutual survivor, a chicken, and dead, respectively.

The Hawk-Dove game (Maynard Smith and Price 1973), an independently developed version of Chicken, comes from biology and captures conflicts over resources. The standard payoff matrix for this game is given in table 7.2. In the Hawk Dove, the players are in conflict over a resource of value $V > 0$. If both players are passive (dove), they split the resource equally and each receives $V/2$. If one player escalates the conflict (hawk) and the other remains passive, then the aggressor gets the entire resource. However, if they both escalate the resource is again split evenly, but each must also pay a cost, C, tied to the mutual conflict. In the game, $C > V$, implying that the resource value is overwhelmed by the conflict cost, so if they both fight each receives a negative payoff.

The one-shot Hawk Dove has three Nash equilibria. Two pure equilibria exist with the players taking opposite actions, namely, one being a dove and the other a hawk. The game also has a mixed strategy where a player becomes a dove with probability $\frac{C-V}{C}$ (this mixed strategy is also the only Evolutionarily Stable Strategy of the game). Here, we assume that the game is symmetric, but asymmetric versions with one player stronger than the other are easily derived.

Games of conflict exist in an interesting part of the space of two-player games. While the game captures a fundamental

COLUMN

PLAYER

		0 (dove)	1 (hawk)
ROW	0 (dove)	$V/2, V/2$	$0, V$
PLAYER	1 (hawk)	$V, 0$	$(V - C)/2, (V - C)/2$

Table 7.2. Payoff matrix for Hawk Dove. Players must decide whether to back down from the conflict and acquiesce as a dove (action 0) or escalate it as a hawk (action 1). The payoffs reflect the value of the contested resource, V, and the cost of mutual conflict, C, with $C > V > 0$. This framework captures a version of Chicken, where the dove and hawk actions are replaced by swerve and straight, respectively.

view of conflict, it also incorporates other key social behaviors. Part of the challenge facing players of a conflict game is a coordination problem (see Chapter 8), as they want to coordinate their actions (either by both not engaging in the conflict or by taking dissimilar actions). These games are also closely related to the Prisoner's Dilemma used in the study cooperation (see Chapter 9). If the cost of conflict falls below the value of the resource (that is, if $V > C > 0$), Hawk Dove transforms into a Prisoner's Dilemma,[1] where the dove and hawk actions correspond to cooperate and defect, respectively. Thus, this model of social conflict incorporates elements of coordination and, as the value of the resource increases or the cost of conflict decreases, cooperation.

7.1 Coevolving Conflict

To explore conflict we deploy the Coevolving Automata Model (CAM) with automata playing variations of a repeated Hawk Dove. The repeated version of Hawk Dove has the same two

---

[1] There is a secondary constraint for the Prisoner's Dilemma, namely $R > (S + T)/2$, and this does not hold here since $R = V/2 = (V + 0)/2 = (T + S)/2$. A slight modification of the payoffs resolves this issue.

		COLUMN PLAYER	
		0 (dove)	1 (hawk)
ROW PLAYER	0 (dove)	2.5, 2.5	0, 5
	1 (hawk)	5, 0	$(5-C)/2, (5-C)/2$

Table 7.3. Parameterized payoff matrix for Hawk Dove. The Hawk Dove shown in Table 7.2 is parametrized by setting $V = 5$ and allowing C to range from 5.25 to 12.0 in increments of 0.25. The dove (hawk) action is indicated by output 0 (1).

players interacting over multiple rounds of the game, each with information about what action the opponent took in the prior round. This information allows agents to condition their future behavior on past actions and, potentially, acquire mutually beneficial strategies. As discussed in Chapter 2, the Folk theorem implies that Nash equilibria abound in repeated games, though it provides little guidance as to which of these equilibria are likely to emerge. The main question below is whether adaptive systems can resolve the challenges presented by conflict over resources and avoid the devastation implied by mutual aggression.

As previously discussed, while games are typically specified by a set of ordinal relationships among the payoffs, in a repeated game the cardinality of payoffs is important. Thus, we parametrize the generalized Hawk-Dove payoffs shown in table 7.2 using the scheme outlined in table 7.3. We set $V = 5$ and allow C to range from 5.25 to 12 in increments of 0.25 to form different Hawk-Dove payoff matrices.

To explore adaptive behavior in the game, we use the CAM described in Chapter 6. We sweep through the values of C in table 7.3 for games of one, four, and ten repeated rounds, across coevolving populations of automata having from one to five states. For each set of game parameters we coevolve the

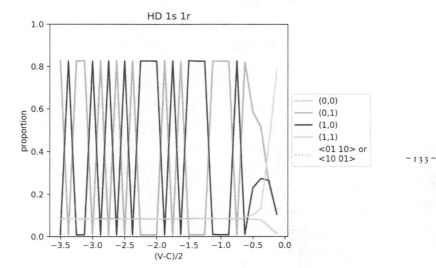

Figure 7.1. Coevolution of one-state automata playing a one-round Hawk Dove with payoffs as described in table 7.3. The x-axis gives the payoff to mutual hawk actions. For each value of $(V - C)/2$ on the x-axis, the y-axis gives the proportion of all observed plays across the 10,000 generations with the indicated joint outcome (with 0 = dove and 1 = hawk). (Since the C values are at discrete intervals, the lines connecting the points provide visual clarity, but are otherwise meaningless.) The dotted line indicates the proportion of games with terminal cycles of either $\langle 0,1\ 1,0 \rangle$ or $\langle 1,0\ 0,1 \rangle$, that is, cycles that imply perfect anti-coordination across each repeated round. In a one-round game with one-state automata no such cycles are possible, so the dotted line is at zero. *Please refer to the Github repository (https://github.com/SantaFeInstitute/ExMachina) for full-sized, full-color versions of all images in this book.*

machines for 10,000 generations. Outputs 0 and 1 imply taking the dove and hawk actions, respectively.

Figure 7.1 shows the results for one-state automata playing a one-round Hawk Dove, with the payoff to each player of mutual hawk actions, $(V - C)/2$, given by discrete values on the x-axis. We find that for values of $(V - C)/2 \leq -0.5$, the system converges to the same set of actions for over 80% of the possible plays across the 10,000 generations. This dominant set of actions has one population always playing dove and the other always playing hawk throughout the entire 10,000 generations (with most of the residual joint actions being either mutual dove ($\{0,0\}$) or hawk ($\{1,1\}$) in roughly equal amounts). This result implies that the two populations receive unequal payoffs, with one population of agents getting 5 per game and the other getting 0—an outcome that is superior for both over mutual-hawk play. The spiky nature of the graph suggests that one-state, one-round systems converge to one of two possible pure equilibria, with one population being hawks and the other doves throughout the 10,000 generations. Which of these two equilibria arise is due to chance, thus additional runs of the experiment might result in the alternate equilibrium, but whichever equilibrium prevails arises early in the trial and persists throughout the remaining generations. As the value of $(V - C)/2$ goes above -0.5, the observed play changes with the mutual hawk outcome taking over. These higher values of $(V - C)/2$ are near the region where Hawk Dove transforms into the Prisoner's Dilemma, suggesting that mutual defection might arise under similar conditions in that game.

The system behaves in a very different way with three-state automata playing four-round games (see fig. 7.2). While the system still tends to be characterized by anti-coordination, with one machine playing hawk and the other playing dove, the proportion of these two outcomes across all generations is near 50%, implying that the agents in both populations, at least over long time scales, receive mean payoffs of around 2.5 each. Indeed, as indicated by the dotted line, even *within* a given generation there are instances that arise in these systems where the players alternate between the two pure anti-coordination equilibria each round. That is, a round of hawk-dove behavior

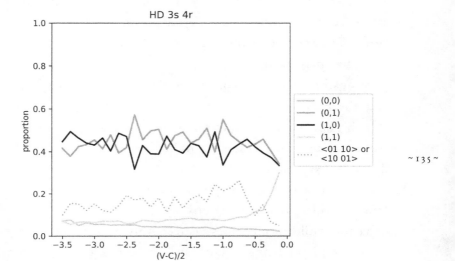

Figure 7.2. Coevolution of three-state automata playing a four-round Hawk Dove with payoffs as described in table 7.3. With the exception of the number of machine states and game rounds, the construction of the figure is the same as figure 7.1. *Please refer to the Github repository (https://github.com/SantaFeInstitute/ExMachina) for full-sized, full-color versions of all images in this book.*

is followed by one of dove-hawk, and so on, implying that the players receive the same payoff (averaging 2.5 per round) *within* a given repeated game.

Therefore, in a system with more computationally capable agents interacting for four rounds, agents achieve the maximum possible equitable payoff either on average across the entire set of generations or, less often, within a given generation. This equity occurs not by both machines always playing dove (which, given the payoffs, would result in the same mean payoff of 2.5 per round with 0 variance), but rather by the machines trading off the two extreme actions. As $(V - C)/2$ increases, hawk-hawk play begins to dominate, especially as this value nears 0.

Figures 7.1 and 7.2 indicate that the number of machine states, repeated rounds, and payoff parameters can result in very different coevolutionary paths for Hawk Dove. One-state machines playing one-round games across a wide swath of payoff parameters lead to one population always playing hawk and the other always playing dove across the generations. Which population becomes dominant is a matter of chance, tied to random events early on in the coevolution of this path-dependent system.

Systems with more computationally capable automata and longer within-game interactions display very different overall behavior: while the machines again coevolve to anti-coordinate with one player being a hawk and the other a dove, which population dominates alternates over time. Typically, this alternation happens over generational time scales, that is, an epoch forms with one population dominating the other for many consecutive generations, followed by a quick transition into a new epoch where the roles are reversed. How such reversals arise when driven by small incremental changes is discussed in section 7.1.1.

We also observe, on occasion, that in systems with larger machines and longer interactions, epochs can arise where the machines learn to alternate between hawk-dove and dove-hawk play within a given repeated game, implying an equitable distribution of payoffs to the players over both the short and long term.[2]

---

[2] This within-game alternation may not always be perfect, as it can entail patterns where the players trade-off their preferred action pairs in unequal amounts, say, three to one.

Figure 7.3 provides a more holistic view of our coevolving conflict system. Each subgraph in the figure (each identical in construction to figures 7.1 and 7.2) represents the behavior of a coevolving system with different sizes of automata (columns) and numbers of repeated rounds (rows). The automaton sizes go from one (left-most column) to five (right-most column) states and the number of repeated rounds in the game is either one (top row), four (middle row), or ten (bottom row). As can be seen from the figure, systems either in the top row (one-round repeated games) or left column (one-state machines) display lock-in behavior similar to what was observed in figure 7.1, while systems in the interior of the figure more closely resemble figure 7.2.

Systems with automata restricted to one state *or* one round of interaction lead to worlds in which one population dominates as hawk to the other's dove across all generations for a wide range of payoff parameters. Systems with automata of at least two states interacting for four or ten rounds result in populations that, at least over long time scales, alternate between the two pure Nash equilibria of Hawk Dove. This alternation often takes the form of one population dominating across many generations followed by a rapid transition to a new state of the system where the other population becomes dominant. Finally, in systems with larger automata having longer repeated interactions, the coevolving machines can fall into epochs where they alternate between the two pure equilibria *within* a given repeated game, allowing the players to achieve equitable payoffs even in the short term.

Thus, as machines become more computationally capable and interactive, we find that the system coevolves in such a way that the players begin to "share" the potential gains in the system, at least over the long run. This behavior produces,

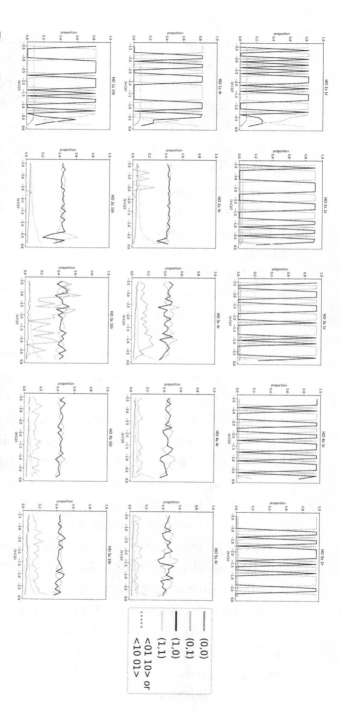

Figure 7.3. Parameter sweep of the Hawk Dove. For each configuration of automaton states, repeated rounds, and payoff parameters, the associated system underwent evolution for 10,000 generations. The number of automaton states and repeated rounds is given in each subplot's title: states go from one (leftmost column) to five (rightmost column) and rounds are either one (top row), four (middle row), or ten (bottom row). The subplots are identical in construction to figures 7.1 and 7.2, with the payoff values given in table 7.3 and the value of hawk-hawk, $(V - C)/2$, shown on the x-axis of each subplot. The solid lines show the proportion of $\{0,0\}$, $\{0,1\}$, $\{1,0\}$, and $\{1,1\}$ plays (with dove = 0 and hawk = 1) during the 10,000 generations. The dotted line shows the proportion of time that play resulted in a terminal cycle of either $\langle 0,1\ 1,0 \rangle$ or $\langle 1,0\ 0,1 \rangle$. Please refer to the Github repository (https://github.com/SantaFeInstitute/ExMachina) for full-sized, full-color versions of all images in this book.

on average, an equitable division of payoffs between the populations. Of course, another way to achieve this end would be for both players to adopt the dove action, an issue we address in section 7.2.

Next, we explore how a system that is locked into, say, dove-hawk ($\langle 0,1 \rangle$) can transition, through a series of small changes, into a system that is locked into hawk-dove ($\langle 1,0 \rangle$). That is, how is it that evolution allows a hawk, in a dominant position, to acquiesce and become a dove?

7.1.1 EXTREME TRANSITIONS

Section 6.3 provided a general discussion and motif for extreme transitions in our coevolving system. Here we provide a detailed example.

Figure 7.4 shows two consecutive system transitions with the first shown on the left- and the second on the right-hand side. The upper two graphs on each side of the figure show the number of each type of machine in the two populations. (Fig. 7.5 provides a summary of the resulting actions and payoffs for the various pairings of the key strategies that arise in this system.) The bottom graph of each transition shows the observed actions of the players over time.

The first transition (left-hand side) starts around generation 500 and takes the system from the consistent play of hawk-dove ($\langle 1,0 \rangle$) to dove-hawk ($\langle 0,1 \rangle$) for the next couple of hundred generations. Thus, the system moves from an outcome favoring the machines in population 0 to one favoring those in population 1. The second transition (right-hand side) returns the system to its previous norm.

The initial phase of the first transition begins with the emergence of a trigger strategy in population 0. This strategy, known as 1Trigger1, plays 1 and continues to do so unless

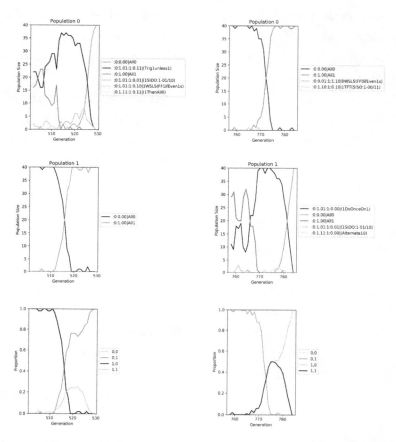

Figure 7.4. Two consecutive transitions moving a system from Hawk-Dove to Dove-Hawk play and back again (two-state machines, four rounds, $C = 10$, and low mutation of 0.033). The top and middle panels show the frequency of the different strategies in the two populations, with the associated legends ordered from top to bottom by the maximum population size observed during any generation of the transition period. The bottom panel shows the distribution of actions over time. These transitions were observed in a single run of the system, with the left-hand transition taking it from $\langle 1,0 \rangle$, the hawk-dove outcome that favors population 0, to $\langle 0,1 \rangle$, the dove-hawk outcome that favors population 1. This state of the world persists until the transition shown on the right half of the figure reverses the fortunes of the populations as an epoch of hawk-dove ($\langle 1,0 \rangle$) begins anew. *Please refer to the Github repository (https://github.com/SantaFeInstitute/ExMachina) for full-sized, full-color versions of all images in this book.*

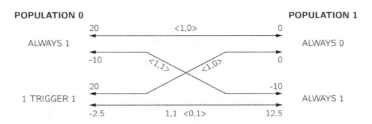

$$
\begin{array}{c}
\quad\quad\quad 0\ D \quad\quad 1\ H \\
\begin{array}{c} 0\ D \\ \\ 1\ H \end{array}
\left[
\begin{array}{cc}
2.5, 2.5 & 0, 5 \\
\\
5, 0 & -2.5, -2.5
\end{array}
\right]
\end{array}
$$

POPULATION 0   POPULATION 1

20   ⟨1,0⟩   0

ALWAYS 1   ALWAYS 0

-10   ⟨1,1⟩   ⟨1,0⟩   0

20   -10

1 TRIGGER 1   ALWAYS 1

-2.5   1,1 ⟨0,1⟩   12.5

Figure 7.5. Payoff relationships in a Hawk Dove transition (two-state machines, four rounds, and $C = 10$). The Hawk-Dove game shown in the upper half of the figure is played for four rounds. The lower half of the figure shows the resulting play and payoffs to the specified machine pairings, with the respective payoffs given at each end point and the sequence of play given in the middle of the links. For example, when 1Trigger1 in population 0 plays Always 0 in population 1, the resulting actions are ⟨1,0⟩ and 1Trigger1 receives a payoff of 20 while Always 0 receives 0. If 1Trigger1 plays Always 1, the resulting actions are 1,1 ⟨0,1⟩ with 1Trigger1 receiving -2.5 and Always 1 receiving 12.5 during the four-round interaction. The evolutionary dynamics are driven by the relative payoffs *within* a population, so the emergence of enough 1Trigger1 in population 0 can allow a mutant Always 1 to outcompete an Always 0 in population 1.

the opponent plays 1, at which point it switches to playing 0 for the remainder of the game. When either the 1Trigger1 or the incumbent Always 1 strategies in population 0 play against the Always 0 machines in population 1, they both receive the payoff for a hawk playing a dove during each round of the game. 1Trigger1 behaves identically to Always 1 *as long as* they both face Always 0, making 1Trigger1 environmentally neutral under these circumstances. Therefore, 1Trigger1's proportion in population 0 can drift about given the stochastic nature of reproduction. Indeed, just before the transition becomes apparent in the observed play of the game, 1Trigger1 has taken over slightly more than half of population 0. This neutral drift places the system in a critical state.

The emergence of a mutant Always 1 in population 1 tips this critical state and begins the observable transition. When population 0 was composed of only Always 1, a mutant Always 1 emerging in population 1 had no chance of survival relative to the incumbent Always 0, since an Always 1 playing against an Always 1 generates $\langle 1,1 \rangle$ and receives a total payoff of -10 (-2.5×4, given $C = 10$) over the four rounds, while an Always 0 playing against an Always 1 generates $\langle 0,1 \rangle$ and receives a payoff of 0. Thus, in population 1, a mutant Always 1 receives a lower payoff than an Always 0 when facing a population composed of only Always 1.

However, the neutral drift of 1Trigger1 in population 0 during the first phase of the transition has inexorably altered the payoff landscape facing population 1. As we saw before, Always 0 playing either Always 1 or 1Trigger1 generates $\langle 0,1 \rangle$ and receives a payoff of 0 while an Always 1 playing against another Always 1 generates $\langle 1,1 \rangle$ and receives a payoff of -10. However, Always 1 playing against 1Trigger1 results in 1,1 $\langle 1,0 \rangle$, giving Always 1 a payoff of 12.5. Thus, the rise of enough 1Trigger1s in population 0 can create a new niche for the Always 1 in population 1. This niche allows the Always 1 in population 1 to outcompete its Always 0 incumbents—an Always 0 receives a payoff of 0 against either Always 1 or 1Trigger1, while an Always 1 receives -10 against Always 1 and 12.5 against a 1Trigger1. If population 0 is composed of at least $\approx 44\%$ (10/22.5) 1Trigger1 machines, then an Always 1 in population 1 receives a higher average payoff than an Always 0. The second phase of the transition, that began with the emergence of a mutant Always 1 in population 1, ends with that mutant displacing its incumbent Always 0 machines.

Once Always 1 gains a foothold in population 1, the third phase of the transition starts. In this phase, the rise of Always

1 in population 1 now forms a new niche for population 0. In population 0, Always 1 does worse than 1Trigger1 when facing only Always 1 (since Always 1 versus Always 1 leads to $\langle 1,1 \rangle$ with a payoff of -10, while 1Trigger1 versus Always 1 generates 1,1 $\langle 0,1 \rangle$ with a payoff of -2.5). Thus, in population 0 1Trigger1 now outcompetes Always 1, allowing it to take over its population during this phase of the transition.

The final phase of this transition is a consolidation that happens in population 0. Note that population 0's 1Trigger1 machines now face only Always 1, giving the 1Trigger1 machines a payoff of -2.5. This makes them vulnerable to invasion by Always 0 (which, by always playing dove, receives a payoff of 0). Thus, the transition ends with population 0 composed of Always 0 and population 1 composed of Always 1. During this transition, the composition of strategies has completely flipped between the two populations, as have their fortunes, with population 1 now getting the dominant payoff by playing hawk to population 0's dove.

The subsequent transition (right-hand side of fig. 7.4) starts around generation 760 and follows a similar motif that returns the system back to its initial state. This second transition is primed by the rise of an environmentally neutral mutant in population 1 that plays hawk unless the other agent plays hawk, in which case, it plays dove once and resets back to hawk. This neutral strategy (when facing Always 0) drifts and eventually becomes a large enough proportion of population 1 that Always 1 can outcompete Always 0 in population 0, leading to a sequence of population dynamics that eventually flips the system from dove-hawk back to hawk-dove play.

7.1.2 A TRANSITION TO EQUAL SHARING

Another behavior that can arise in this system is one where the machines learn to alternate plays of hawk-dove with dove-hawk *within* a given set of repeated rounds. This outcome results in both players maximizing their potential aggregate payoffs from the game and equitably splitting these gains in the short term.

Figure 7.6 illustrates a system of two-state machines that transitions from always playing dove-hawk to alternating plays of dove-hawk and hawk-dove during the repeated rounds of a given game. At the start of the transition, populations 0 and 1 are filled with Always 0 and Always 1, respectively. During the initial phase of the transition, an environmentally neutral Flip-Flop strategy (1WSLS) enters population 1 and through neutral drift displaces over half of the Always 1 machines. This creates a productive niche in population 0 for a machine that sends out an alternating sequence of hawk and dove actions. This Alternating machine achieves a different set of actions when playing Flip Flop versus Always 1, and as long as population 1 has more than 50% Flip Flops, Alternating displaces Always 0 in population 0.

This leads the system into the final phase of the transition where a machine appears in population 1 that begins with action 0 and then takes action 1 and continues to do so unless a 0 is observed, in which case it takes action 0 once and resets to action 1. This latter machine, when facing population 0, outperforms both Always 1 and Flip Flop in population 1 and takes over, leading the system to converge on alternating between the actions of hawk-dove and dove-hawk. (At the end, an environmentally neutral strategy enters population 0 and its proportion relative to Alternating is due to chance.)

The above transition, albeit more elaborate than the previously discussed transitions, follows the same motif outlined in section 6.3: a world with an outcome strongly favoring one of the populations is transformed by a neutral invader establishing a foothold in the dominant population, and as this invader's population drifts upwards a new niche

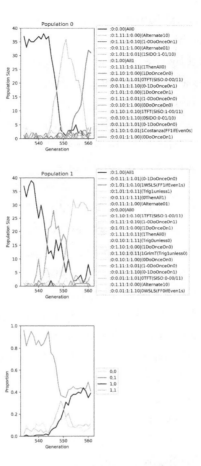

Figure 7.6. A transition to alternating actions in a Hawk Dove (two-state machines, four rounds, and $C = 10$). The top two panels show the frequency of the different strategies in the two populations, with the associated legends ordered from top to bottom by the maximum population size observed during any generation of the transition period. The bottom panel shows the distribution of actions over time. Prior to entering the transition, the system plays $\langle 0,1 \rangle$ where population 0 acquiesces and plays dove while population 1 plays hawk. The transition moves the system to where the interactions lead to the sequence $\langle 1,0 \ 0,1 \rangle$ with population 0 alternating between hawk and dove and population 1 alternating between dove and hawk, equilibrating the payoffs to each agent within a given repeated game. *Please refer to the Github repository (https://github.com/SantaFeInstitute/ExMachina) for full-sized, full-color versions of all images in this book.*

emerges that is exploited by a mutant in the subordinate population. As this latter mutant grows, it creates a new niche that is exploited by the original neutral invader, transitioning the system into a new equilibrium that improves the position of the originally subordinate population. In the case above, the transition resulted in both populations receiving the same payoff, while in the two prior transitions the subordinate population became the dominant one.

7.2   Why Can't We All Just Get Along?

An outcome that we don't see emerging in the coevolving conflict system is both machines playing dove for extended periods of time. Across the various parameters we investigated, the vast majority of observed actions concentrated on either hawk-dove or dove-hawk, with only minor amounts of dove-dove or hawk-hawk (and, as discussed, an increase in hawk-hawk play as the payoff parameter $(V - C)/2$ nears 0 and converges on a Prisoner's Dilemma). At one level, the dove-dove outcome seems far more "sensible" than outcomes that alternate between hawk-dove and dove-hawk, since dove-dove guarantees each player an even split of the maximum total payoff during each round, versus having to employ more elaborate coordination schemes either during a given repeated game or across epochs.

One advantage of the CAM is the ease with which one can perform experiments to investigate such questions. In this case, we can initiate a Hawk-Dove system with both populations filled with dove-loving machines and see what happens. When we do this we find that the populations are quickly overrun by invading mutants of Always Hawk. This is not surprising, as Always Dove is a ready feedstock for any hawkish strategy (and Always Hawk is a likely mutant of Always Dove).

Could more reactive strategies than Always Dove establish dove-dove play? Suppose we initiate the populations with strategies such as Tit For Tat or Grim Trigger that both begin by playing dove and continue to do so unless the opponent plays hawk, at which point they switch to playing hawk to different degrees. Even with such strategies we still find both populations being invaded by hawks. This occurs because a mutant Always Dove is environmentally neutral relative to the more reactive strategies, and thus it can gain a foothold via neutral drift. Moreover, Always Dove outperforms other dove-loving machines in the face of hawkish strategies (as total acquiescence to a hawk provides a higher payoff than fighting). Both of these effects put the system back into the precarious position where populations of Always Dove become vulnerable to mutant hawks.

7.3 Conclusions

Games of conflict are predicated on the existence of a scarce resource that can either be shared or fought over. Fights are costly, and if both sides choose to fight it leads to the worst possible outcome for all. A seemingly obvious social solution here is for the agents to share the resource and split the gains evenly. Unfortunately, this solution is confounded by the ever-present incentive for an agent to fight to acquire the entire resource for itself in hope that the other agent will acquiesce.

The CAM provides some interesting, albeit challenging, insights into the problem of social behavior in environments characterized by resource conflicts. Systems that have agents with either limited processing ability or interactions fall into a persistent state that has one population always oppressing the other. Which population becomes dominant is a matter of chance, but once that die has been cast the dominance persists throughout subsequent generations.

As agents gain more processing ability and participate in longer, repeated interactions, the system is still characterized by one population dominating the other but, at least over the long term, the potential gains from beneficial social behavior are shared. In these latter systems, innate coevolutionary instabilities occasionally arise that can—after a sufficient accumulation of barely noticeable small events—rapidly alter the system's behavior. Such coevolutionary instabilities solve the social problem of sharing the scarce resource over evolutionary time.

As machines gain additional computational power and interact for even longer periods, a new solution emerges to the problem of conflict. This solution has agents, over the course of a repeated game, not only avoiding direct fights, but also alternating between the dominant and subordinate roles each round, providing each agent with the highest possible payoffs consistent with an equitable division of the resource even in the short run. The coordination needed to implement such a solution requires a carefully constructed set of machines that are far more elaborate than, say, machines that just share the resource equally each round by both playing dove—unfortunately, this latter solution is incompatible with the coevolutionary forces governing the system. Thus, coevolution must engineer a more elaborate solution to get around its own limitations.

Summarizing the results of coevolution and social conflict in Hawk Dove, we find:

(i) Coevolving automata quickly adapted and concentrated their joint actions on either of the two possible pure Nash equilibria, with one population playing hawk and the other playing dove.

(ii) Systems composed of either one-state machines *or* one-round interactions quickly locked into one of the two pure Nash equilibria and remained in that equilibrium for subsequent generations.

(iii) Systems with machines of more than one state *and* four or ten repeated rounds of play resulted in both pure equilibria arising roughly equally, on average, across the generations.

(iv) The equitable division of payoffs observed in these latter systems was often due to long epochs where one population gets its preferred pure equilibrium, followed by a rapid transition to an epoch where the other population gets its preferred equilibrium.

(v) Systems with more computationally capable machines and longer interactions were sometimes able to coevolve machines that coordinated their actions so that agents received equitable payoffs during each set of repeated interactions, rather than across epochs.

(vi) There is some evidence that larger machines and longer repeated games were more conducive to the system achieving equitable outcomes in the short term.

(vii) Transitions between the two pure equilibria were facilitated by neutral mutations that arose in the dominate population. As these mutants grew via neutral drift they created a niche that could be exploited by new mutants in the subordinate population. Once mutants from the subordinate population occupied this niche, the environment facing the formerly dominant population began to favor the previously neutral mutants, allowing the outcome of the game to flip to favor the previously subordinate population. ✒

8

COORDINATION

*Instructed by experience that the love of happiness is the
sole principle of all human actions, he found himself
in a condition to distinguish the few cases, in which
common interest might authorize him to build upon
the assistance of his fellows, and those still fewer, in
which a competition of interests might justly render it
suspected. In the first case he united with them in the
same flock, or at most by some kind of free association
which obliged none of its members, and lasted no longer
than the transitory necessity that had given birth to it.
In the second case every one aimed at his own private
advantage, either by open force if he found himself
strong enough, or by cunning and address if he thought
himself too weak to use violence.*

JEAN-JACQUES ROUSSEAU
*A Discourse Upon the Origin and the Foundation of the
Inequality Among Mankind* (1755)

One of the potential benefits of social life is the ability of agents to
coordinate with one another and multiply their advantages. Even
the most basic social interaction often requires coordinating of
the time and place for that interaction. As interactions increase,
the need to coordinate increases as well, whether it is "keeping to
the right" when using a roadway or developing norms that allow
communication signals to take on common meanings. At the heart
of coordination is a need to synchronize among multiple possible

COLUMN

PLAYER

		0	1
ROW	0	C, C	$0, 0$
PLAYER	1	$0, 0$	c, c

Table 8.1. Payoff Matrix for dominant Pure Coordination. The payoffs are such that $C > c > 0$. Thus, both players prefer the $\{0,0\}$ to the $\{1,1\}$ outcome to mis-coordinating, suggesting an obvious coordination point.

options, often with limited information about the choices of others and, in more complicated scenarios, with a divergence of interests across the coordinated outcomes that adds a degree of conflict to the interaction.

Some fundamental models of coordination are captured by two player games.[1] In most of these games, the pure Nash equilibria become the obvious coordination points. At the simplest level, consider the game in table 8.1 with two pure equilibria, one of which ($\{0,0\}$) gives higher payoffs to both agents. For example, two agents might want to meet with each other at one of two possible locations, with one of the locations being superior for both agents. Of course, if they find themselves at the $\{1,1\}$ equilibrium, neither would want to unilaterally switch their decision without the other following suit. Notwithstanding such possibilities, there is an obvious focal point in this game at the Pareto dominating set of actions given by $\{0,0\}$.

To make coordination slightly more challenging, consider the game in table 8.2. Again, the players benefit by coordinating their actions, but they are indifferent between the two pure coordination points. An example of this type of problem is deciding on a convention for driving on either the right or left side of the road. While coordination is needed to avoid accidents,

---

[1]Variants where more than two players must coordinate also exist.

COLUMN

PLAYER

		0	1
ROW	0	C, C	$0, 0$
PLAYER	1	$0, 0$	C, C

Table 8.2. Payoff matrix for Pure Coordination. The payoffs are such that $C > 0$. Both players receive the same payoff of C if they can coordinate at either of the two pure coordination points, $\{0,0\}$ and $\{1,1\}$. Mis-coordination results in each player receiving a lower payoff of 0.

either choice works equally well. Of course, unlike the previous game, neither of the pure equilibria are focal and without some prior history or pre-game communication initial coordination is difficult. Sometimes, focal choices can be deduced by behavior in other contexts, for example, whatever side of the road cars adopt to drive on might influence how pedestrians use a sidewalk.

While the previous examples capture some important coordination scenarios, they are (relatively) easy to solve given the common interest of the agents, with a bit more effort required when the pure equilibria provide identical payoffs.

Coordination becomes more interesting, and difficult, when the agents want to coordinate, but also disagree about the best coordination point.[2] A simple game capturing this situation is known as the Battle of the Sexes (BOS) (see table 8.3). In this game, coordinating at either $\{0,0\}$ or $\{1,1\}$ is superior to not coordinating, but the agents conflict over which of these

---

[2]Even this model can be elaborated on in various ways, for example, by the addition of an outside signal that the agents could use to improve coordination. Such signals are the basis for the idea of correlated equilibria. If, say, before each play of the game agents have access to a commonly observed random coin flip, then they might incorporate this outcome into their strategies, such as playing population 0's preferred equilibrium on a head and population 1's on a tail. While one can include such signals in the model, we find that coevolutionary systems coordinate even without such signals.

COLUMN

PLAYER

		0	1
ROW	0	R, r	$0, 0$
PLAYER	1	$0, 0$	c, C

Table 8.3. Payoff matrix for Battle of the Sexes. The payoffs are such that $R > c > 0$ and $C > r > 0$. Both players are better off if they coordinate their actions (either at {0,0} or {1,1}) than if they fail to coordinate, but they differ in their preferred coordination point. The row player prefers to coordinate at {0,0} (since $R > c$) while the column player prefers {1,1} (since $C > r$). Typically, the payoffs are symmetric with $R = C$ and $r = c$.

coordination points is best. An example of such a scenario is, say, when both agents are more successful if they coordinate their food gathering activities, but they prefer different foods.

8.1 Coevolving Coordination

Coordination games offer a nice test of social behavior, as the presence of multiple equilibria might place a premium on thoughtful, interactive behavior. The difficulty of coordination depends on the game. For example, when the environment consists of a dominant pure coordination game like that shown in table 8.1, coevolving automata quickly settle on the obvious coordination point. In the pure coordination game given in table 8.2, the machines also quickly arrive at, and maintain, one of the two equally valued pure coordination points. These results hold even with single-state machines interacting for only one round. In either of these games, agents that coordinate are more likely to be reproduced and, even with two equally good coordination points, the randomness inherent in the system breaks the symmetry and leads to a bandwagon effect that causes the populations to converge on a common coordination point.

COLUMN

PLAYER

		0	1
ROW	0	5, M	0, 0
PLAYER	1	0, 0	M, 5

Table 8.4. Parameterized payoff matrix for Battle of the Sexes. The value of M ranges from 1.0 to 5.0 in increments of 0.25. As M increases, the incentive to coordinate on one's preferred outcome versus that of the other player decreases.

While the above results seem intuitive, many of the standard solution proposals from game theory make different predictions. For example, in the dominant pure coordination game (table 8.1) the inferior {1,1} outcome is a Nash equilibrium, an Evolutionary Stable Strategy, and a stable attractor with a nontrivial basin of attraction under replicator dynamics.

The BOS game, containing elements of both coordination and conflict, is a more interesting experimental substrate for exploring coordination. Given that the incentives to coordinate are buffeted by agents desiring different coordination points, the resolution of this tension places a premium on thoughtful social behavior. To explore this model, we parameterize the BOS payoffs as shown in table 8.4. The payoff value M is set between 1.0 and 5.0 in 0.25 increments. As M increases, the incentive to coordinate at one's preferred equilibrium decreases, since the loss caused by coordinating at the other player's preferred point $(5 - M)$ diminishes. When $M = 5.0$ the game becomes one of pure coordination.

As before, for each parameterized game we run the Coevolving Automata Model (CAM) with automata using from one to five states playing a repeated game of either one, four, or ten rounds. The automata coevolve according to the CAM specified in Chapter 6.

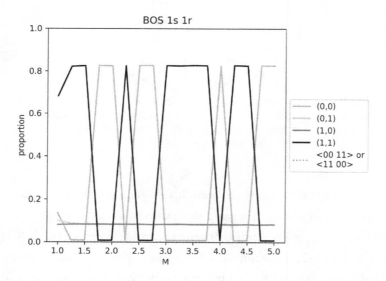

Figure 8.1. Coevolution of one-state automata playing a one-round Battle of the Sexes with payoffs as described in table 8.4. The x-axis gives the payoff of coordination to the subordinate player. For each parametric value on the x-axis, the y-axis gives the proportion of all observed plays across the 10,000 generations with the indicated joint outcomes. (Since the M values are at discrete intervals, the lines connecting the points provide visual clarity but are otherwise meaningless.) The dotted line indicates the proportion of games with terminal cycles of either $\langle 0,0\ 1,1 \rangle$ or $\langle 1,1\ 0,0 \rangle$, that is, cycles that alternate between the two pure coordination points each repeated round. No such cycles are possible under one-state machines or one-round games.

Figure 8.1 shows the results for one-state automata playing one-round BOS games. Regardless of the value of M, the system coordinates at one, and only one, of the two pure equilibria over 80% of the time, with the remaining plays resulting in miscoordination. While either of the pure equilibria can arise, the one that does (depending on stochastic forces during the initial generations) is maintained for all subsequent generations.

Once we allow larger machines and more repeated rounds, more interesting behavioral regimes emerge in this system. In a world of three-state machines playing repeated games of four rounds, coordination becomes more complex (see fig. 8.2). For low values of M, that is, for games where accepting the other player's preferred equilibrium comes at a higher cost, the agents are still able to coordinate during most plays across all of the generations, but rather than concentrating actions at only one of the pure equilibria, the populations roughly divide the two outcomes. This division is typically imperfect in the short run, as the system tends to lock into long epochs focused on only one of the pure equilibria, but over the long run transitions occur leading to epochs focused on the alternative pure equilibrium.

Thus, on average, the system produces an equitable division of payoffs between the two populations. Sometimes, agents are able to achieve equity even in the short run, as indicated by the dotted line in figure 8.2 that gives the proportion of outcomes that have terminal cycles that alternate between the two equilibria during each round of a given repeated game (either $\langle 0,0\ 1,1 \rangle$ or $\langle 1,1\ 0,0 \rangle$).

The payoff parameter M has an important influence on the behavior of the system. For $M \geq 4$, that is, when the cost of accepting the other player's preferred equilibrium is relatively low, the system coordinates on only one of the pure equilibria more than 90% of the time. Which of the two pure equilibria is chosen depends on early stochastic events, but once one becomes the norm it persists throughout the remaining generations.

Figure 8.3 shows the BOS results across varying levels of automaton size (columns) and repeated rounds of the game (rows), where each subgraph is identical in construction to figures 8.1 and 8.2. Across all conditions, the level of mis-coordination is low. Thus, these systems are able to coevolve toward a mutually beneficial outcome during almost

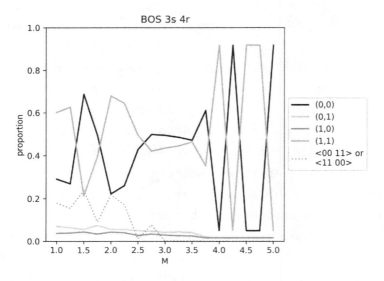

Figure 8.2. Coevolution of three-state automata playing a four-round Battle of the Sexes with payoffs as described in table 8.4. With the exception of the number of machine states and game rounds, the construction of this figure is the same as figure 8.1.

all interactions. Sometimes, this coordination is due to one population of agents always receiving its preferred outcome across all generations, that is, the system locks into one of the pure equilibria and stays there throughout. Such behavior characterizes the systems with one-state machines *or* one round of play. It also emerges in systems with larger machine sizes and longer interactions when the payoff parameter M is above 4.0 or so (as M nears 5.0, the BOS resembles a game of pure coordination).

When the machines have more than one state *and* four or ten rounds of repeated play, new regimes of coordination emerge. In these new regimes the machines not only coordinate on the two pure equilibria, but alternate between them. This alternation is often across long time scales, that is, the system

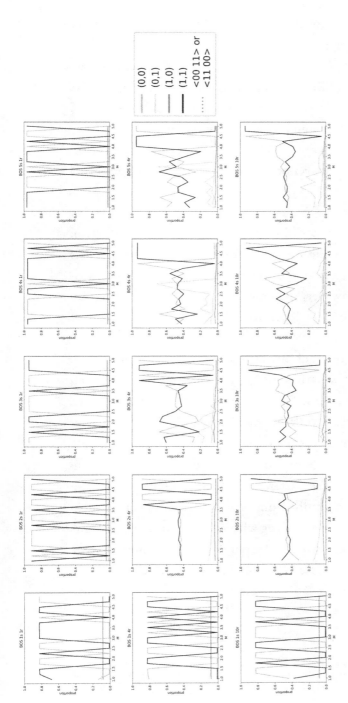

Figure 8.3. Parameter sweep of the Battle of the Sexes. For each configuration of automaton states, repeated rounds, and payoff parameters, the associated system underwent evolution for 10,000 generations. The number of automaton states (columns) and repeated rounds (rows) is given in each subplot's title: states go from one (leftmost column) to five (rightmost column) and rounds are either one (top row), four (middle row), or ten (bottom row). The subplots are identical in construction to figures 8.1 and 8.2, with the payoff values given in table 8.4 and the value of M shown on the x-axis of each subplot. The solid lines show the proportion of {0,0}, {0,1}, {1,0}, and {1,1} plays during the 10,000 generations. The dotted line shows the proportion of time that repeated play resulted in a terminal cycle of either $\langle 0,0\ 1,1 \rangle$ or $\langle 1,1\ 0,0 \rangle$. *Please refer to the Github repository (https://github.com/SantaFeInstitute/ExMachina) for full-sized, full-color versions of all images in this book.*

spends a number of contiguous generations at one of the pure equilibria and then transitions to the other pure equilibrium for multiple generations. Sometimes, the agents alternate between the two pure equilibria within a given repeated game (as indicated by the dotted line). On occasion,[3] such short-term alternation occurs at high levels. Finally, whenever agents miscoordinate, the errors tend to favor actions of {0,1} versus {1,0}, a bias tied to each player wanting to end up at its preferred coordination point.

Thus, agents in these systems concentrate their joint actions on the pure coordination points. This coordination begins early on in the evolution of the system and persists throughout the remaining generations with low levels of miscoordination. However, the exact details of this coordination vary in interesting ways depending on the processing power of the machines.

With one-state machines, the coevolving automata lock into a pure coordination point and remain there for all subsequent generations. This implies that the two populations receive asymmetric payoffs, with one averaging 5 and the other M per play. Either of the pure coordination points are equally likely to arise—which one dominates depends on random events early on in the system's evolution. Once the system begins to favor an equilibrium, a bandwagon effect locks in that coordination point. Along with the computational results above, the one-state machine system is simple enough that we can use standard models of evolutionary dynamics to analyze the system (Appendix C discusses these models using BOS as an illustrative example).

---

[3] See, for example, some of the results that arose using three states and ten rounds, as well as four or five states and four rounds.

As the number of states in the machines increases, that is, as the agents become more capable processors of information, the coordination patterns become more interesting. The first major change, observed with two or more states, is that the evolving automata become more equitable over the long run. With machines of two or more states the automata still lock into a pure coordination point when M is large. However, for smaller values of M, that is, when the relative benefit of coordinating on one's preferred coordination point increases, the system alternates between the two pure coordination points in such a way that, on average, the time spent at each one is roughly equal. The equity that arises here is typically on the time scale of generations rather than play within a given generation. That is, the system enters into long epochs where only one of the pure equilibria is played for many contiguous generations and, on occasion, these epochs are disrupted by a rapid transition that flips the system into a new epoch focused on the other coordination point.

8.1.1 EXTREME TRANSITIONS

Transitions between an epoch with, say, a cycle of $\langle 0,0 \rangle$ to one of $\langle 1,1 \rangle$, raise an interesting question: how does a population of agents that finds itself at its less-preferred coordination point get the other population of agents to transition away from their preferred point? Figure 8.4 illustrates two such transitions in a single run of two-state machines playing a four-round game with $M = 2$.

In section 6.3 we provided a general explanation of these types of extreme transitions. In section 7.1.1 we gave an example of such a transition in Hawk Dove. Based on these previous accounts we now trace an extreme transition in BOS.

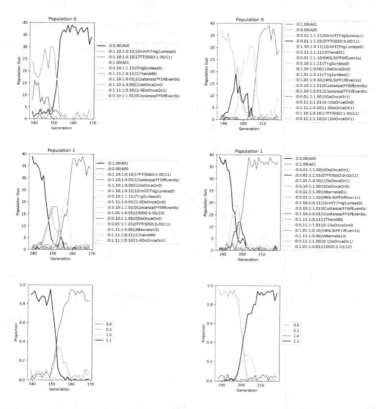

Figure 8.4. Transitions between pure equilibria in a Battle of the Sexes (two-state machines, four rounds, and $M = 2$). The top two panels show the frequency of the different strategies in the two populations, with the associated legends ordered from top to bottom by the maximum population size observed during any generation of the transition period. The bottom panel shows the distribution of actions over time. The transition on the left-hand side took the system from coordinating on $\{1,1\}$, the equilibrium favoring population 1, to coordinating on $\{0,0\}$, favoring population 0. The right-hand side shows the subsequent transition that returned the system to the equilibrium favoring population 1. *Please refer to the Github repository (https://github.com/SantaFeInstitute/ExMachina) for full-sized, full-color versions of all images in this book.*

Suppose that both populations in BOS are composed of Always 0 machines. Given this, the system concentrates all plays on the {0,0} pure equilibrium and population 0 receives its preferred payoff. This outcome is relatively stable, since isolated mutations attempting to move the system to the other equilibrium do poorly. For example, an Always 1 arising in either population quickly dies off since it always mis-coordinates when playing Always 0—it is better to coordinate at the inferior equilibrium, than to not coordinate at all.

Now, introduce an environmentally neutral mutant in population 0 that plays like Always 0 when facing Always 0, but also has the ability to play action 1 under alternative inputs. Strategies like Tit For Tat (TFT) or Grim Trigger that begin by playing 0 meet these criteria, since against Always 0 the resulting play is $\langle 0,0 \rangle$ while against Always 1 the play is 0,1 $\langle 1,1 \rangle$.

Such an environmentally neutral strategy can undergo neutral drift and its representation in population 0 can begin to crowd out the incumbent Always 0 machines.[4] For the discussion below we will assume that TFT is the environmentally neutral machine.

If TFT takes over enough of population 0, a niche opens up for population 1 that favors invasion by a mutant Always 1. If, in turn, this mutant takes hold in population 1, it creates a niche in population 0 that allows the entire system to flip into playing the {1,1} equilibrium.

Figure 8.5 gives the payoffs for the various machine pairings involved in such a transition. When either Always 0 or (the environmentally neutral) TFT in population 0 plays an Always

---

[4] A Moran process (see Appendix C) can be used to calculate the likelihood of this drift. For example, a neutral mutation has a $1/P$ chance of taking over the entire population, where P is the total population size. However, taking over the entire population is not necessary for the neutral mutant to catalyze a transition.

0 in population 1 the outcome is $\langle 0,0 \rangle$, so the population 0 machines receive payoff $r\Pi$ and the population 1 machines receive payoff $r\pi$, where r is the number of repeated rounds (here, four) and Π and π are the payoffs from the preferred (here, five) and less-preferred (here, two) equilibria, respectively. If population 0 is only composed of Always 0, then an invading Always 1 in population 1 is nonviable as it will always mismatch actions and receive a payoff of 0 versus the $r\pi > 0$ received by the incumbent Always 0 machines in population 1. However, an Always 1 in population 1 outcompetes an Always 0 in that population when $(P - \delta)0 + \delta(r - 1)\Pi \geq Pr\pi$, where P is the total population size and δ is the number of TFT machines in population 0. This viability condition simplifies to $\frac{\delta}{P} > \frac{r\pi}{(r-1)\Pi}$, where $\frac{\delta}{P}$ gives the proportion of TFT in population 0. For example, in the game shown in figure 8.5 we have $r = 4$, $\pi = 2$, and $\Pi = 5$, implying that $\frac{\delta}{P} = 8/15 \approx 0.53$. Therefore, if the total size of population 0 is 40, Always 1 has a payoff advantage over Always 0 in population 1 when there are more than 21 TFT machines in population 0.

Moreover, with the rise of Always 1 in population 1 the evolutionary landscape for population 0 changes. Always 0 does worse than TFT in population 0 if there are any Always 1 machines in population 1, since Always 0 and TFT get the same payoff against Always 0, but TFT has a payoff advantage over Always 0 when facing Always 1. Thus, once Always 1 invades population 1, the previously environmentally neutral machines in population 0 (here, TFT) are no longer neutral and take over that population.

The above dynamics result in the system undergoing a dramatic transition from always playing {0,0} to almost always (with the exception of the mis-coordination on the first round) playing {1,1}. The system will eventually consolidate to always

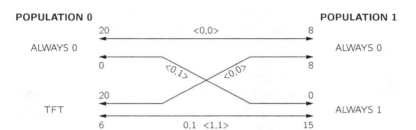

Figure 8.5. Payoff relationships in a Battle of the Sexes transition (two-state machines, four rounds, and $M = 2$). The Battle-of-the-Sexes game shown in the upper half of the figure is played for four rounds. The lower half of the figure shows the resulting play and payoffs to the specified machine pairings, with the respective payoffs given at the end points and the sequence of play given in the middle of the links. For example, when Tit For Tat in population 0 plays Always 1 in population 1, the resulting actions are 0,1 $\langle 1,1 \rangle$ and Tit For Tat receives a payoff of 6 while Always 1 receives 15. If Tit For Tat plays Always 0, the resulting actions are $\langle 0,0 \rangle$ with Tit For Tat receiving 20 and Always 0 receiving 8 during the four-round interaction. The evolutionary dynamics are driven by the relative payoffs *within* a population, so the emergence of enough Tit For Tat in population 0 can allow a mutant Always 1 in population 1 to outcompete its incumbent Always 0.

playing {1,1} when a mutant Always 1 (which coordinates across all rounds) arises in population 0 and crowds out TFT. This leaves the system completely transformed with two homogeneous populations of Always 1 coordinating on {1,1}—a complete flip of the system's behavior from its pre-transition state of two homogeneous populations of Always 0 coordinating on {0,0}. Once this new epoch of {1,1} begins, it can persist for long periods, though it too is vulnerable to a parallel sequence of events[5] that flip it back to an epoch of {0,0}.

The actual machine dynamics captured in the top two panels of figure 8.4 are a bit more complicated than the above description. For example, multiple neutral mutations and other nonviable mutants arise. Nonetheless, the essence of the transition follows the process outlined above.

The ability to reconcile a seemingly paradoxical event—a rapid transition of the system between two radically different states, driven by a series of small changes—illustrates just one of the advantages of using the CAM. The mere occurrence of such an event is surprising given normal intuitions, and without the CAM we may not have even considered this transition possible—again, we note Boulding's (1978b) first law: "anything that exists is possible." Once the model displayed this phenomenon, it also provided a means by which to examine it in enough detail to formulate and test a useful theory about how it occurred and, in the process, give us new insights and understanding about the behavior of not only this, but other systems.

Of course, once the various pieces are observed, assembled, and distilled, if the consilience is complete the insights often seem obvious in hindsight.

The epochal shift of the system-wide behavior observed here is initiated by a seemingly innocuous, environmentally neutral mutation that slowly propagates in the dominant population. These neutral machines require more than one state since they need to embody an alternative behavior conditional on their input.

---

[5]This sequence would begin with the invasion of population 1 by a neutral machine such as a TFT or Grim Trigger that begins by playing 1 rather than 0.

Thus, these transitions are initiated by an increase in the complexity of the dominant population's machines. The neutral mutation takes a simple machine that always plays for its own best equilibrium and elaborates it with some new actions that only get invoked if the opponent does something different than expected. Such neutral machines rarely have their alternative behavior tested by the heretofore docile subordinate population, and even if they were tested they would have a slight advantage over their incumbents. Once the proportion of neutral mutations in the dominant population reaches the critical threshold, a single mutant in the subordinate population can invade that population and, in turn, alter the environment facing the dominant population enough that adaptive forces align to rapidly transform both populations, putting the system into a new epoch with radically different behavior. This rapid and cataclysmic shift forces an entire population to cede its superior position, driven only by small adaptive changes.

In BOS with machines of more than one state, there is the potential for transitions to move the system from one pure coordination equilibrium to the other. This implies that, at least over longer time scales, the gains from coordinated social behavior are shared in an equitable manner even when there are asymmetric preferences for coordination.

Some of the evolutionary systems we observed were also capable of equitable play even on short time scales. That is, cycles such as $\langle 0,0 \; 1,1 \rangle$ emerged during repeated rounds of play. When this happens the machines alternate their preferred coordination points *within* a given game, leading to equitable payoffs during the repeated game itself and, consequently, during each generation of the epoch.

The likelihood of short-term equitable play is tied to the number of states in the machines. In theory, two-state machines are capable of achieving perfect alternation. And, if we initiate a two-state system with populations of alternating strategies we find that the resulting epoch is extremely long lasting. However, such machines are difficult to coevolve in the model *de novo*. The difficulty of generating alternating two-state machines, and their robustness once this behavior is acquired, is due to the mutation space that surrounds such machines. Only a small set of two-state machines are capable of supporting alternating behavior, and these machines occupy local maxima where one-step mutations make the agents worse off, with additional mutations leading up a gradient that embraces non-alternating outcomes. Thus, discovering alternating machines is difficult, but once they are found they are robust.

Once machines have more than two states, within-repeated-game alternation can arise spontaneously. With three-state machines such epochs tend to be long lasting, while with more than three states the alternating epochs don't last as long, but arise more frequently. Machines with three or more states can develop asymmetric patterns of alternation, such as a cycle of $\langle 0,0\ 0,0\ 1,1 \rangle$.[6]

Figure 8.6 shows two sequential transitions from a single CAM run of a four-round BOS with low mutation. The left-hand transition takes the system from an epoch where the machines play only {0,0} during the four rounds to an epoch with an asymmetric pattern where over the four rounds the machines play {0,0} twice, {1,1} once, and mis-coordinate at

---

[6]Asymmetric alternation cannot arise with two-state machines, since every coordinated play requires the machine to devote one state, so having more than one same-state outcome in a mixed sequence requires more than two states.

{0,1} once. The right-hand transition takes place not long after the asymmetric epoch began, and has the machines evolving to an epoch where they alternate between the two coordination points during each round. In this new epoch, the two populations perfectly split the gains from coordination.

As we saw earlier, transitions from one epoch to another are often driven by the emergence of neutral mutations that precondition the environment for a rapid transition. This transition mechanism also holds in the within-round sharing cases above when the three-state machines move from an epoch with one population being dominant, to one with asymmetric sharing, to one characterized by symmetric sharing.

For example, the movement of the system into asymmetric sharing began with a population of Always 0 facing a population of TFT, resulting in ⟨0,0⟩ and giving the Always 0 its preferred equilibrium. The population of Always 0 gets invaded by an environmentally neutral mutant that always plays 0 if it sees only 0, but will play 1 on occasion given a different input sequence. Once this mutant grows enough, a mutation among the TFT machines that takes a slightly different set of actions gets the neutral mutant to play the sequence {0,0 0,1 0,0 1,1}, tipping the system into the epoch of asymmetric sharing. A related analysis can explain the movement from asymmetric to symmetric sharing.

8.2 Conclusions

We find that coevolving systems easily achieve social coordination. Even one-state machines quickly evolve coordination, though one population dominates the other throughout the generations in such worlds. Nonetheless, such dominant outcomes are mutually beneficial as the machines are better off coordinating than not, even though one population benefits more than the other.

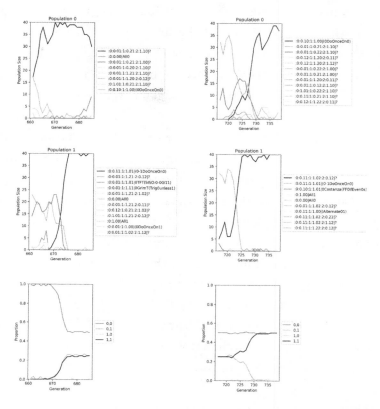

Figure 8.6. A transition to within-game sharing of the pure equilibria in a Battle of the Sexes (three-state machines, four rounds, $M = 2$, and low mutation of 0.033). The top two panels show the frequency of the different strategies in the two populations, with the associated legends ordered from top to bottom by the maximum population size observed during any generation of the transition period. The bottom panel shows the distribution of actions over time. These transitions were observed in a single run of the system, with the left-hand transition taking it from populations always coordinating on {0,0} to asymmetric coordination where the machines play {0,0 0,1 0,0 1,1} during the four-round game, resulting in twice coordinating on population 0's preferred outcome, once on that of population 1, and one mis-coordination. The transition on the right-hand side takes the system to an epoch where the machines perfectly alternate between the two preferred coordination points via ⟨0,0 1,1⟩. *Please refer to the Github repository (https://github.com/SantaFeInstitute/ExMachina) for full-sized, full-color versions of all images in this book.*

As machines become more sophisticated and interactions become longer, we see a shift in the system's behavior whereby not only does coordination arise, but it does so in an equitable manner across the two populations. At first this equity is on long time scales rather than individual games, as the system enters into coordinated regimes where one population dominates the other. These regimes eventually get disrupted by cataclysmic transitions wherein the oppressed population becomes the oppressor. In such systems, on average, both populations of machines receive a payoff equivalent to alternating between the two pure coordination points.

For machines with more than two states engaging in multiple rounds of repeated play, coevolution can create systems that are equitable even on short time scales. While two-state machines are capable of such short-term fairness, this is unlikely to occur in the regular course of coevolution, though it is extremely robust if it does happen. As the number of states in the machines rises above two, the likelihood of epochs characterized by short-term equity increases, though the expected length of such epochs decreases.

Thus, we note the following observations for the coevolution of social coordination:

(i) Evolving automata quickly concentrated their joint actions on the pure coordination points, with low rates of mis-coordination.

(ii) Systems of one-state machines locked into one of the pure equilibria, and remained in that equilibrium for all subsequent generations.

(iii) Systems with machines of more than one state playing four or ten repeated rounds resulted in both of the pure equilibria arising equally, on average, across the generations, leading to equitable coordination. This equitable division was often the result of alternating epochs where, within each epoch, one of the pure coordination points was maintained.

(iv) With machines of two or more states playing four or ten repeated rounds, equitable coordination became possible on even short time scales with machines alternating between the two pure coordination points during each round of repeated play, leading to cycles such as $\langle 0,0 \ 1,1 \rangle$.

(v) While two-state machines were capable of short-term alternation, it was unlikely to arise in the normal course of coevolution. However, if it did arise, it was extremely robust.

(vi) With machines of more than two states, short-term alternation could spontaneously arise, with the frequency of such behavior increasing, and the length of the resulting epoch decreasing, as machine size increased.

(vii) With machines of more than two states playing four or ten repeated rounds, the within-game patterns of alternating between the coordination points can become asymmetric. For example, one player might receive its preferred coordination point twice as often as its less preferred point.

(viii) Transitions between, say, epochs of $\langle 0,0 \rangle$ and $\langle 1,1 \rangle$ were facilitated by environmentally neutral mutations that complicated the strategy of the incumbent machines in the dominant population. If this population of neutral machines increased enough via drift, a niche opened up for an invading mutant in the subordinate population and this, in turn, create another niche that allowed the previously neutral mutant to outcompete its incumbents as well. ✦

9

COOPERATION

In such condition, there is no place for Industry; because the fruit thereof is uncertain: and consequently no Culture of the Earth; no Navigation, nor use of the commodities that may be imported by Sea; no commodious Building; no Instruments of moving, and removing, such things as require much force; no Knowledge of the face of the Earth; no account of Time; no Arts; no Letters; no Society; and which is worst of all, continuall feare, and danger of violent death; And the life of man, solitary, poore, nasty, brutish, and short.

THOMAS HOBBES
Leviathan ([1651]1982)

From bacteria coordinating the release of toxins to humans avoiding an arms race, cooperation is an important social behavior. Its existence is often surprising, since even though mutual cooperation is preferred to mutual defection, individual incentives often favor defection. How can cooperation emerge, and be maintained, under such conditions?

Cooperation can take many forms. In Chapter 8 we considered models of agents coordinating their actions. The focus here is on situations where cooperative arrangements must weather incentives to defect. For example, bacteria are all better off if they coordinate their attack and simultaneously release their toxins, but as long as the other bacteria release their toxins, any given bacterium is better off not attacking to save internal resources and avoid external threats.

The classic game for analyzing cooperation is the Prisoner's Dilemma. Melvin Dresher and Merrill Flood, while working at the RAND Corporation, developed this game as part of a suite of games designed to illustrate some anomalies tied to Nash's equilibrium concept in non-zero-sum games. The first formal write up of the Prisoner's Dilemma was due to Albert Tucker (1950). This version had two co-conspirators being arrested for a capital crime. The suspects are placed in separate cells and each is given the following choice (that must be made without knowledge of what the other will choose): if neither confesses there is enough evidence that both will be jailed for a year, however, if both confess then both will be jailed for ten years and, finally, if one confesses and the other does not, the one who confessed goes free while the one who kept quiet is put to death.

The prisoners face a difficult dilemma. If they cooperate with each other, that is both keep quiet, they go free in a year. If they both defect and confess they are jailed for ten years. Thus, mutual cooperation makes each co-conspirator better off than mutual defection. However, they both have an individual incentive to defect regardless of what the other player does: if the other player confesses then confessing yields ten years rather than death and if the other player stays quiet then confessing leads to going free rather than being jailed for a year.[1] Either way, each prisoner is individually better off confessing, leading to mutual defection (the only pure Nash equilibrium of this game), which makes them both worse off than if they had cooperated and remained quiet. It is this result that first intrigued Dresher and Flood, and it has

---

[1] In game theory, a choice that is superior regardless of what the other player does is known as a (strictly) dominant strategy. While arguments for focusing on Nash equilibria may require subtle reasoning, pursuing a dominant strategy is an obvious, fail-safe choice.

		COLUMN PLAYER	
		0 (cooperate)	1 (defect)
ROW	0 (cooperate)	R, R	S, T
PLAYER	1 (defect)	T, S	P, P

Table 9.1. Payoff matrix for Prisoner's Dilemma. Both the row and column players must choose to either cooperate (action 0) or defect (action 1). The payoffs are given by the ordered pairs in the table separated by commas, with the first value going to the row and the second to the column player. A Prisoner's Dilemma requires $T > R > P > S$ and $R > (T + S)/2$ (this latter condition ensures that alternating plays of $\langle 0,1 \ 1,0 \rangle$ do not result in a higher expected payoff than mutual cooperation $\langle 0,0 \rangle$).

kept subsequent generations of social scientists deeply engaged with the Prisoner's Dilemma and the issue of cooperation more generally.

The classic Prisoner's Dilemma is formalized in the payoff matrix given in table 9.1. The payoff values are known as the reward (R) for mutual cooperation, the punishment (P) for mutual defection, the temptation (T) to defect, and the sucker (S) payoff for cooperating. For a Prisoner's Dilemma we require $T > R > P > S$ and $R > (T + S)/2$. The first condition produces the needed incentive structure of the game, with defecting always being a strictly dominant strategy and mutual defection being worse than mutual cooperation. The second condition ensures that having the players taking turns exploiting one another is not superior to mutual cooperation.

The predicted outcome of mutual defection in the Prisoner's Dilemma assumes rational, self-interested players who cannot communicate, and who play the game for a single round. Altering any of these assumptions might make cooperation more likely. If the players are not entirely self-interested, for example, their opponents are kin with shared genetics, then the implicit payoffs tied to the survival of the shared genes could resolve the dilemma, but invoking such a mechanism creates a different game. If players can communicate ahead of time and form binding contracts, then there is the potential for cooperation to emerge if the players recognize the advantage of mutual cooperation and can contract to avoid the incentive to defect from such an agreement. If the players engage in repeated rounds of the game, then the incentives might be altered by the shadow of the future—short-term gains from defection can be overwhelmed by the long-term value of mutual cooperation.

Of these various paths to cooperation, repeated play is of the most interest in our study of the origins of social behavior. As noted, if agents are not self-interested, either due to kinship (which evolution would embrace) or some higher-level notion of altruism, the cooperative dilemma is resolved by changing the payoffs in the one-shot game enough to sidestep the challenge of cooperating. Resolving cooperation by contracting is also interesting, but such "advanced" behaviors need to emerge from the origins we wish to explore. This leaves repeated play as the most likely mechanism for initiating cooperation.

The Folk theorem admits the possibility of repeated play leading to a large class of potential equilibria. This theorem assumes that players first agree on a specific sequence of mutual actions, and then adopt strategies that follow this sequence with the proviso that any deviation by the opponent results in an alternative set of future actions that maximizes the harm to the violator (in the case of the Prisoner's Dilemma, defecting thereafter). As long as future payoffs matter, any sequence of plays can be supported as a Nash equilibrium under such conditions.[2] Thus, the Folk theorem provides little predictive

---

[2]Note that this result is predicated on a game that repeats either an infinite number of times or has an unknown endpoint. If this is not the case,

power in repeated games (even if one could justify the needed levels of pre-game coordination).

As discussed in Chapter 2, an often underappreciated aspect of repeated games is that the cardinal values of the payoffs are important. The primary constraint on the Prisoner's Dilemma's payoffs is ordinal: $T > R > P > S$, and meeting this constraint ensures the needed incentives for a one-shot game. However, if the game is repeated the cardinal values of the payoffs matter. For example, many definitions of the Prisoner's Dilemma add the condition that $R > (T + S)/2$, which makes mutual cooperation superior to agents exploiting one another on alternate plays. However, even this constraint leaves a lot of latitude for defining the game. For example, $(T + S)/2$ could be greater than, equal to, or less than P, and the game is still a Prisoner's Dilemma.

Games other than the Prisoner's Dilemma have also been used to study cooperation. In particular, the Stag Hunt models a situation where there is a tension between social cooperation and individual safety, and it provides an interesting testbed for both cooperation and coordination. The Stag Hunt was inspired by a passage from Rousseau's *Discourse on the Origin of Inequality* ([1755] 2018, pp. 29–30):

> *Was a deer to be taken? Every one saw that to succeed he must faithfully stand to his post; but suppose a hare to have slipped by within reach of any one of them, it is*

---

rationality can lead to a somewhat paradoxical outcome. Suppose that rational agents play a repeated Prisoner's Dilemma for, say, exactly ten rounds. When the players arrive at the last round of the game, it is as if they are playing a one-shot game, so they both should defect. Given that play in the final round is now determined, then the penultimate round is as if they are playing a one-shot game, and they should defect in that round as well. Continuing such reasoning unravels the game to its beginning, implying mutual defection in every round. This argument holds whether the known endpoint is at ten or ten-million rounds. In human experiments, while cooperation does fall off as the game gets closer to a known endpoint, one does not see the complete unraveling predicted here.

COLUMN

PLAYER

		0 (stag)	1 (hare)
ROW	0 (stag)	A, A	C, B
PLAYER	1 (hare)	B, C	D, D

Table 9.2. Payoff matrix for Stag Hunt. The payoffs are such that $A > B \geq D > C$. Both players cooperating and hunting for a stag ($\{0,0\}$) leads to the highest payoff (A) for each agent. A player hunting hare receives either B (if the other player hunts stag) or D (if they both hunt hare). Thus, while mutually cooperating and hunting stag leads to a Pareto dominant outcome, a player may still want to hunt hare as receiving payoffs of either B or D may be "safer" than hunting stag and receiving payoffs of either A or C.

not to be doubted but he pursued it without scruple, and

when he had seized his prey never reproached himself

with having made his companions miss theirs.

The payoff matrix for a two-person Stag Hunt is given in table 9.2, with $A > B \geq D > C$. Hunting for stag leads to either the highest possible payoff (A) if the partner cooperates and also joins the stag hunt, or the lowest (C) if the partner defects and hunts for hare. Hunting for hare pays either D if both agents hunt for hare, or a potentially higher amount B if the other player hunts for stag and makes it easier to find a plump hare. Thus, hunting for stag involves the highest payoff risk, resulting in either the highest or lowest possible payoff (depending on what the other player does) versus receiving one of the two intermediate payoffs by hunting hare. In the Stag Hunt, both mutual cooperation and mutual defection are pure Nash equilibria in the one-shot game (in the Prisoner's Dilemma, the only one-shot pure Nash equilibrium is mutual defection).

While we are casting both the Prisoner's Dilemma and Stag Hunt as games of cooperation, other classes of social behavior are inherent in these games. For example, one could view achieving the Pareto dominant outcomes in both games as a problem of coordinating on the appropriate actions. Moreover, the Prisoner's Dilemma is related to the Hawk Dove explored in Chapter 7 and the Stag Hunt has a similar structure to some of the coordination games we considered in Chapter 8.

9.1 Coevolving Cooperation

To explore the origins of cooperation we investigate both the Prisoner's Dilemma and Stag Hunt using the Coevolving Automata Model (CAM). As in our previous studies, we explore the impact of the processing ability of the agents and their repeated interactions on the emergence of cooperation. Thus, we use automata ranging from one to five states playing repeated games of either one, four, or ten rounds. The automata coevolve according to the CAM specified in Chapter 6.

9.1.1 PRISONER'S DILEMMA

The payoffs for the Prisoner's Dilemma are parameterized using the scheme outlined in table 9.3. We first fix the values of the two extreme payoffs (the Temptation and Sucker payoffs) and then sweep through game-compatible values of both the Reward and Punishment.

Figure 9.1 shows the results for one-state automata playing a one-round Prisoner's Dilemma. Regardless of the values of R or P, we find that agents mutually defect (shown in black) around 80% of the time, with the remainder of the plays having one player cooperate and the other defect. If the machines are limited to a single state, then the only strategies that can be implemented are Always Cooperate or Always Defect. In such an environment, Always Defect prevails and (other than mutational accidents) cooperation does not arise. Even if more elaborate strategies are available to a machine, in a single round

		COLUMN PLAYER	
		0 (cooperate)	1 (defect)
ROW	0 (Cooperate)	R, R	$0, 5$
PLAYER	1 (Defect)	$5, 0$	P, P

Table 9.3. Parameterized payoff matrix for Prisoner's Dilemma. To meet the underlying constraints of the Prisoner's Dilemma (see Table 9.1) we let $T = 5 > R > P > S = 0$. We let R range from 2.75 to 4.75 in increments of 0.25, with the lowest value of R guaranteeing that the secondary payoff condition $(R > (T + S)/2 = 2.5)$ always holds. The value of P ranges from 0.25 to $R - 0.25$, also in increments of 0.25.

of play only its initial output matters. Thus, in the one-state, one-round world cooperation fails to emerge. Indeed, as we will see, mutual defection predominates whenever machines have one state *or* interact for one round.

The results of three-state automata playing four-round repeated games are shown in figure 9.2. We find that cooperation (shown in gray) emerges under certain payoff parameters, in particular, when R is relatively high and P is relatively low (the upper left region of the figure). As we move away from this cooperative region there is a transitional boundary where some systems achieve high levels of cooperation and some don't, and beyond this boundary the system is dominated by defection. Recall that for each set of payoff parameters the system coevolved for 10,000 generations, so in the transition region the data may be driven by alternating epochs of cooperation and defection or long initial periods of defection before cooperation is discovered—both have been observed.

The fact that the emergence of cooperation is tied to the cardinal values of the payoffs has some interesting implications. First, with more data one could derive hypotheses tying the emergence of cooperation to simple relationships among the

PD 1s 1r (R/P)

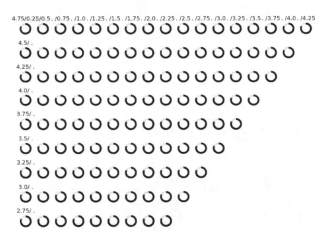

Figure 9.1. Coevolution of one-state automata playing a one-round Prisoner's Dilemma with payoffs as described in table 9.3. Each row of the figure represents a different value of R (reward), starting at 4.75 in the top row and decreasing by 0.25 in each subsequent row until reaching a value of 2.75 in the bottom row. Each column of the figure gives a different value of P (punishment), starting at 0.25 in the left-most column and incrementing by 0.25 in each subsequent column until reaching a value of 4.25 in the right-most column. Each ring in the diagram gives the proportion of all observed plays across 10,000 generations of coevolution, with black indicating plays of $\{1,1\}$ (mutual defection) and light gray indicating plays of either $\{0,1\}$ or $\{1,0\}$ (one agent cooperates and the other defects). The imposition of the constraint that $R > (T+S)/2 = 2.5$ accounts for the missing rings in the figure.

PD 3s 4r (R/P)

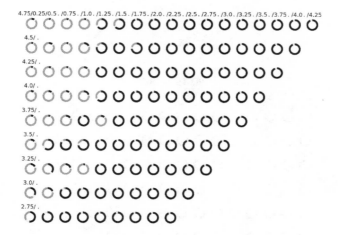

Figure 9.2. Coevolution of three-state automata playing a four-round Prisoner's Dilemma with payoffs as described in table 9.3. With the exception of the number of machine states and game rounds, the construction of this figure is the same as figure 9.1, where gray indicates plays of {0,0} (mutual cooperation). *Please refer to the Github repository (https://github.com/SantaFeInstitute/ExMachina) for full-sized, full-color versions of all images in this book.*

payoff parameters. For example, there is some evidence that cooperation requires $P < (T + S)/2$ and $R - P > \tau$, where τ is a critical threshold. Second, a lot of experimental studies— both human and computational—use a single set of payoff parameters ($T = 5$, $R = 3$, $P = 1$, and $S = 0$) introduced by Axelrod (1984) in his influential work on this game. The CAM's results suggest that payoff choices may influence the likelihood of observing mutual cooperation.

Behavioral epochs are a common feature in this coevolutionary system. We can define an epoch based on the consistency of the joint actions (here, {0,0}, {0,1}, {1,0}, and {1,1}) during contiguous generations. Generations where these frequencies do not vary too much from one generation to the next constitute an epoch. For example, in a run of 10,000 generations using three-state machines playing four-round games with payoff parameters $T = 5$, $R = 4$, $P = 1$, and $S = 0$, thirteen epochs were observed ranging in length between 6 and 8,228 generations (with a mean of 847.3 and median of 29). These thirteen epochs could be reduced to six different prototypical epochs, for example, epochs where mutual cooperation dominated (two of the thirteen, including the epoch that lasted for 8,228 generations) or where mutual defection was the norm (five of the epochs). The transition periods ranged from 0 to 16 generations in length (with a mean of 5.2 and median of 4). Over the 10,000 generations, this system was in epochs more than 99% of the time.

In section 6.2 we saw how the CAM generates relatively long epochs of consistent behavior punctuated by rapid transitions between epochs, and section 6.3 provided a common motif for such transitions. Moreover, while the actual transitions from one behavioral regime to another are rapid, it can take many generations (and attempts) to realign the machines in a population to make such transitions possible. During this realignment there is little observable change in the system's overall behavior.

Thus, the short transition period is the observed realization of a much longer period of the system accumulating incremental changes that poise it on the edge of being destabilized by another incremental change—like a house of cards completely collapsing after the addition of a seemingly innocuous card and then, like a phoenix rising, magically reforming itself into a completely different house.

The coevolutionary results across different machine sizes and repeated rounds of play are shown in figure 9.3. The number of states available to the machines is given by each column, starting at one on the left and rising to five on the right. The number of repeated rounds in each game is given by the row, with a single round played in the top row, four in the middle, and ten in the bottom. The subplots are identical in design and interpretation to the previous figures.

We find that with either one-state machines *or* one-round games, the coevolutionary system results in mutual defection across the entire set of payoff parameters. However, as the machines become larger than one state *and* the games become longer than one round, cooperation begins to emerge. As we saw in figure 9.2, this emergence is tied to the payoff parameters. In general, cooperation is more likely for low values of P. As R increases, the range of cooperation-compatible P values also increases. We also find that as the number of repeated rounds or machine states increases, the cooperative regimes embrace larger regions of the payoff-parameter space, except when four- or five-state machines play four-round games. In these latter cases, cooperation emerges for only the lowest values of P. Why this happens is an open question. Perhaps, to establish cooperation in a repeated Prisoner's Dilemma strategies must develop a way to cooperate, yet not tolerate (at least for too long) defection. In a four-round game, smaller-sized machines have access to only a few strategic schemata—a few of which embrace strategies like Tit For Tat (TFT). As the machines become larger many more schemata become available and, given the relatively short length of the game, it may be difficult for evolution to evaluate these increased options.

As previously observed, there is a dramatic difference in the system's behavior when we move away from one-state

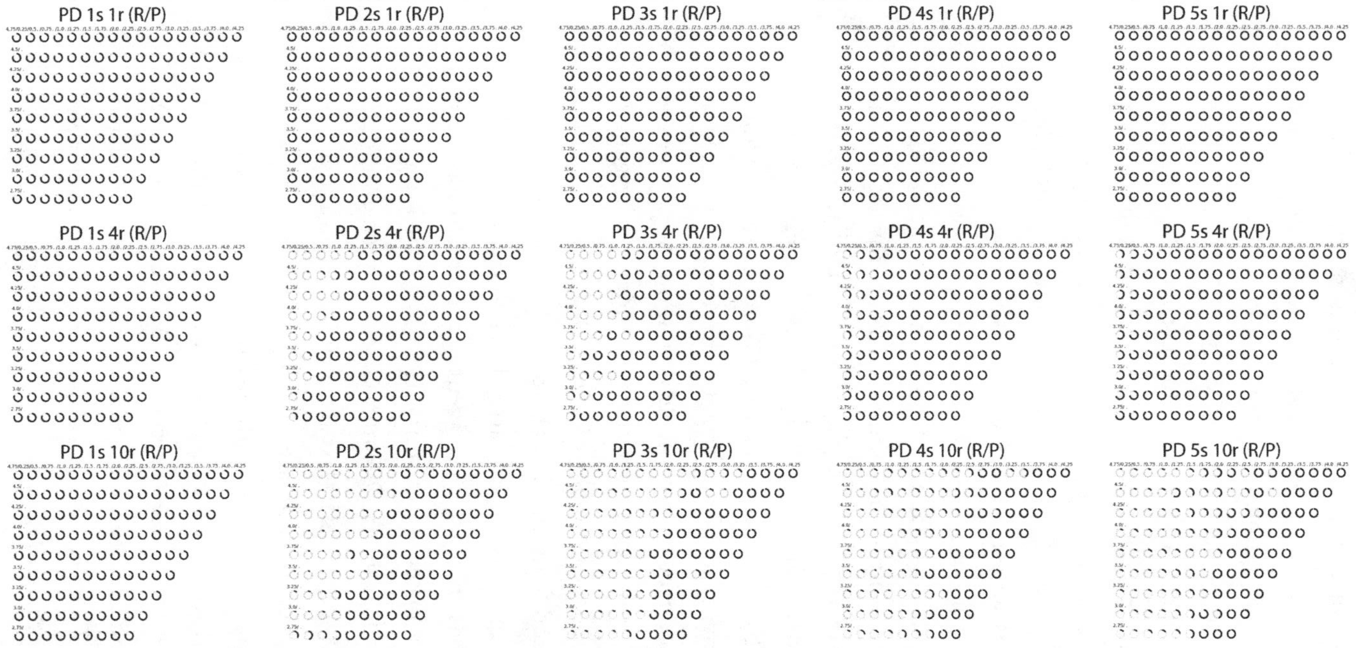

Figure 9.3. Parameter sweep of the Prisoner's Dilemma. For each configuration of automaton states, repeated rounds, and payoff parameters, the associated system underwent coevolution for 10,000 generations. The number of automaton states and repeated rounds is given in each subplot's title: states go from one (leftmost column) to five (rightmost column) and rounds are either one (top row), four (middle row), or ten (bottom row). The subplots are identical in construction to figures 9.1 and 9.2, with the payoff values given in table 9.3 and the value of R and P given by the rows and columns of each subplot. The individual rings show the proportion of $\{0,0\}$ (gray), $\{0,1\}$ and $\{1,0\}$ (light gray), and $\{1,1\}$ (black) plays during the 10,000 generations. *Please refer to the Github repository (https://github.com/SantaFeInstitute/ExMachina) for full-sized, full-color versions of all images in this book.*

machines. This is not surprising, as one-state machines face a severe constraint since they must commit to a single action during the entire game, ignoring all inputs. Given that defection is a dominant strategy, it always yields a higher payoff than cooperation in a one-state environment. Even when games are repeated, increasing the shadow of the future, the inability of one-state strategies to condition their actions on the observed play of the opponent is a fatal flaw. A one-state cooperative machine, unable to change its action, is vulnerable to exploitation.

Moving from one- to two-state machines adds twenty-four new possible computations (as enumerated and classified in figure 3.3). Among these twenty-four computations are the archetypal strategies (see fig. 9.4) that have played an outsized role across hundreds of Prisoner's Dilemma studies. These strategies include TFT (that begins by cooperating and then mimics the previous action of its opponent) and Grim Trigger (that cooperates as long as the opponent cooperates, but any defection on the part of the opponent results in defection for the remainder of the game). Strategies like Win Stay Lose Shift (WSLS) a.k.a. Pavlov (see, for example, Nowak and Sigmund 1993) are also possible using two states. In WSLS the agent has an aspiration level, a, and as long as its current payoff meets this target the agent is content to stay with its previous action, otherwise it shifts its action. The aspiration level for WSLS in a Prisoner's Dilemma is set between R and P, implying that WSLS stays with its last action if it receives a payoff of either T or R (since both are greater than a) and shifts otherwise. Thus, if WSLS cooperated it will continue to do so if the opponent also cooperated (since it received R) or switch to defection if the opponent defected (since it received S). Similarly, if WSLS defected it will continue to defect if the opponent cooperated (since it received T) or switch to cooperating if the opponent defected (since it received P). Figure 9.4 also illustrates a strategy

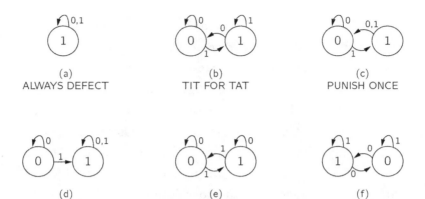

Figure 9.4. Two-state archetypal Prisoner's Dilemma strategies. Each machine is capable of playing a Prisoner's Dilemma where action 0 is cooperate and 1 is defect. Automaton (a) is a single-state machine that always defects. Automaton (b) implements Tit For Tat that begins by cooperating and then mimics the most recent action of the opponent. Automaton (c) implements Punish Once that cooperates unless it is defected upon, at which point it defects once and returns to cooperation. Automaton (d) implements Grim Trigger that begins by cooperating and continues to do so as long as the opponent cooperates, however, any defection by the opponent triggers defection for the remainder of the game. Automaton (e) implements Win Stay Lose Shift that switches its action whenever its payoff is below an aspiration level, here set between the Reward and Punishment payoff values. Finally, (f) implements the opposite behavior of (e) by initially defecting and then following a Win Shift Lose Stay strategy (a.k.a. 1Costanza).

that does the opposite of WSLS (to avoid confusing acronyms, hereafter known as 1Costanza), that begins by defecting and then implements a Win Switch Lose Stay strategy that switches when it exceeds its aspiration level and otherwise stays put. While the design of 1Costanza does not seem ideal, it occasionally facilitates transitions in this system.

The introduction of two-state automata results in a much richer behavioral world. Strategies can now begin to condition their behavior on the actions of their opponents. The lifting of this processing constraint allows the system to embrace a radically different and productive social behavior, in particular, the establishment and maintenance of mutual cooperation.

Defection is still a viable strategy in the two-state machine world. As previously discussed, defection is a dominant strategy insofar as it yields higher payoffs regardless of what the opponent does in a single-shot game. Even in a repeated game, Always Defect is productive when an agent faces a world of unpredictable and unresponsive opponents. In our coevolutionary model, the early generations of evolution are populated by a random selection of strategies, so Always Defect is likely to be optimal during this initial period. Moreover, Always Defect can easily arise as twenty of the sixty-four possible two-state machines implement this strategy. Thus, we find that during the early generations of coevolution, the system devolves into a Hobbesian state of nature with mutual defection "and the life of [automata], solitary, poore, nasty, brutish, and short."

How does the system escape this fate?

9.1.1.1 Transitioning to Cooperation in the Prisoner's Dilemma

In section 6.3 we discuss how environmentally neutral mutations can trigger a transition. A variant of this scenario can play out in the Prisoner's Dilemma (see fig. 9.5). Suppose that the two populations are composed of only Always Defect strategies, resulting in mutual defection on every play of the game. Now, introduce into the first population defect Grim Trigger (dGT), that is, a strategy that defects as long as the opponent does, but if the opponent ever cooperates it switches and cooperates thereafter. This new strategy is environmentally neutral since when it plays against Always Defect it also always defects.

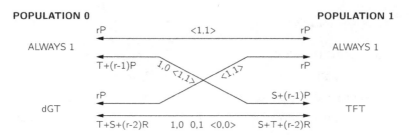

$$\begin{array}{c c} & \begin{array}{c c} 0 & \quad 1 \end{array} \\ \begin{array}{c} 0 \\ 1 \end{array} & \left[\begin{array}{c c} R,R & S,T \\ T,S & P,P \end{array} \right] \end{array}$$

Figure 9.5. Payoff relationships in a Prisoner's Dilemma transition (two-state machines playing r rounds). The Prisoner's Dilemma game shown in the upper half of the figure is played for r rounds. The lower half of the figure shows the resulting play and payoffs to the specified machine pairings, with the respective payoffs given at the end points and the sequence of play given in the middle of the links. For example, when a dGT in population 0 plays a Tit For Tat in population 1, the resulting actions are 1,0 0,1 $\langle 0,0 \rangle$ and dGT receives a payoff of $T + S + (r - 2)R$ and Tit For Tat receives $S + T + (r - 2)R$. The evolutionary dynamics are driven by the relative payoffs *within* a population, so the emergence of enough dGT in population 0 can allow a mutant Tit For Tat in population 1 to outcompete its incumbent Always Defect.

Given that dGT is environmentally neutral in the first population, its proportion, ρ_{dG}, can increase through neutral drift. As its proportion increases, the environment facing the second population changes, though as long as the second population continues to always defect this change is not apparent. However, the emergence of a strategy like TFT in the second population can trigger a cascade that allows cooperation to be established in both populations. A TFT in the second population gets an average payoff of $\Pi_T = (1 - \rho_{dG})(S + (r-1)P) + \rho_{dG}(S + T + (r - 2)R)$, where r is the number of repeated rounds and the first and second parts of the equation give the expected payoffs when playing Always Defect and dGT, respectively. Always Defect in the second population receives $\Pi_D = rP$ per game given that dGT is environmentally neutral. Therefore, the mutant TFT will have a payoff advantage if $\Pi_T > \Pi_D$ or

$$\rho_{dG} > \frac{P - S}{T + P + r(R - P) - 2R} \ \forall\, r > 1. \qquad (9.1)$$

The critical threshold given by this equation is decreasing in R (for $r > 2$) and r, and increasing in P, implying that as we move either down or to the right in the payoff-parameter space shown in the previous figures, a cooperative cascade requires that the neutral invader constitutes a higher proportion of the first population. For game parameters $T = 5$, $R = 4$, $P = 1$, $S = 0$, and a four-round game, the critical value of $\rho_{dG} = 1/10$. So, in a population of size 40 there needs to be more than four dGT before a TFT in the other population can outcompete its incumbent Always Defect. Moreover, dGT in the first population is able to outcompete its incumbent Always Defect as long as it receives a higher payoff than Always Defect when playing TFT.[3] This requires that $T + S + (r - 2)R > T + (r - 1)P$ which, given the parameter values above, holds.[4]

Figure 9.6 illustrates a transition of the Prisoner's Dilemma system in a ten-round game using a low mutation rate of 0.033. This transition begins around generation 84,314 and was proceeded by 240 other transitions. Of these 240 transitions, twenty-two of them lead to brief epochs of high cooperation (lasting between five and twenty-two generations in length, with a median of 7.5 and mean of 8.2 generations, with only two of the twenty-two epochs exceeding ten generations). The epoch starting in generation 84,314 lasted for over 15,000 generations (and

---

[3] dGT and Always Defect receive the same payoff from playing Always Defect—this is why dGT was environmentally neutral to begin with.
[4] However, there are game parameters that would not meet this requirement, for example, when $r < 3$.

was ongoing when the CAM ended after 100,000 generations). At the start of this transition, both populations were composed of Always Defect. In generation 84,304 a mutant dGT strategy arose in population 1. This environmentally neutral strategy reproduced and grew over the next few generations, reaching a population of eleven by generation 84,310. At this time, a mutation arose in population 0 that began by defecting, and then cooperated unless the opponent defected, in which case it would defect once and return to cooperation. This strategy does well against dGT as they mutually cooperate after the third round following their uncoordinated play, though it loses to Always Defect, receiving the punishment payment for half the rounds and being a sucker for the remainder. However, with enough neutral drift of dGT in population 1 it becomes viable. In generation 84,315 a mutation in population 0 produced a variant of WSLS that begins by defecting (rather than cooperating) and then implements the WSLS rule. This new defecting WSLS (dWSLS) strategy does well and takes over population 0 (after some brief insurgencies by Always Defect and standard WSLS). Population 1 also experiences various runs on the strategic throne, though it also converges on a long-lasting population of dWSLS.

The previous transition illustrates the importance of niche construction in these systems. The initial world appeared to be hopelessly trapped in mutual defection. The system escapes this trap by the emergence of an environmental neutral mutation, though its presence is undetectable in the observed behavior of the system. By chance, this neutral mutation drifts enough to reach the population density necessary to form a new niche for the other population whereby a previously untenable mutant can thrive. Once this new mutant becomes established, it creates a niche that favors the previously neutral mutant. These events rapidly transform both populations and alter the system's behavior. A

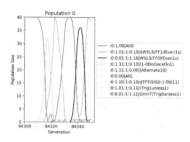

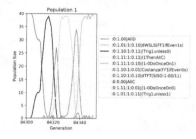

~194~

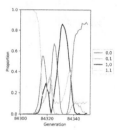

Figure 9.6. A transition to cooperation in a Prisoner's Dilemma (two-state machines, ten rounds, $T = 5$, $R = 4$, $P = 1$, $S = 0$, and low mutation of 0.033). The top two panels show the frequency of the different strategies in the two populations, with the associated legends ordered from top to bottom by the maximum population size observed during any generation of the transition period. The bottom panel shows the distribution of actions over time. In this transition, the system moves from mutual defection ($\{1,1\}$) to mutual cooperation ($\{0,0\}$) as shown in the bottom panel. Both populations are initially dominated by Always Defect. As the transition is completed, both populations are dominated by a variant of Win Stay Lose Shift that begins by defecting rather than cooperating. *Please refer to the Github repository (https://github.com/SantaFeInstitute/ExMachina) for full-sized, full-color versions of all images in this book.*

series of minor changes lead to a self-reinforcing sequence of niche creation events that quickly moves the system from a world mired in defection to one bountiful in cooperation.

There are other routes to the emergence of cooperation in these systems. Figure 9.7 shows an example where the simultaneous emergence of *non*-environmentally neutral mutants in *both* populations is enough to push the system into a new equilibrium. In this example, two populations composed of only Always Defect get invaded by (regular) Grim Trigger strategies that become self-reinforcing once they simultaneously arise in both populations.[5] When facing Always Defect, Grim Trigger receives a payoff of $S + (r - 1)P$, with the initial round of trying to cooperate putting Grim Trigger at a disadvantage relative to the rP that an incumbent Always Defect would receive. However, with enough Grim Triggers in the other population, this disadvantage can be overcome by getting rR when facing other Grim Triggers. Let the opposing population be composed of proportion ρ_G of Grim Triggers and $1 - \rho_G$ of Always Defect. The expected payoff to a Grim Trigger facing that population is $\Pi_G = (1 - \rho_G)(S + (r - 1)P) + \rho_G rR$, while an Always Defect receives $\Pi_D = (1 - \rho_G)rP + \rho_G(T + (r - 1)P)$. Therefore, $\Pi_G > \Pi_D$ when

$$\rho_G > \frac{P - S}{2P + r(R - P) - S - T}, \qquad (9.2)$$

if the denominator is positive. As before, the critical threshold of ρ_G is decreasing in R and r, and increasing in P (for $r > \frac{T-S}{R-S}$), suggesting that the payoff regions in the parameter sweeps where cooperation is most likely to emerge coincide with the regions that require the lowest joint populations of cooperative strategies to ensure their survival. For game parameters $T = 5$, $R = 4$, $P = 1$, $S = 0$, and a four-round game, the critical value of $\rho_G = 1/9 \approx$

---

[5] These Grim Triggers are eventually replaced by Tit For Tat.

0.11. Thus, in a population of size 40, if more than four Grim-Trigger agents exist in a population otherwise composed of Always Defect, a Grim Trigger opposing that population outperforms any Always Defect incumbents.

Thus, even without environmentally neutral strategies there is a path to cooperation. If, in *both* populations, mutation results in enough cooperative strategies simultaneously arising, these cooperative mutants can survive and grow in their respective populations. Moreover, these systems can bootstrap this type of transition when, say, a lone mutant cooperator in one population happens upon multiple cooperative mutants in the other population. In this case, the lone mutant outperforms its incumbents and increases in population size, even though the multiple mutants in the other population may decline. However, the situation is reversed in the next generation, and the dynamics can seesaw back and forth, eventually leading to both populations bootstrapping the critical mass needed to sustain mutual growth and flip the system into cooperation.

Figure 9.7 shows such a transition in a ten-round Prisoner's Dilemma (with $T = 5$, $R = 4$, $P = 1$, $S = 0$, and mutation of 0.333). Before the transition, both populations are dominated by Always Defect strategies resulting in a world of mutual defection. However, within a span of ten generations the system undergoes a transformation to mutual cooperation. As hypothesized above, the transition required a sufficient population of TFT-like strategies to emerge in both populations, and once these populations crossed the critical threshold the transition took off.

This system shows an ecological succession akin to grasslands becoming forested, where the system is initially dominated by the opportunistic Always Defect, moves on to Grim Trigger, and ultimately forms a climax community composed of TFT.

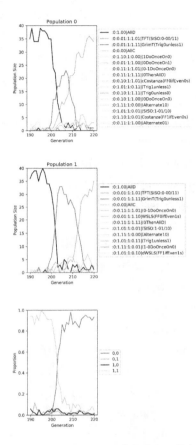

Figure 9.7. A transition to cooperation in a Prisoner's Dilemma (two-state machines, ten rounds, $T = 5$, $R = 4$, $P = 1$, $S = 0$, and mutation of 0.333). The top two panels show the frequency of the different strategies in the two populations, with the associated legends ordered from top to bottom by the maximum population size observed during any generation of the transition period. The bottom panel shows the distribution of actions over time. In this transition the system moves from mutual defection ($\{1,1\}$) to mutual cooperation ($\{0,0\}$) as shown in the bottom panel. Both populations (top two panels) are initially dominated by Always Defect. The transition begins with a wave of Grim Trigger arising in both populations, quickly followed by a rise in Tit For Tat. As the transition is completed, both populations are dominated by Tit For Tat. *Please refer to the Github repository (https://github.com/SantaFeInstitute/ExMachina) for full-sized, full-color versions of all images in this book.*

The general patterns observed in the previous transitions appear in various guises across the Prisoner's Dilemma CAMs. Worlds of mutual defection populated by Always Defect get transformed into cooperative worlds populated by TFT and Grim Trigger. The rise of TFT and Grim Trigger is not too surprising, as both strategies take a "trust but verify" approach to cooperation by being friendly to cooperation but not tolerating defection. TFT is quick to forgive a defection, as long as the opponent is willing to give up a Temptation payoff to re-establish cooperation, while Grim Trigger is less tolerant. Smaller numbers of other strategies often arise during transitions, most of which have some ability to cooperate, albeit some less well than others. Of course, other machines come and go with even lower frequencies, likely the result of nonviable mutations.

The dynamics of the transitional ecosystem out of mutual defection are closely linked to the possible mutations. Recall that twenty of the sixty-four possible two-state, two-action automata are behaviorally identical to Always Defect (see fig. 3.3). Every two-state, two-action machine has six possible single mutations (by either changing the action in one of its two states or altering one of its four possible transitions). Thus, there are 120 possible mutations of the twenty possible Always-Defect machines. Of these 120 mutations, eighty result in another Always Defect. Eight of the 120 mutations result in Always Cooperate, though this strategy, while promoting cooperation, is also a super food (yielding a continuous stream of temptation payoffs) for Always Defect. The remaining thirty-two mutations generate the other twenty-four unique two-state, two-action strategies, each of which arises either once or twice. For example, of the 120 possible mutations of the twenty possible Always Defect machines, TFT and Grim Trigger each show up only once.

STATE 0	STATE 1	NAME
0:0,1	1:0,1	Tit For Tat
0:0,0	1:0,1	Always Cooperate
0:0,1	0:0,1	Always Cooperate
1:0,1	1:0,1	Always Defect
0:0,1	1:1,1	Grim Trigger
0:1,1	1:0,1	Cooperate then defect thereafter with a restart on a cooperation
0:0,1	1:0,0	Cooperate and punish once on a defection

Table 9.4. One-mutant neighbors of a two-state Tit-For-Tat machine. Each state is coded as action:transition-state-on-0,transition-state-on-1, where action 0 = cooperate and 1 = defect.

Cooperative epochs, once they begin, often persist. There are six possible mutations of a two-state TFT (see table 9.4). Five of these mutants (Always Cooperate (twice), Grim Trigger, cooperate and punish once on a defection, and cooperate then defect thereafter with a restart on a cooperation) are relatively cooperative and responsive to defection to various degrees. The remaining mutant is Always Defect. The six possible mutations of a two-state Grim Trigger (see table 9.5) are quite similar to those of TFT, with two of them always cooperating, two cooperating more strategically (TFT and WSLS), and the remaining two either always defecting or defecting after the first round.

The limited mutation space for two-state TFT and Grim Trigger gives cooperative systems composed of such machines a certain degree of robustness. However, such systems can succumb to behaviorally neutral mutants. For example, if Always Cooperate takes over enough of a population of TFT, an Always Defect mutant can buckle the system and take over.[6]

---

[6]Always Defect gets rT from playing Always Cooperate and $T + (r - 1)P$ from playing Tit For Tat, while Tit For Tat gets rR from its cooperative partners.

STATE 0	STATE 1	NAME
0:0,1	1:1,1	Grim Trigger
0:0,0	1:1,1	Always Cooperate
0:0,1	0:1,1	Always Cooperate
1:0,1	1:1,1	Always Defect
0:0,1	1:0,1	Tit For Tat
0:1,1	1:1,1	Cooperate Once, Defect Thereafter
0:0,1	1:1,0	Win Stay, Lose Shift

Table 9.5. One-mutant neighbors of a two-state Grim-Trigger machine. Each state is coded as action:transition-on-0,transition-on-1, where action 0 = cooperate and 1 = defect.

Having cooperative populations continually tested by invaders like Always Defect can keep the number of potentially dangerous neutral mutants suppressed to low enough levels that the population can avoid invasion. If the world is too sanitized and rarely faces Always Defect, potentially ruinous Always Cooperate mutations will not be culled and the system may become vulnerable to invasion. Like an immune system, if these machine ecosystems constantly face outside threats they tend to remain strong and are able to fight off new infections, but if they avoid the threats entirely their ability to respond to new threats is compromised.

By carefully studying the various "natural" histories that arise in the CAM, we can abstract from the particular details that drive a given transition and develop more general concepts. As we saw above, there may be different mechanisms that drive cooperative transitions. In the Prisoner's Dilemma, happy accidents can occur that produce enough of a change in both populations during a given generation to initiate a transition to cooperation. Even under extremely low mutations, mechanisms such as the accumulation of environmentally neutral strategies can allow a small mutation in the other population to quickly transform the system.

The Prisoner's Dilemma is an important challenge for social behavior since individual incentives are at odds with social incentives. Notwithstanding such incentives, we find that there are conditions under which social behavior can prevail and improve the welfare of the cooperative agents while also preventing the system from devolving into its original, individualist state.

9.1.2 STAG HUNT

Another key game involving cooperation is Stag Hunt. While the Prisoner's Dilemma holds interest because the individual incentives are at odds with the social incentives, the Stag Hunt is intriguing for a different reason: the cooperative choice, while Pareto dominant, is risky.

We parameterize Stag Hunt payoffs as outlined in table 9.6. While cooperating and hunting stag provides the highest possible payoff to both players (5 points each), it entails the risk that the opposing player defects and the stag hunter receives nothing. The underlying riskiness of this situation is tied to the expected values of the two actions. Let ρ give the probability of the opponent hunting stag. Then, the expected payoff from also hunting stag is $\rho 5 + (1-\rho)0 = \rho 5$, while that from hunting hare is $\rho B + (1 - \rho)D$. Therefore, hunting stag yields a higher expected value than hunting hare when $\rho > D/(5 + D - B)$. Increasing either B or D increases the required ρ, that is, as the hare-related payoffs increase, one requires a higher expectation that the opponent will hunt stag to be willing to do so as well.

Figure 9.8 shows the CAM's behavior for Stag Hunt when one-state automaton play one-round games. As seen in the figure, the payoff parameter space splits into two regions, one

COLUMN

PLAYER

		0 (stag)	1 (hare)
ROW	0 (stag)	5, 5	0, B
PLAYER	1 (hare)	$B, 0$	D, D

Table 9.6. Parameterized payoff matrix for Stag Hunt. To meet the constraints of the Stag Hunt (see table 9.2) we let $5 = A > B \geq D > C = 0$. We then sweep through values of B and D. We let B range between 0.5 and 4.5 and the value of D range between 0.5 to B, both in increments of 0.5.

where the players cooperate and jointly hunt stag and one where they both defect and pursue hare. The dividing line between these two regimes is roughly where the sum of B and D equals 5. When $B + D = 5$ (or, equivalently, $B = 5 - D$) the minimum probability of the opponent hunting stag that favors hunting stag as well is $\rho = D/(5 + D - B) = D/2D = 1/2$, that is, as long as the players expect that the opponent will hunt stag at least 50% of the time, they also want to hunt stag.[7] Table 9.7 provides the threshold probabilities needed to hunt stag under different payoff parameters. As shown in the table, the payoff parameters consistent with a one-state one-round CAM converging on cooperation with both players hunting stag imply that ρ is around 0.5 or less.

If we increase the number of states in the machines to three and the number of repeated rounds to four, the space of payoff parameters that support cooperation expands to cover almost the entire payoff parameter space (see fig. 9.9). The small set of payoffs that still lead to defection are consistent with expectations of stag play on the part of the opponent that are around 80% or higher (see table 9.7), versus the 50% we observed in the one-state one-round

---

[7]A similar condition can be used to define the basin of attraction under replicator dynamics.

STAG 1s 1r (B/D)

Figure 9.8. Coevolution of one-state automata playing a one-round Stag Hunt with payoffs as described in table 9.6. Each row of the figure represents a different value of B, starting at 4.5 in the top row and decreasing by 0.5 in each subsequent row until reaching a value of 0.5 in the bottom row. Each column of the figure gives a different value of D, starting at 0.5 in the left-most column and incrementing by 0.5 in each subsequent column until reaching a value of 4.5 in the right-most column. Each ring in the diagram gives the proportion of all observed plays across the 10,000 generations of coevolution with gray indicating plays of {0,0} (mutual stag), black indicating plays of {1,1} (mutual hare), and light gray indicating plays of either {0,1} or {1,0} (one agent going after stag and the other pursuing hare). The requirement that $B \geq D$ accounts for the missing rings in the figure. *Please refer to the Github repository (https://github.com/SantaFeInstitute/ExMachina) for full-sized, full-color versions of all images in this book.*

system. Thus, as machines become more capable and interactions become longer, the system is able to support cooperation even when the required level of expected cooperative behavior on the part of the opponent is higher.

The observations above capture the essence of the observed CAM behavior across a wide range of system parameters. Figure 9.10 provides data across a range of machine sizes and repeated

		D							
	0.5	1.0	1.5	2.0	2.5	3.0	3.5	4.0	4.5
4.5	0.50	0.67	0.75	0.80	0.83	0.86	0.88	0.89	0.90
4.0	0.33	0.50	0.60	0.67	0.71	0.75	0.78	0.80	
3.5	0.25	0.40	0.50	0.57	0.63	0.67	0.70		
B 3.0	0.20	0.33	0.43	0.50	0.56	0.60			
2.5	0.17	0.29	0.38	0.44	0.50				
2.0	0.14	0.25	0.33	0.40					
1.5	0.13	0.22	0.30						
1.0	0.11	0.20							

Table 9.7. Probability of hunting stag equalizing the expected payoff between the two possible actions. The table provides the minimum probability of hunting stag by the opponent that equalizes the expected value of playing stag or hare for the payoff parameters B and D in the game defined in table 9.6. These probabilities provide a threshold, above which hunting stag leads to a higher expected payoff than hunting hare and below which hunting hare dominates.

interactions. Systems with one-state machines (left-most column) *or* one round interactions (top row) are similar to one another, with comparable regions of payoff parameters that support cooperation versus defection (roughly bisected by the line given by $B + D = 5$). As we increase the size of the machines *and* the rounds of interaction the space of payoff parameters supporting cooperation expands, with some evidence that this space is slightly larger for ten- versus four-round games.

9.1.2.1 Transitioning to Cooperation in the Stag Hunt

An example of a transition to cooperation in Stag Hunt is shown in figure 9.11. The parameters used in this experiment were chosen to favor a system that supports both cooperation and defection. Prior to the transition, the system was characterized by both players defecting and chasing hare ({1,1}). Two strategies dominated the populations at the start of the transition: dGT that begins by

STAG 3s 4r (B/D)

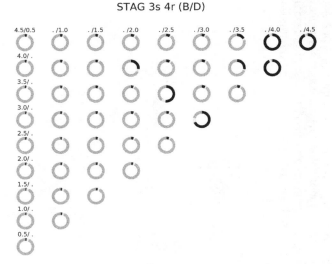

Figure 9.9. Coevolution of three-state automata playing a four-round Stag Hunt with payoffs as described in table 9.6. With the exception of the number of machine states and game rounds, the construction of the figure is the same as figure 9.8.

defecting and continues to do so unless a cooperation is observed, at which point it cooperates thereafter, and a variant of TFT (dTFT) that begins by defecting and then mimics the previous action of the opponent. (Both of these strategies also arose in one of the Prisoner's Dilemma transitions analyzed earlier.) These two strategies, when either playing themselves, each other, or Always Defect, result in mutual defection across all rounds of the game (giving each strategy a payoff of 14 in a four-round game under the given payoff parameters). As we saw previously, the emergence and growth of these two strategies comes from environmentally neutral drift. Once a sufficient number of these strategies propagate in the two populations, the system is poised for a transition. This transition is catalyzed by the emergence of Always Cooperate.

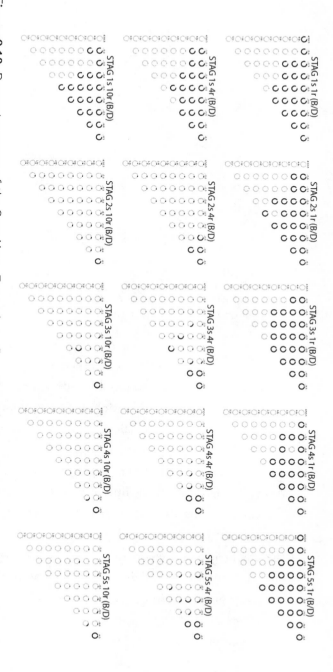

Figure 9.10. Parameter sweep of the Stag Hunt. For each configuration of automaton states, repeated rounds, and game parameters, the associated system underwent coevolution for 10,000 generations. The number of automaton states and repeated rounds is given in each subplot's title: states go from one (left-most column) to five (right-most column) and rounds are either one (top row), four (middle row), or ten (bottom row). The subplots are identical in construction to figures 9.8 and 9.9, with the payoff values given in table 9.6 and the values of B and D given by the rows and columns of each subplot. As before, the individual rings show the proportion of {0,0} (gray), {0,1} and {1,0} (light gray), and {1,1} (black) plays during the 10,000 generations. *Please refer to the Github repository (https://github.com/SantaFeInstitute/ExMachina) for full-sized, full-color versions of all images in this book.*

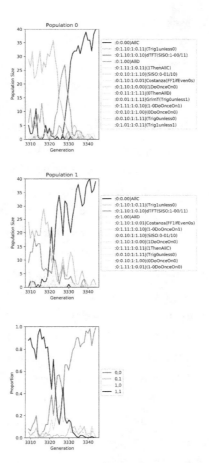

Figure 9.11. A transition to cooperation in a Stag Hunt (two-state machines, four rounds, $A = 5$, $B = 4.5$, $C = 0$, and $D = 3.5$). The top two panels show the frequency of the different strategies in the two populations, with the associated legends ordered from top to bottom by the maximum population size observed during any generation of the transition period. The bottom panel shows the distribution of actions over time. The parameters used here were chosen based on figure 9.10 to result in worlds that can generate epochs of either cooperation or defection. Prior to the transition, both players chased hare ($\{1,1\}$). The system transitioned around generation 3,330 (bottom panel) to where both players pursue stag ($\{0,0\}$) and remained in that state when the CAM ended at generation 10,000. *Please refer to the Github repository (https://github.com/SantaFeInstitute/ExMachina) for full-sized, full-color versions of all images in this book.*

Figure 9.12 tracks a transition for a similar system with the mutation rate one-tenth the size (0.033 versus 0.333) to make the transition easier to track. Here, the transition begins with population 0 being dominated by Always Defect and population 1 being dominated by dTFT. A mutation in population 0 at generation 2,247 introduces an Always Cooperate strategy[8] that thrives against dTFT opponents, reproduces, and drives out Always Defect in population 0. As Always Cooperate grows in population 0, the environment facing population 1 is altered enough to where Always Cooperate can invade that population, which happens with a fortuitous mutation at generation 2,253. Eventually, Always Cooperate takes over both populations, leaving the system in a robust state of mutual cooperation.

The ability for Always Cooperate to prevail over Always Defect is counterintuitive, since Always Cooperate loses in a direct contest with Always Defect (0 versus 18), or for that matter, with any of the strategies that drive the transition (see fig. 9.13). But, performance here depends on how a strategy does relative to its incumbent strategies when playing against the mix of opponents in the *other* population, and on this criterion Always Cooperate thrives as long as Always Defect is suppressed in the other population. For example, if the other population is composed solely of, say, dTFT, then Always Cooperate receives a payoff of 15 while Always Defect in that *same* population receives 14, and on such thin payoff margins cooperative destinies can arise. So, in a world where both populations are composed of Always Defect, a dTFT mutant can arise and propagate since it is environmentally neutral when facing Always Defect. With enough drift of the dTFT, Always Cooperate becomes viable in the other population and it can drive out its Always Defect incumbents. In a four-round

---

[8] Recall that Always Cooperate is the second most numerous one-step mutant of Always Defect.

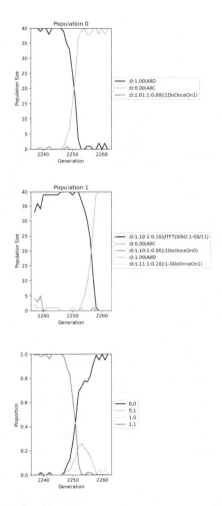

Figure 9.12. A transition to cooperation in a Stag Hunt (two-state machines, four rounds, $A = 5$, $B = 4.5$, $C = 0$, $D = 3.5$, and low mutation of 0.033). The top two panels show the frequency of the different strategies in the two populations, with the associated legends ordered from top to bottom by the maximum population size observed during any generation of the transition period. The bottom panel shows the distribution of actions over time. The game is identical to that in figure 9.11, with the exception that reproduced agents undergo a single mutation with probability 0.033 instead of 0.333. As discussed in the text, the transition motif between the two systems is similar, albeit simpler in this system.

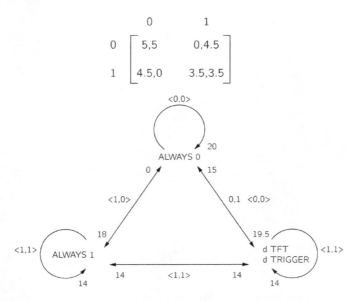

Figure 9.13. Payoff relationships in a Stag Hunt transition (two-state machines, four rounds, $B = 4.5$, and $D = 3.5$). The Stag-Hunt game in the upper half of the figure is played for four rounds. The lower half of the figure shows the resulting play and payoffs to pairings of the machines often involved in transitions to cooperative outcomes, with the respective payoffs given at the end points and the sequence of play given in the middle of the links. For example, when Always 0 plays defect Tit For Tat (dTFT), the resulting actions are $0,1 \langle 0,0 \rangle$ and Always 0 receives a payoff of 15 and dTFT receives 19.5 over the four rounds. Since populations coevolve separately, it is the relative payoff to other machines in an agent's own population when facing another population that drives the coevolutionary dynamics.

game, Always Cooperate and dTFT are able to mutually cooperate in three out of four rounds. Even though the actual play is not random, from the perspective of Always Cooperate, it is as if the probability of the opponent pursuing stag is 75%—a likelihood that greatly mitigates the risk of cooperating.

The final piece of the dynamics of this system is the flipping of the first population composed of dTFT, dGT, and Always Defect, to a population of only Always Cooperate. As noted above, prior to any observable change in the system's behavior, dTFT and dGT invaded the first population, crowding out Always Defect and allowing Always Cooperate in the second population to gain enough traction to begin displacing its incumbents. As Always Cooperate takes over the second population, the environment facing the first population changes enough so that Always Cooperate becomes viable.[9] Once this new environment facing the first population shifts enough, Always Cooperate takes over the first population as well, leading the system to a state of mutual cooperation.

Once the Stag Hunt system has converged on mutual cooperation, it is stable under reasonable mutation rates. While a population entirely composed of Always Cooperate can be invaded by an environmentally neutral mutant, such as TFT, that does not open up a niche for a less cooperative mutant in the rival population. This is due to the structure of the game, as mutual cooperation provides the highest possible payoff for both players in the game.

9.2 Conclusions

Cooperation is a fundamental social behavior that improves the welfare of agents that can form the necessary alliances. What makes cooperative phenomena interesting is that such productive

---

[9]Under the game parameters used here, Always Cooperate in the first population receives a mean payoff of $\Pi_C = \rho_C 20 + \rho_D 0 = \rho_C 20$, where ρ_C and ρ_D are, respectively, the proportion of Always Cooperate and Always Defect strategies in the second population. Always Defect in the first population has a mean payoff of $\Pi_D = \rho_C 18 + \rho_D 14$ and dTFT (or dGT) receives $\Pi_{dT} = \rho_C 19.5 + \rho_D 14$. First, $\Pi_{dT} > \Pi_D$ as long as there is at least one Always Cooperate in the second population, implying that dTFT and dGT will grow relative to Always Defect in the first population once an Always Cooperate appears in the second population. Second, $\Pi_C > \Pi_D$ when $\rho_C > 7\rho_D$ and $\Pi_C > \Pi_{dT}$ when $\rho_C > 28\rho_D$. Thus, Always Cooperate in the first population outcompetes Always Defect once the the ratio of Always Cooperate to Always Defect in the second population exceeds seven, and Always Cooperate out competes dTFT (or dGT) when that ratio exceeds twenty-eight.

alliances are often at odds with individual incentives. In both the Prisoner's Dilemma and Stag Hunt, while cooperation leads to gains for both players, each individual has an incentive (whether in terms of direct gain or decreased risk) that makes defecting attractive. Indeed, there are regions of the payoff spaces where defection is the norm. However, when more computationally capable agents interact with one another for longer periods of time, the system can transition to epochs of mutual cooperation.

As we observed in our previous explorations of social behaviors, niche construction can be important here as well. A world dominated by mutual defection can get transformed into a cooperative world when seemingly innocuous mutants begin to displace the incumbents in one of the populations. These new mutants respond to defection with defection, and thus they are undetectable to an outside observer watching the system's outcomes. However, when these mutants are exposed to cooperation they behave differently than the incumbents and cooperate. Chance events may allow the proportion of innocuous mutants in a population to grow large enough so that a niche is created that can support cooperative strategies in the rival population. If such cooperative strategies arise, they quickly propagate across their own population and this, in turn, creates a cooperative niche that reinforces the presence of the previously innocuous mutants, allowing them to invade as well.

As before, sequences of niche creation events allow the system to bootstrap itself out of asocial and into social behavior—here allowing cooperation to emerge from a world seemingly locked into defection.

Studying the "natural" histories that arise in the CAM gives us new insights into how systems seemingly locked into a bad equilibrium can be rapidly transformed. Such transformations can be driven by different mechanisms. Sometimes, simultaneous sequences of happy accidents in both populations provide enough of a push to transform the system directly, much like how the addition of just the right amount of energy allows a chemical system to overcome a barrier and synthesize a new reaction. We saw such a transformation in the Prisoner's Dilemma when, by chance, just enough cautiously cooperative strategies emerged in both populations to achieve the critical mass necessary to generate system-wide cooperation. Alternatively, transformations can be brought about by a long sequence of small chance events that encourage the propogation of environmentally neutral agents that eventually put the system into a state where the addition of a small spark leads to a radical transformation.

The origins of cooperative social behavior are inexorably tied to such transitions. Life may well have begun "solitary, poore, nasty, brutish, and short" without an obvious path forward. However, as the CAM demonstrates, adaptive systems can break out of such unfortunate states of nature through a series of small changes that eventually lead the system to rapidly transform itself into a sustainable, cooperative social world where agents can flourish.

We have observed the following for the coevolution of social cooperation:

(i) Systems of one-state machines *or* games with only one round of play tended toward defection. Under these conditions, mutual defection coevolved quickly in the Prisoner's Dilemma, while in the Stag Hunt it tended to arise in a large region of the payoff-parameter space.

(ii) Systems with machines of more than one state *and* four or ten repeated rounds promoted the emergence of mutual cooperation over large parts of the payoff-parameter space. For the Prisoner's Dilemma, these cooperative regimes were somewhat reduced as machine sizes moved past three states in four-round games. In the Stag Hunt, the cooperative regime extended to all but the most extreme payoff parameters.

(iii) Cardinal values of the payoffs mattered in these systems, especially in regimes with larger machines and more repeated rounds. This implies that not all Prisoner's Dilemmas or Stag Hunts have the same coevolutionary potential for cooperation.

(iv) These systems tended to be characterized by long epochs of relatively stable behavior, punctuated by transitions between epochs taking place over only a few generations. These transitions were driven by ecological dynamics that embraced various mechanisms ranging from simultaneous changes that supported new behavioral regimes to the slow accumulation of neutral changes that created a cascade of niches that promoted the rapid emergence of strategies that altered the system's behavior. ❧

10

COMMERCE

The first difficulty in barter is to find two persons whose disposable possessions mutually suit each other's wants. There may be many people wanting, and many possessing those things wanted; but to allow of an act of barter, there must be a double coincidence, which will rarely happen ... Sellers and purchasers can only be made to fit by the use of some commodity, some marchandise banale, as the French call it, which all are willing to receive for a time, so that what is obtained by sale in one case, may be used in purchase in another. This common commodity is called a medium of exchange, because it forms a third or intermediate term in all acts of commerce.

W. STANLEY JEVONS
Money and the Mechanism of Exchange (1875)

The exchange of goods is a powerful way for agents to better their existence. Exchange allows agents to trade goods that they can easily acquire for goods that are not as readily available. It also allows agents to specialize in the production of one good in anticipation of being able to trade it for another. Ultimately, trade is a way to extend the pool of resources available to all agents. Given this potential, it is not surprising that trade likely arose early in the history of life. Around 320,000 years ago in the Rift Valley of Africa, there is evidence of exchange as hand axes[1] gave way to smaller and more refined tools (Brooks *et al.* 2018). As for other organisms, there is fossil evidence of microbial mats forming around 3,500 million years ago (Schopf 2006), a time period early in the history of life on Earth. Microbes living in such mats could have been involved in the exchange of various resources. Social behaviors surrounding exchange provide an enormous benefit to those agents that adopt them, whether those agents are multicellular organisms or online shoppers.

Exchange was a preoccupation of economics long before Jevons's discussion of the double coincidence of wants. Smith (1776) noted how the potential for specialization could, via international trade, improve the wealth of nations. Ricardo (1817) developed the theory of comparative advantage, one of the more counterintuitive (certainly to politicians) results in economic theory. At the heart of Ricardo's contribution is the idea that it is the relative, not absolute, tradeoffs between the production of goods that drive trade. Thus, trade is still beneficial even when one of the agents is, in absolute terms, "better" at producing every good than its potential trading partners.

The act of trade or commerce embraces many social behaviors. Along with a willingness to trade, commerce requires both coordination and cooperation (see Chapters 8 and 9, respectively). Coordination is needed for the agents to meet at the appropriate time and place, and have on hand the appropriate goods to trade. Cooperation is needed for the actual exchange—each agent is better off trading than not, yet each may have an incentive to cheat by misrepresenting or failing to deliver the promised good or payment.

---

[1] A technology that predates *H. sapiens* by over a million years.

In the models explored here, we intentionally increase the difficulty of exchange by forcing agents to make their decisions about whether to send a good or not *prior* to knowing the decision of the other agent. Thus, agents can only react to their trading partner's actions from previous rounds. This makes the usual notion of voluntary exchange with the ability for each agent to veto a trade more complicated.

10.1 Coevolving Commerce

To explore commerce we consider a simple model of exchange. We assume that there are two goods in the world: α and β. Moreover, these two goods are complements to one another and must be consumed together to have any value, thus an agent's payoff is given by $\min\{\alpha, \beta\}$. A classic example of complementary goods is left and right shoes, where an agent wants to consume them together with the more complete pairs of shoes the better. In biology, α and β could represent two metabolites needed for a vital chemical reaction.

Suppose that there are two groups of agents, one of which has an unlimited amount of α and the other of which is flush in β. Agents from the two groups meet and must simultaneously decide whether to send a good to the other agent (action 0) or keep it (action 1). Table 10.1 shows the payoff matrix for this game. The game is unusual since each agent's own action makes no direct difference to its own payoff—an agent's payoff is solely determined by the action chosen by its opponent. Since an agent's action does not directly impact its own payoff the single-shot game has Nash equilibria everywhere—any set of pure strategies or any possible mixing over the strategies is a Nash equilibrium. Notwithstanding this abundance of equilibria, only the outcome where both players send their goods is Pareto dominant.

		COLUMN PLAYER	
		0 (send)	1 (keep)
ROW	0 (send)	1, 1	0, 1
PLAYER	1 (keep)	1, 0	0, 0

Table 10.1. Payoff matrix for Simple Trading. There are two types of goods in the world that must be consumed together to generate a unit of payoff. Each agent has access to an unlimited amount of the complementary good needed by the other agent. The agents meet and each must simultaneously decide whether to send its good to the other player (action 0) or keep it (action 1).

To explore coevolution in this simple game of trade we apply the Coevolving Automata Model (CAM) described in Chapter 6. Two populations of automata are matched in a tournament and play the repeated version of Simple Trading given in table 10.1. During each round, machines must decide whether to send a good (action 0) or keep it (action 1). Sending a good comes at no cost to the agent as it has an unlimited supply of its own good. As per the CAM, the action taken by a machine in a given round becomes the input to the other machine prior to the next round, thus each automaton receives information about, and responds to, the previous actions of its opponent. Each experiment runs for 10,000 generations with automata of a fixed size (ranging from one to five states) playing repeated games of various lengths.

A priori, it is hard to predict the likely outcome here. Given that any set of pure or mixed actions results in a Nash equilibrium, this might suggest that the observed play will be essentially random. However, the Pareto dominance of the send-send actions might favor that outcome—since sending a good is costless perhaps trade will be pervasive. Or, given that the actions of an agent have no direct impact on its own payoff, this might suggest that trade will be more happenstance.

Predicting the likely behavior of this system is even more difficult when we allow varying levels of computational ability for the agents and differing amounts of repeated play. Given the lack of *a priori* intuitions associated with this game, the CAM provides a useful way to formulate predictions and sharpen our understanding of adaptive behavior in this basic model of exchange.

Table 10.2 gives the proportion of each possible pair of actions that arose during the 10,000 generations of each experiment. For one-state automata, trade is rather happenstance with each of the four possible pairs of actions equally likely. Even with machines that have more than one state, if there is only one round of trade, actions are also uniformly distributed. However, once machines with more than one state begin to trade for more than one round, mutual trade ($\{0, 0\}$) becomes more likely. There is a slight increase in such trade in two-round games, but once rounds are repeated more than twice mutual trade begins to dominate the system. For larger machines playing longer games, the system often achieves mutual trade around 90% of the time. There is also some evidence that once machines get larger than two states, mutual trade is suppressed for some intermediate-length games (a point we return to below).

The results of the simple trade system form an intriguing set of patterns. In simple worlds, associated with either one-state machines *or* one- or two-round repeated games, mutual trade is a random event even though it is costless and both agents would be better off if it occurred. As the number of interactions increases above two *and* machines become more computationally capable by having at least two states, the system undergoes a transformation and mutual exchange becomes the norm.

STATES	ROUNDS	{0,0}	{0,1}	{1,0}	{1,1}
1	1	0.25	0.25	0.25	0.25
	2	0.25	0.24	0.25	0.25
	3	0.25	0.24	0.26	0.25
	4	0.25	0.25	0.25	0.25
	10	0.26	0.25	0.25	0.24
2	1	0.24	0.25	0.25	0.26
	2	0.27	0.26	0.24	0.23
	3	0.89	0.04	0.04	0.03
	4	0.88	0.04	0.04	0.04
	10	0.87	0.04	0.04	0.05
3	1	0.26	0.25	0.24	0.24
	2	0.27	0.24	0.27	0.22
	3	0.72	0.11	0.09	0.08
	4	0.88	0.04	0.04	0.04
	10	0.86	0.04	0.04	0.06
4	1	0.26	0.25	0.25	0.24
	2	0.31	0.25	0.24	0.20
	3	0.60	0.14	0.16	0.10
	4	0.90	0.04	0.04	0.03
	10	0.93	0.02	0.02	0.02
5	1	0.24	0.24	0.26	0.26
	2	0.29	0.23	0.26	0.22
	3	0.50	0.18	0.19	0.13
	4	0.80	0.07	0.08	0.05
	10	0.91	0.02	0.03	0.03

Table 10.2. Proportion of time in each outcome in a simple model of exchange. The standard Coevolving Automata Model was run once for each condition for 10,000 generations, using machines of various sizes (first column) playing repeated games of different lengths (second column). The remaining columns show the proportions of the chosen game actions (where 0 = send, 1 = keep) observed across all of the rounds and generations of the associated experiment.

The oddity of the simple trade system is that it operates very indirectly. Since an agent's actions have no direct impact on its own payoff, it is via indirect impacts, both in the short (during a given game) and long term (during coevolutionary time), that the system's behavior can be deciphered.

Coevolution occurs when one population's actions alter the evolutionary landscape facing another population. Here, coevolution takes an extreme form, akin to evolutionary farming.

To hone some intuitions about this system, consider an agent facing a population of one-state machines. Since one-state machines do not condition their outputs on inputs, there is no way to influence their behavior in the short term during a repeated game. That is, regardless of what an agent does, the behavior of its one-state opponent will not change during a given game. It is only when the opposing machine has more than one state and the game is for more than one round that an agent's behavior can potentially alter its opponent's within-game behavior.

The behavior of the system on coevolutionary time scales — that is, how the evolutionary landscape imposed by one population determines what types of machines are reproduced in subsequent generations in the other population—is also important here. Given that the payoffs in Simple Trading are determined solely by the actions of the opponent, coevolutionary landscapes can lead to some unusual behavior. For example, consider an agent facing a population of one-state machines. Since one-state machines always take the same action (regardless of their opponent's action) and payoffs are solely determined by such actions, all of the agents in the opposing population receive the same payoff when playing against a population of one-state machines. This implies that the evolutionary landscape facing agents playing against a population of one-state machines is flat, that is, since every agent receives the same payoff as any other agent in its own population, selection is random.[2] Under a flat evolutionary landscape, reproduction is driven solely by neutral drift.

In the Simple Trading system, whenever a machine sends a good to an opponent it increases that opponent's payoff by one, altering that opponent's evolutionary prospects. Therefore, even though sending goods may not directly change one's own payoff, it indirectly influences what opponents are likely to arise in the future—sending goods is a way of rewarding a particular strategy and increasing its likelihood of being reproduced in future generations.[3]

Such evolutionary farming must be carefully done. For example, encouraging the proliferation of *any* strategy that sends goods might result in a coevolutionary anomaly in one's *own* population. As noted, if one population becomes filled with, say, Always Send, the evolutionary landscape facing the other population becomes flat, allowing any strategy in that population to do as well as any other. Such indiscriminate farming results in the devolution of the population of farmers, destroying their ability to successfully manipulate the strategies in the other population.

---

[2] The converse is not true—the two types of one-state machines may receive different payoffs when facing a population with conditional strategies for more than one round of play.

[3] This form of coevolution can often lead to unusual evolutionary outcomes. For example, one would not expect tasty, slow-moving, and relatively defenseless animals like cattle and chickens to excel in an evolutionary race, yet there are around 1.5 billion cattle and upwards of 20 billion chickens in the world. Obviously, this success is due to humans creating selective forces that override the usual evolutionary imperatives. Edward Abbey (1975, p. 185) concisely captured this issue when he (nefariously) referred to cows as "slow elk."

In Simple Trading, evolutionary dynamics can be driven by small subpopulations of strategies. For example, suppose a population is composed of some mix of Always Send and Always Keep. Every machine in the opposing population, regardless of its structure, receives the same payoff and therefore the evolutionary landscape facing that population is flat allowing strategic drift. However, having multiple rounds and adding just a single conditional strategy to the population of Always Send and Always Keep is sufficient to impose selection on the other population, since play against that single conditional strategy will differentiate payoffs. This can lead to unusual dynamics, for example, take a population of Always Send and Tit For Tat (TFT) facing a population composed of only Always Send. The presence of TFT in the first population protects the second population from being invaded by Always Keep, however, Always Send and TFT in the first population get the same payoff, so neutral drift could allow TFT to disappear.

The above intuitions help explain the Simple Trading results. In a world of one-state machines playing any number of repeated rounds, both populations face a flat evolutionary landscape. Without any selection, machines drift across random structures resulting in random play, making mutual trade a chance event.

The same lack of selective pressure also emerges in one-round games played with machines of any size. Automata issue their first move without seeing any input from the opponent, so the initial action of a machine is identical regardless of the opponent. Thus, in a one-round game automata of any size display unconditional behavior, resulting in the same payoff for all opponents. Again, both populations face flat evolutionary landscapes, coevolution has no bite, and machines randomly drift in and out of both populations.

Therefore, a necessary condition for coevolution to matter in this system is to have machines with at least two states (which are capable of conditional behavior) playing more than one-round games (which provide an opportunity for the players to condition on previous actions). However, the CAM results suggest that this is not a sufficient condition for trade, since two-round games, even with machines with more than one state, also devolve into random trade.

In a two-round game, each agent commits to its first action and then decides on its second action based on the opponent's initial action. This limited interaction raises an interesting problem in Simple Trading given that one's actions don't directly influence one's payoff. Suppose a machine reciprocates an initial send by an opponent with a send in the second round, thereby encouraging the proliferation of those initial-send machines in the other population. Unfortunately, the increase of initial-send machines in the other population adds fitness to every machine (regardless of structure) in the reciprocator's population, since they all benefit from the opponent's initial send. Thus, reinforcing initial senders does not provide a selective advantage to the reciprocator. It is only with more than two rounds that strategies can impact their *relative* fitness.

As games get longer than two rounds machine size begins to matter. Two-state machines playing three rounds or more achieve mutual trade almost 90% of the time. With larger machines, mutual trade approaches or exceeds this value in longer-length games. However, larger machines playing fewer rounds often result in a lower proportion of trade than systems with smaller machines. For example, in three-round games, mutual trade arises in 89%, 72%, 60%, and 50% of the possible interactions, for two-, three-, four-, and five-state machines, respectively. It is only when the larger machines encounter longer-length games that high levels of mutual trade occur.

Therefore, constraining processing ability appears to benefit trade. Smaller machines must base their behaviors on simple patterns, such as mimicking the opponent's last action, and such constraints may improve performance in repeated games of moderate length. Larger machines can invoke far more sophisticated patterns, such as taking a particular set of three actions regardless of the opponent's moves, and these unconstrained possibilities likely hamper such machines in moderate-length games. The longer the game relative to the size of the machine, the more evolutionary pressure there is on identifying concise and productive schemata.

There is an unusual tension in this simple trading system. In the short term, agents want to encourage the opposing population to always send goods. However, if that opposing population becomes filled with strategies that send goods unconditionally, the coevolutionary pressure on an agent's own population is lost and strategies drift. For long-run stability the system needs strategies that send goods, but in a way that differentiates between strategies that also differentiate. This result is consistent with other observations of this system—we often see large populations of conditional senders (like TFT or Grim Trigger) emerging in this system versus unconditional strategies like Always Send.

Above, we considered a very simple model of trade: agents have an unlimited amount of one of two necessary goods and are matched with an agent holding the other good. Agents can either send one of their goods at no cost or hold on to it. This scenario is unusual as an agent's actions have no direct impact on its own payoff so, *a priori*, one might think that the system will always trade (given that it comes at no cost) or never trade (given that it comes at no direct benefit). The results were more subtle and tied to the dynamics of coevolution in both the short term—the action of sending may induce the other player to send in the next round—and long term—the payoffs one agent gives to the other allow that agent to thrive (or wither) during subsequent generations of coevolution. We found that mutual trade does not arise (over chance) in systems with one-state machines and any number of repeated rounds, or in systems of machines with more than one state and either one or two repeated rounds. However, once systems have machines of more than one state playing for more than two rounds, mutual trade becomes the norm, approaching rates of around 90% for some systems.

10.2 Trade with Constraints

The Simple Trading model above provides a benchmark for exchange in an adaptive system under (at least *a priori*) favorable conditions. Unfortunately, even under seemingly favorable conditions the social gains of trade did not always accrue. Next, we explore a more classic model of exchange.

10.2.1 SYMMETRIC COMPLEMENTS

Most exchange occurs under conditions where the endowments of the agents are limited. For example, take the previous model, but endow each agent with only ten units of its own good. Now, the potential social gain embodied in this system is, at most, the creation of ten complementary pairs of goods. If the system produces less than ten such pairs, then an opportunity is lost for improving the welfare of at least one of the agents without diminishing the welfare of the other—that is, there is a potential Pareto improvement in the system. Once all ten pairs of goods are held by the agents the system is Pareto efficient. Of course,

Pareto efficiency does not imply equity—any outcome where the total holdings of the agents add up to ten pairs, including the one where one agent gets all ten, is Pareto efficient.

Edgeworth (1881) introduced the classic analysis of this model of two-agent exchange in his delightfully named treatise *Mathematical Psychics*. His analysis can be visualized using the "Edgeworth box" shown in figure 10.1. In this figure, two agents are endowed with ten units of two different goods. Agent A's perspective is given by the traditional origin of the graph, with the amount of A's holdings of goods α and β given by the standard x- and y-axis values, respectively. Agent B's perspective is generated by reflecting A's perspective, that is, by starting at the top-right corner and looking toward the traditional origin. Whatever goods that are not held by agent A are held by agent B. Thus, any point in the box provides an allocation of the ten units of the two goods between the two agents. For example, point $(10, 0)$ (using the traditional origin) is where agent A gets ten units of good α and no units of good β, and agent B gets no units of good α and ten units of good β.

As in the previous section, we assume that the agents want to consume the two goods in pairs. Such preferences are given by the symmetric Leontief utility function $U(\alpha, \beta) = \min\{\alpha, \beta\}$. Given these preferences, the set of Pareto efficient allocations of the goods, known as the contract curve, is given by the 45° line[4] where all ten complementary pairs of goods are allocated across the agents.

The most general social prediction arising out of the Edgeworth box is that the final allocation of the system should be on the contract curve. Since the contract curve contains

---

[4] Using a line assumes that the goods are infinitely divisible. Here, goods are discrete, so technically the contract curve is given by the discrete unit points on the diagonal.

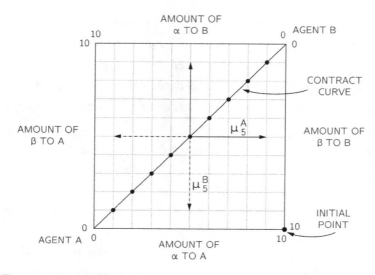

Figure 10.1. Edgeworth box for exchange. This Edgeworth box captures the potential allocations of two goods in fixed supply between two agents. Agent A's perspective is from the origin of the graph, while agent B's perspective is a reflection of A's from the opposite corner. The system begins with agent A having ten units of α and no units of β, and agent B having ten units of β and no units of α. Each agent's final utility is tied to the number of completed pairs of the two goods that they obtain, with the more completed pairs the better (thus, each agent has symmetric Leontief preferences given by $\min\{\alpha, \beta\}$). The resulting contract curve, containing all of the allocations that are Pareto efficient, is given by the 45° diagonal.

the possible Pareto efficient outcomes, any allocation not on this curve implies that there exists an alternative allocation where at least one agent is better off and the other is no worse off. If we add the additional condition that exchange is always voluntary, namely, that either agent can veto a proposed trade, we can refine the prediction of the final allocation of goods by eliminating points on the contract curve that have lower utility than either agent's initial endowment. In this system, with symmetric Leontief preferences and initial endowments that give each agent ten of their namesake good and none of the other, the entire contract curve represents

Pareto improvements since the endowed utility of each agent is 0.

To explore this system we implement the CAM used in the previous section. As before, social behavior is reflected in the properties of the final allocation of goods between the agents. The first signature of social behavior is a Pareto efficient allocation of goods as reflected in the system ending up somewhere on the contract curve.[5] A second (and perhaps "higher") level of social behavior might incorporate equity concerns. In the models below, the agents begin in symmetric positions (each endowed with an equivalent amount of the needed complementary good), so a redistribution of the goods where each agent receives five complementary pairs is possible.

Given that agents can only exchange one good per round, it takes at least one round for agents to acquire a complementary pair of goods. Since agents are endowed with ten goods each they can create at most ten possible complementary pairs of goods. Therefore, if trade is somehow directed so that the system ends up on the contract curve this requires a minimum of five (if the agents always exchange goods each round, giving each a final allocation of five pairs) to ten (if one agent is able to acquire all ten pairs by getting the other agent to blindly send all of its goods) rounds. Given the need for sustained periods of trade, computations may be more taxing, requiring larger-sized machines, especially if nontrivial counting is involved. For example, computations such as "send exactly four goods regardless of what your opponent does" or "reciprocate at most two of your opponent's sends," require at least five-state automata. Thus, useful strategies may require larger machine sizes in this system.

---

[5] In Simple Trading, the contract "curve" requires mutual trade in every round.

We consider two systems, one where the agents are each endowed with four units of the complementary good and another where the endowment is equal to ten. In each round of the game, agents can either send (action 0) a unit of their endowed good or keep it (action 1). After each round of trade, agents process information about what the opponent did in the previous round. Experiments are conducted for systems with from one- to five-state machines playing from one to ten repeated rounds.

Figure 10.2 shows the Edgeworth box resulting from an experiment using three-state machines playing ten-round games, with each agent being endowed with ten units of the complementary good associated with its population. The system coevolves the agents for 5,000 generations, and the figure shows the density of the final allocation of goods across the last 4,000 generations of trading. The contract curve here is the diagonal from the lower-left to upper-right corners of the box.

In this experiment, the modal outcome implied trade where each agent traded five units. This resulted in each agent having five complementary pairs of goods, and thus the system was able to achieve the efficient *and* equitable outcome. Most of the remaining outcomes ended up on either the bottom or right-side borders, implying that only one of the agents sent (some) goods to the other.

To investigate the impact of the various trading parameters, a series of experiments was conducted. First, consider a system where each agent is endowed with four units of the complementary good associated with its population. Again, agents coevolve for 5,000 generations and the final allocations at the end of each game from generation 1,000 on are averaged and put into the Edgeworth boxes shown in figures 10.3 and 10.4. As in the other experiments, a single run of (in this case) 5,000 generations needs to be interpreted

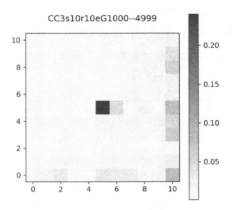

Figure 10.2. Edgeworth box of three-state coevolving machines trading with equal endowments of ten goods and symmetric complements. The two agents had endowments that initially placed them in the lower-right corner of the Edgeworth box, with one population of agents having ten units of the x-axis and none of the y-axis good, and the other population having no units of the x-axis and ten units of the y-axis good. Agents received one unit of payoff for each pair of x-axis and y-axis goods that they hold in the final round. Two populations of agents coevolved for 5,000 generations playing ten-round games, and the figure displays the density of the final allocations at the end of the ten rounds of trading averaged over the last 4,000 generations of the coevolution. The contract curve connects the lower-left and upper-right corners of the diagram.

with some caveats if path dependence occurs. The initial endowment point is the bottom-right of each Edgeworth box.

In one- and two-round games, regardless of machine size, final allocations were spread randomly over the possible ending allocations—a similar result to what we saw in the Simple Trading game. As the game was iterated for more than two rounds with one-state machines, typically no trade was observed and the system remained at the original endowments. With machines of more than one state and an intermediate number of rounds, final outcomes spread across the triangular region below the contract curve, but as the number of rounds increased, trade concentrated on the bottom and right-side boundaries. Thus, longer periods of interaction led to less equitable outcomes. This latter result is tied to machine size, as smaller machines have a harder time navigating longer interactions given innate limits on computation.

Figures 10.5 and 10.6 show the parallel results for a system with an initial endowment of ten units of the two goods. The results here are less murky than those with the lower endowment, as the larger endowment aligns better with the number of available rounds. As before, one- or two-round games led to random final allocations and one-state machines either resulted in random allocations (if the number of rounds was less than or equal to half the endowment) or no trade (if the number of rounds was greater than half the endowment). However, with more than two rounds and with machines of more than one state, the final allocations appeared to converge to the efficient and equitable outcome with five pairs of goods for each agent.[6] As the number of rounds exceeded six, machines of three or more states continued to maintain the efficient and equitable outcome (with a bit more noise under higher rounds), while those with two states adopted a pattern similar to what was observed in the four-endowment system in this region (with none or only one of the populations sending goods).

To gain more insight into the population dynamics driving the Edgeworth model, we analyzed two-state machines with endowments of ten goods playing a range of rounds. For games with less than three rounds, the final allocation in this system was essentially random, for reasons related to those explaining the Simple Trading results, namely, in a two-round game machines

---

[6]When the number of rounds is less than five, this final allocation is not feasible and the agents appear to trade to the nearest feasible equitable allocation.

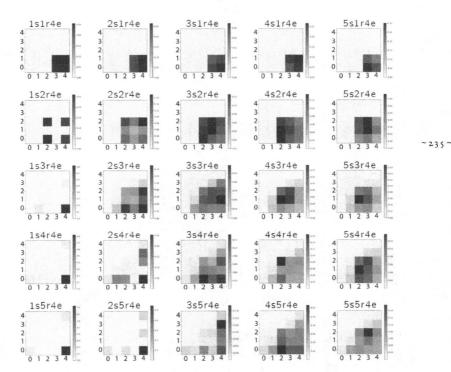

Figure 10.3. Parameter sweep of Edgeworth trade with equal endowments of four goods and symmetric complements (1/2). For each configuration of automaton states and repeated rounds, the associated system underwent evolution for 5,000 generations, starting from the lower-right point in the Edgeworth box where one agent had four units of α and none of β, and the other agent had four units of β and none of α. The number of automaton states and repeated rounds is given in each subplot's title: states go from one (leftmost column) to five (rightmost column) and rounds go from one (top row) to five (bottom row). Each subplot shows the Edgeworth box of the outcome density observed at the end of the repeated game over the last 4,000 generations of the experiment. (Note that the density scale can vary across the diagrams.) *Please refer to the Github repository (https://github.com/SantaFeInstitute/ExMachina) for full-sized, full-color versions of all images in this book.*

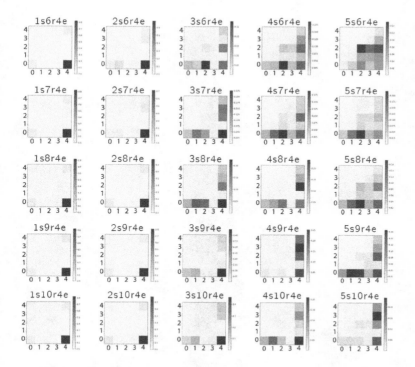

Figure 10.4. Parameter sweep of Edgeworth trade with equal endowments of four goods and symmetric complements (2/2). The conditions and construction are identical to figure 10.3, with the exception that the number of rounds goes from six (top row) to ten (bottom row).

cannot reinforce the productive behavior of an opponent in a way that impacts relative fitness. Once we have more than two rounds, conditional strategies begin to exert themselves. In games of three and four rounds, we find that exchange is driven by the presence of conditional strategies such as TFT, Grim Trigger, 0 and Punish Once, and 0WSLS (do 0 if there are an even number of 1's). All of these strategies begin by trading and continue to do so as long as the opponent trades, but if the opponent fails to trade the machines (in various ways) limit their own trading. This results in systems that achieve mutual exchange for each round,

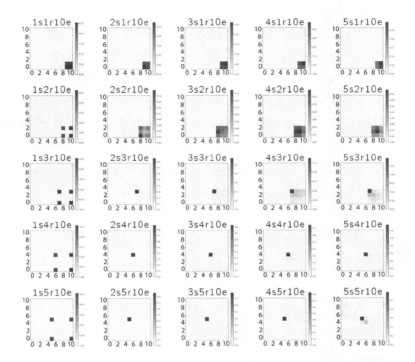

Figure 10.5. Parameter sweep of Edgeworth trade with equal endowments of ten goods and symmetric complements (1/2). For each configuration of automaton states and repeated rounds, the associated system underwent evolution for 5,000 generations, starting from the lower-right point in the Edgeworth box where one agent had ten units of good α and none of good β and the other player had ten units of good β and none of good α. The number of automaton states and repeated rounds is given in each subplot's title: states go from one (leftmost column) to five (rightmost column) and rounds go from one (top row) to five (bottom row). Each subplot shows the Edgeworth box of the outcome density observed at the end of the repeated game over the last 4,000 generations of the experiment. (Note that the density scale can vary across the diagrams.)

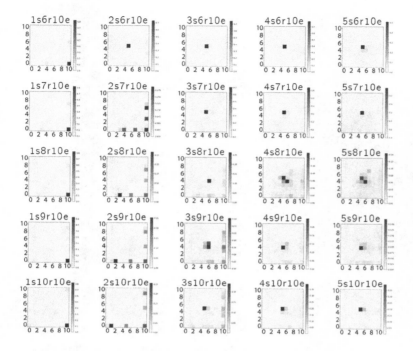

Figure 10.6. Parameter sweep of Edgeworth trade with equal endowments of ten goods and symmetric complements (2/2). The conditions and construction are identical to figure 10.5, with the exception that the number of rounds goes from six (top row) to ten (bottom row).

with final allocations of either three or four pairs of goods to each agent depending on the number of rounds.

A wider range of behavior emerges when the game has five rounds. One possibility here is the same behavior that arose in the three- and four-round games, where the previously discussed conditional strategies emerge and the agents trade five goods, resulting in both an efficient and equitable outcome. Such systems tend to be robust once they arise. However, another dynamic can arise that involves strategies such as play 1 when an even number of 1s has been input (1WSLS), play 1 unless a 1 is input, in which case only play 0 (Trigg1Unless1), and play 1 then all 0s. Populations composed of these strategies have agents begin by not trading and then switch to trading for the remainder of the game, implying a meta-cycle of 1,1 ⟨0,0⟩. Such a cycle results in four trades leading to each agent obtaining four complementary sets of goods rather than the five that arose in the first dynamic. The strategies driving this second dynamic do better than the previous strategies against a randomly selected strategy from the twenty-six unique two-state machines, so evolution may promote their rise. If they do take over, the resulting world is hard to escape as the four strategies all begin by not trading, which tends to confound the set of trade-and-reciprocate-trade strategies that characterized the first dynamic.

Once the game is played for six rounds the second dynamic we saw in the five-round game dominates. In a six-round game, the meta-cycle of 1,1 ⟨0,0⟩ is ideal as it allows exactly five trades to be completed over the six rounds, leading to both efficient and equitable outcomes. With two-state machines, the aforementioned meta-cycle is the only way to trade exactly five goods in six rounds. There are only four two-state machines that can create a cycle of 1,1 ⟨0,0⟩ (1WSLS, Trig1unless1, 1-0DoOnceOn1, and 1ThenAll0)—some of the same machines we saw in the alternative five-round dynamic above. In the six-round system, 1WSLS, which keeps when the opponent has kept for an even number of times (or, alternatively, trades as long as the opponent has kept for an odd number of times), tends to dominate the populations. This strategy gets the maximum expected payoff of the twenty-six possible strategies when playing against a random opponent. It also dominates the other three aforementioned strategies by getting at least as high of a score against all but three of the other strategies (0TFT, 1TFT, and 0-1DoOnceOn0, all of which are weak performers overall).

The six-round system provides a nice example of coevolution productively using external constraints. Two-state machines are inherently limited when it comes to counting, yet the reward in this system comes from sending five goods over *six* rounds as long as the opponent reciprocates. Interacting two-state machines have a difficult time trading in all but one round—indeed, the only way to do so is to not trade in the first round and trade thereafter, since not trading once in some round after the first one requires more computation than a two-state machine can muster. If the machines had access to more states, there is the potential for developing alternative strategies that could implement the required behavior. However, under the constraint of two states, machines must implement an imprecise strategy that hijacks regularities of the environment (here, playing exactly six rounds) to produce a "second-best" machine.

The second-best machine that arises in the six-round game fails in the seven-round game, since there is no way for it to only trade for five of the seven rounds. Thus, trade begins to break down as other machines become competitive. The coevolution in these high-round worlds tends to support machines that always keep, along with various other strategies that come in and out, resulting in either no or one-sided trade. Such machines push the system to the bottom or right-side borders of the Edgeworth box.

While seven rounds is too much for two-state machines, Figure 10.6 shows that larger-state machines can navigate games of seven to ten rounds. For example, a three-state machine can use its first state just to keep the good and then transition into the two-state machine that arose in the six-round game—this leads to meta-play of 1,1 1,1 ⟨0,0⟩, which keeps for two rounds and sends thereafter, resulting in five trades over seven rounds. This approach fails for eight rounds, but other possible machine interactions result in meta-plays that provide new opportunities to solve the counting problem. For example, we observe populations of three-state machines that create meta-play of 1,1 1,0 0,1 1,1 $\langle 0,0 \rangle$, so during the initial four rounds each agent acquires a single complementary good and then in the remaining four rounds goods are always exchanged, leading to five complementary pairs being created for each agent. Machines resulting in meta-play of $\langle 1,0\,0,1 \rangle$ do relatively well in nine-round games (with one machine receiving five and the other getting four complementary pairs) and they achieve the efficient and equitable outcome in ten-round games with each receiving five pairs of goods.

Thus, as machines become larger, the set of possible meta-plays increases to the point where computational challenges can be solved in *ad hoc* ways that exploit environmental regularities.

10.2.2 ASYMMETRIC COMPLEMENTS

In the Edgeworth experiments above the two goods were perfect complements, implying that one-to-one exchanges give each agent a complementary pair of goods. The exchange ratio can be thought of as a price—the amount of one good that has to be given up for the other. In Appendix G we investigate what happens to the system when prices are less trivial. We apply the identical CAM above in an environment where unequal amounts of the two goods are needed to form the payoff-providing, complementary set: agents gain one unit of payoff by acquiring *two* units of α and one unit of β. We modify the endowments so that twice as many αs are endowed to the A agent at the start of the game, keeping the total number of possible complementary sets of goods in the system at ten. We also double the maximum number of rounds so that either agent could acquire all of the goods in the system. The automata have the same construction and actions as before, implying that only a single good (of either type) can be exchanged in any given round even though the price needed for efficient and equitable trade is two for one.

As before, social outcomes require that the agents realize at least some of the potential gains to trade. One way to do this involves the inequitable outcome where only one agent sends its goods to the other. A more socially interesting outcome embraces both efficiency and equity, where agent A sends two α goods in return for one β good.

The overall results of the asymmetric system had more noise and less equity in the final outcomes than we saw in the symmetric system. The final allocations in this system typically favored the A agents (each endowed with twenty units of the good that was needed twice in every bundle). In a similar way to the symmetric Edgeworth system, more machine states and trading rounds encouraged greater efficiency, and too many rounds could result in the system breaking down under smaller-sized machines. Overall, while the asymmetric system did not achieve equity, it did display regimes that realized the full gains from trade.

10.3 Conclusions

Exchange is a fundamental part of social life. At its simplest level, exchange arises when one agent's trash is another agent's treasure. The models above, however, explored a more active notion of exchange where agents had to explicitly consent to send a good. One added difficulty in our system was that the agents had to send their goods without knowing what the other agent would do in a given round, and thus agents could only react to what their trading partner did in the prior round.

Even under conditions that would seem favorable to such exchange—unlimited amounts of the trade good with no costs of sending it to the other—productive exchange required a minimal level of computational ability and interaction.

When we imposed constraints on the number of goods in the system, the behavior of the coevolutionary system became more subtle. At low levels of computation and interaction, exchange was either nonexistent or haphazard. However, once the system crossed critical thresholds, the potential gains of trade began to be realized as the interacting agents exchanged enough goods to achieve Pareto efficient outcomes. As the system moved beyond these thresholds, new regimes emerged where exchange led to both efficient *and* equitable outcomes under symmetric complements, though such outcomes began to break down as increased interactions outstripped the computational abilities of the agents. Even under these more demanding conditions, on occasion, coevolution was able to create *ad hoc* solutions by leveraging off regularities in the environment.

The models above capture a very basic notion of exchange that could be extended in many different directions. First, there was no production in these systems. The introduction of production—allowing choices about what goods to produce and how to produce them—would be interesting. For example, the theory of comparative advantage (Ricardo 1817) makes some seemingly anomalous predictions about specialization that would be interesting to test in a coevolutionary model. Second, there are theories about why firms exist (see, for example, Coase 1937; Williamson 1981) tied to the notion that the transaction costs of exchange can be high enough to warrant an alternative solution, such as forming a firm or, in biology, a symbiont or multicellular organism. More advanced models of exchange could embrace such transaction costs and be used to explore the conditions necessary for the formation of social organizations akin to firms, cells, or whole organisms. Theories of transaction costs tend to favor the formation of firms as agents interact more frequently, face higher levels of uncertainty that make contracting over the various contingencies difficult, or must specialize their production to the point where survival outside of the partnership is unlikely. While such ideas have found ready applications in economics, they could be useful for understanding phenomena such as multicellularity in biology.[7]

To summarize our experiments in social exchange:

(i) In the Simple Trading model, where agents can exchange unconstrained amounts of the trade good without cost, systems with one-state agents *or* less than three rounds of trade were unable to establish mutual trade beyond random chance.

(ii) When agents had more than one state *and* traded for more than two rounds, mutual exchange arose in the Simple Trading model.

(iii) A pure form of coevolution drove these previous results, with agents tuning the environment of the other population so as to encourage the proliferation of agents that not only trade, but do so conditionally. This latter

---

[7]Command and control also plays a role in the formation of firms. In particular, the difficulty of gathering and processing the information needed to make, and implement, productive decisions may place a natural limit on the size of social organizations. While this may be true for centralized systems of command and control, there are plenty of examples in the study of complex systems, such as honeybee colonies, where large and productive organizations exist without central control. These latter systems tend to be characterized by agents following simple interaction rules (see, for example, Golman, Hagmann, and Miller 2015). An interesting exercise would be to coevolve collections of machines, where the coevolution is over the individual behavior of the machines, but the payoff is tied to the success of the collective.

requirement prevented neutral drift from devolving one's own population.

(iv) In a model of constrained trade with symmetric Leontief preferences, systems with one-state agents *or* less than three rounds of trade were unable to establish mutual trade beyond random chance.

(v) When agents had more than one state *and* traded for more than two rounds, exchange could drive the constrained system toward efficient and equitable allocations.

(vi) As the number of rounds increased, the exchange in the constrained system began to degrade in consistent ways toward less efficient and more inequitable allocations.

(vii) Sometimes, limits on the computational ability of the agents were overcome in *ad hoc* ways by the system coevolving machines that leveraged off of environmental regularities.

(viii) A constrained trade model with asymmetric Leontief preferences followed similar patterns to that of the symmetric Leontief model, though the asymmetric system tended to converge on less equitable allocations. ✍

II

COMMUNICATION

... then said they unto him, Say now Shibboleth; and he said Sibboleth; for he could not frame to pronounce it right: then they laid hold on him, and slew him at the fords of the Jordan. And there fell at that time of Ephraim forty and two thousand.

Book of Judges 12:6, American Standard Version

One of the hallmarks of social behavior is interaction, and such interactions are often mediated by communication. Most of the communication we think about, from emojis and Morse code to contracts and constitutions, are the result of a long period of refinement combining adaptation and, in many cases, careful thought and curated social norms. Communication occurs throughout the natural world as well, such as quorum sensing in bacteria, ants depositing pheromones, the body postures of wolves, and the whistles and clicks of dolphins. The ubiquity and variety of independently developed forms of communication in human, natural, and artificial systems are a testament to its value in enhancing the fitness of agents. Our interest here is in the origins of communication in primitive social systems.

At the outset, we tie our hands to the systems that we have been exploring in the previous chapters. In the Coevolving Automata Model (CAM) agents interact through actions that get communicated to the other agent as inputs. It is in the context of this very limited action-input channel that we limit our search for communication.

Real-world actions often take on meaning beyond their immediate consequences. For example, at one time the action of raising one's hands to show that no weapons were being concealed was a useful way to avoid an unnecessary conflict. While that action can still be used in that context, it has also been abstracted into our broader communication system. For example, when a computer crashes and you raise your hands in resignation, presumably the computer neither recognizes nor responds to that gesture (at least, not yet).

To understand the emergence of communication in the CAM we seek similar evidence of actions with direct consequences being repurposed to convey additional meaning. Such evidence becomes stronger when the direct consequences of the action come at an immediate cost to the communicative agent, a cost presumably borne in the short term to alter the future behavior of the opponent in a way that will have long-term benefits that outweigh the short-term costs.[1]

In section 3.3 we showed how the interactions between two machines can be captured via a meta-machine. Meta-machines

---

[1] In other work, Miller, Butts, and Rode (2002) and Miller and Moser (2004) used a variant CAM to explore a much more explicit notion of communication. In these models, actions included directly sending communicative tokens that had no *a priori* meaning. Agents evolved machines that sent and responded to such tokens and, in that process, decided on a move to take when playing a single-shot game such as a Prisoner's Dilemma. This system was equivalent to having a strategic conversation with an opponent and, based on that conversation, deciding how to play the game. One surprising result from this work was that even in situations where communication was not enforceable (known as cheap talk) and thus, at least theoretically, should have been ignored, agents paid attention to it. For example, in the Prisoner's Dilemma handshakes developed that distinguished cooperators from defectors, allowing, at least for short periods (until the handshake got nullified by mimics), cooperation to emerge in the system. While this work provides an interesting example of how communication can be refined in an adaptive system, it presupposes the existence of communicative tokens and a structured sequence of talk followed by a single play of the game, leaving open the question of how these elements arose in the first place.

take on the characteristic form of a snake biting its own body, with the sequence of interactions starting at the snake's tail and moving toward its head until it jumps from the head back to the body and cycles anew. Thus, meta-machines potentially begin with a unique sequence of joint actions that eventually transitions into a perpetual cycle.

It is in the nature of the meta-machines that we will search for the origins of communication. When two machines enter a cycle they are locked into a joint set of actions, and the resulting payoffs, for perpetuity. When such cycles are preceded by a sequence of unique actions—that is, when the initial interactions move from the snake's tail to the bite mark—that sequence of initial actions establishes which perpetual cycle the underlying machines will embrace. As such, these initial actions serve as a communicative handshake that determines the nature of the subsequent interactions—the difference between Shibboleth and Sibboleth can be the death of forty and two thousand.

11.1   Coevolving Communication

One of the most dramatic coevolutionary events that we observed in our experiments was the rapid transition of a system from one extreme epoch to another. What role does communication play in such transitions?

Recall that extreme transitions are often characterized by a common motif (see sec. 6.3). Figure 11.1 reproduces this motif. Prior to the transition, the dominant population is composed of α machines interacting with β machines in the subordinate population. Such interactions are characterized by a set of actions that focus on immediate payoffs, rather than communication *per se*.

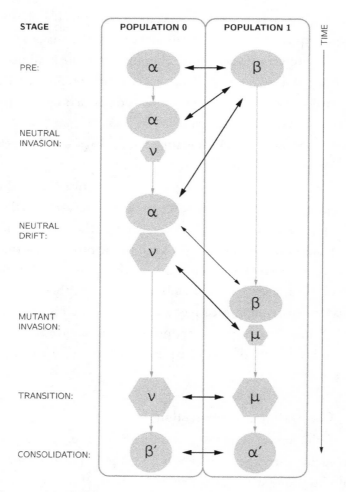

Figure 11.1. Communication in an extreme transition. Pre-transition, the two populations have stabilized into an epoch where communication is unnecessary and the machines exploit the gains from their immediate actions. A mutation in population 0 leads to an environmentally neutral machine, ν, that increases its representation in that population through neutral drift. Though the presence of the neutral mutant doesn't initially alter the observed behavior of the system, it does open up an opportunity for communication by an invading mutant, μ, in population 1. The action (signal) sent by μ establishes a new set of joint actions with ν, eventually resulting in a rapid transition of the system to a new steady state. In this new steady state, like the initial state of the system, communication wanes.

The first phase of the transition is initiated by the emergence of a neutral mutant, ν, in the α population. This mutant performs the identical sequence of actions as α does against β so, again, all actions are focused on exploiting immediate payoffs.

However, ν differs from α in an important way, namely, its response to alternative sequences of (heretofore unseen) actions differs from that of its α brethren. Thus, insofar as alternative actions can communicate different intentions, ν will listen. It is this difference between ν and α that sets the stage for a transition.

Once the preconditions for a transition have been established, a simple communicative catalyst is sufficient to overturn the existing order. The emergence of an appropriate mutant, μ, in β's population serves as this catalyst. The initial actions of μ and β differ, and μ's alternative action signals the ν machines in the other population. When μ interacts with an α, the signal value of μ's alternative action is worthless and, indeed, imparts a cost on μ giving it a lower payoff than if it had avoided the new action altogether. However, the new action (signal) emitted by μ has meaning to ν, and results in these two machines undertaking a different set of subsequent actions that enhances both of their relative payoffs, with ν and μ doing better than their incumbent α and β machines, respectively. Thus, we find that actions with immediate payoff consequences are repurposed as signals that entail an immediate short-term cost, while promoting a long-term gain.

In many of the previous chapters, the details of various transitions have already been explored, though their implications for emergent communication were not highlighted. Now, we reconsider some of these transitions given this new lens.

First, consider a slightly simpler example of one of the transitions in the Prisoner's Dilemma explored in Chapter 9. In this game, the system often finds itself in a world of mutual defection. The emergence of strategies like Grim Trigger (cooperate, but if the opponent ever defects, defect thereafter) and Tit For Tat (cooperate, then mimic the previous action of the opponent) has the potential to flip this system into a world of mutual cooperation. Both of these strategies begin by signaling a willingness to cooperate, and if that signal is acted upon, they cooperate. However, if the resulting action to their communicative overture is a defection, both Grim Trigger and Tit For Tat take that as a signal to defect (to different degrees). In a world of Always Defect, both Grim Trigger and Tit For Tat pay a cost for repurposing their first action as a cooperative signal, since they receive the Sucker rather than the Punishment payoff in the first round, so the attempted communication comes at a short-term cost. Yet if they meet each other, the potential value of establishing cooperation may make such costs evolutionarily tolerable.

The Stag Hunt was also analyzed in Chapter 9 and it provides another example of a communicative transition. In this game there is the Pareto inferior outcome where players hunt hare that, from a risk perspective, can dominate the superior payoffs from hunting stag. Such incentives can lock the system into both players always pursuing hare and receiving an intermediate payoff. Moreover, any agent that unilaterally adopts an Always Stag strategy does poorly, since its actions communicating a desire to play stag are ignored and it receives the lowest possible payoff.

Now, suppose an environmentally neutral mutation such as a variant of Tit For Tat (that begins by playing hare, and thereafter copies the action of the opponent) emerges in one of the populations. This new strategy establishes the same cycle as Always Hare does when playing against Always Hare, so there is no observable change in the outcome of this system. However, if this new Tit For Tat becomes a nontrivial part of its population—a possibility through neutral drift—the world is primed for communication to initiate a transition into a regime where the agents focus their actions on stag-stag play. This occurs when a new strategy in the other population signals its willingness to play stag by taking that action. Even though this results in the new strategy receiving the lowest possible payoff in the first round (as the opponent is sure to play hare), such a communicative overture will be reciprocated by Tit For Tat in the next round and the potential exists for the stag-stag outcome to become the norm.[2] Once a willingness to play stag is communicated and reciprocated, the agents can establish mutual stag play and begin to outcompete their incumbents. Thus, the previously costly communication of wanting to play stag becomes viable with the establishment of the more favorable cycle. As the system moves toward increasing stag-stag outcomes, evolutionary refinements will likely lead to both populations becoming composed of Always Stag machines, at which point the value of communication disappears from the system.

---

[2]In this case, the new strategy must be tolerant of the opponent initially playing hare. Thus, a Tit For Tat that begins by playing stag would not work as the players would fall into a sequence of $\langle 1,0 \ 0,1 \rangle$. Strategies like Tit For Two Tats or a Grim Trigger that begins with stag, then plays hare unless it sees a stag, in which case it plays stag thereafter, could succeed in switching the equilibrium.

As a final example, consider the Battle of the Sexes (see Chapter 8). Unlike the previous two examples, here the ability to communicate opens up a vulnerability as well as an opportunity. Suppose that both populations are playing Always 0, resulting in a cycle of $\langle 0,0 \rangle$, the pure coordination point that favors the row population. If we introduce an environmentally neutral strategy like Grim Trigger into the row population the observable play doesn't change. However, if the proportion of Grim Trigger becomes greater than a critical threshold, a niche opens up for Always 1 in the column population. Always 1 does poorly against Always 0 in the game, since their interactions result in a cycle of $\langle 1,0 \rangle$ and total mis-coordination. However, Grim Trigger responds to the signal generated by Always 1 leading to actions of 0,1 $\langle 1,1 \rangle$, that is, after the initial communication (and mis-coordination) the two agents fall into the pure coordination equilibrium that favors the column players. Here, the communication of a desire to go to the other equilibrium that, prior to the emergence of Grim Trigger had no impact, is sufficient to change the behavior of some opponents. Communication takes over this system as it realigns on the new equilibrium and then it disappears when machines such as Always 1 outcompete their incumbents in both populations.

11.2   Conclusions

In the primitive model of agent interaction represented by the CAM we find hints of the origins of communication. Communication emerges as a natural part of the model, with its signature becoming apparent in the meta-machines generated by the interacting agents. We find that actions with immediate payoff consequences can be repurposed as communicative tokens[3] that, at a cost of not exploiting immediate payoffs, allow the agents to alter their joint actions and gain social benefits.

The above examples of communication facilitating system-wide transitions share a common set of features. First, the importance of communication in the system can wax and wane. In the above systems, we often find long epochs during which action norms are so well defined that little communication is needed and the agents simply experience the direct consequences of their behavior. These epochs are altered by brief, communication-driven transitions. Thus, even though communication is a driver of system-wide behavior, it is a transitory phenomenon and its importance may not always be apparent. Second, for communication to become important, a necessary condition is that at least some of the agents have enough computational ability that their behavior can be conditioned on the actions (signals) they receive. In the examples above, two-state machines had sufficient computational power to allow communication to emerge.

A key role of communication is the facilitation of transitions from one steady state of a system to another. Some of these transitions, such as those in the Prisoner's Dilemma and Stag Hunt, allow the agents to realize a joint social gain by moving from an uncooperative outcome to a cooperative one. In the Battle of the Sexes, transitions moved the agents from one pure coordination point to another, enabling the agents to more equitably share the social gains across long time scales. Thus, communication plays an integral role in catalyzing the origins of various social behaviors, sometimes moving a system from asocial to social and at other times allowing higher-order social behaviors, such as equity, to emerge. ☞

---

[3] Not to beat around the bush, but language is filled with such tokens.

PART III:
CONCLUSIONS

12

EX MACHINA

The universe is no narrow thing and the order within it is not constrained by any latitude in its conception to repeat what exists in one part in any other part. Even in this world more things exist without our knowledge than with it and the order in creation which you see is that which you have put there, like a string in a maze, so that you shall not lose your way. For existence has its own order and that no man's mind can compass, that mind itself being but a fact among others.

CORMAC MCCARTHY
Blood Meridian (1985)

The origins of social behavior come from survival itself. However life began, it became grist for the evolutionary mill once it was able to replicate with some fidelity. The earliest organisms were likely passive players on this new stage of life, relying on chance encounters for survival. In the beginning, mere survival was a triumph.

In the subsequent struggle for existence, the premium on survival began to favor those organisms that could sense and respond to their world. Early on, organisms directed these newfound abilities toward an indifferent environment containing both salvation and peril.

At some point, the environment began to fill with other sensing and responding organisms, and social behavior became not only possible, but productive, and the next act in the play of life began.

The machinery needed for social behavior has been available for billions of years on Earth. The earliest organisms able to sense and respond to their environment likely harnessed "molecular minds" akin to what we see in chemotaxic bacteria like *E. coli*. Receptors on the outside of the cell can identify the shapes of specific molecules and trigger internal cascades of molecular signals that allow the cell to create memories and take actions. Such molecular minds allow *E. coli* to sense the presence of nutrients or toxins and, based on that information, embark on survival-enhancing responses that lead the bacterium toward useful chemicals, and away from those that are harmful. Such molecular minds are sufficient for behavior *ex machina*.

To explore social origins we created the Coevolving Automata Model (CAM) to serve as a time machine. The model uses evolution, a fundamental force of (literally) nature, to adapt coevolving populations of interacting, thoughtful agents. These agents are based on simple computing machines (finite automata) that produce new actions (outputs) in response to the previous actions (inputs) of an opponent. The computational ability of a machine depends on its number of states. With only one state, machines are passive agents that cannot alter their actions. Each additional state produces a quantum leap in a machine's ability to process inputs and generate responses. Perhaps surprisingly, machines with just two states—capable of only the crudest form of conditional behavior—are often sufficient to dramatically shift a system's social behavior.

The ability to make choices is meaningless if the consequences of such choices cannot play out over time. Thus, the amount of interaction between agents is an important determinant of social behavior. If agents interact only once there is no chance to muster a meaningful response. Under such conditions, even the most sophisticated agent dissolves into a rudimentary passive machine.

Therefore, the potential for acquiring social behavior requires two key changes in the system. The first change is giving agents at least the minimum ability to sense and respond to the actions of others. The second entails agents having some sustained interactions with one another. Throughout the (nontrivial) social worlds that we explored, adaptive systems with only one-state machines *or* one-round interactions were incapable of producing and maintaining social behavior. Once systems had machines with more than one state interacting for more than one round, social behavior began to emerge.

Finally, we explored variations across a series of fundamental environments that had the potential, but not the necessity, of social behavior. Most of these environments were drawn from well-known examples from game theory that emphasized interactions where the emergence of social behavior has to overcome significant barriers. We found that within each of these games[1] there were regions of feasible payoffs that led to stark differences in whether the system became social.

In general, the systems generated by the CAM are dominated by epochs of relatively static agent behavior, representing quasi-equilibria of the system. Depending on the environment, these epochs varied in length from tens to occasionally thousands of generations.

Rapid transitions moved the system from one epoch to another. Given that the system is driven by small random events, the rapidity of these transitions and the often extreme differences between adjacent epochs is surprising. However, such transitions are governed by a simple motif. Prior to the start of a

---

[1] As discussed, the cardinal values of payoffs matter when games are repeated. The CAM provides a convenient way to catalog this dependency.

transition both populations seem impervious to change, with the incumbent machines able to outperform all potential invaders. The observable transition is proceeded by the emergence in one of the populations of what appears to be an innocuous agent. This new agent behaves identically to its incumbent machines when facing the current opposing population, but its behavior can diverge under different circumstances. Random events and neutral drift can allow the proportion of the seemingly innocuous agents to grow within its own population. If that proportion increases enough, it creates a niche for the opposing population that can be exploited by a new mutant that causes the previously innocuous agents to alter their behavior in a way that allows this new mutant to thrive relative to its incumbents.

As the new mutant replicates it creates a niche that is exploited by the original innocuous invader, allowing that innocuous invader to take over its own population as well. This self-reinforcing displacement of the two original incumbents rapidly transforms the system into a new epoch of behavior. This new epoch may be further consolidated when simplified versions of the conquering agents take hold.

Extreme transitions exhibit revolution by evolution: small gradual changes set the stage for rapid and dramatic systematic changes. Such (r)evolutions are a potential path for the origin of social behavior: a world of interacting agents seemingly locked into an inferior outcome dominated by simple, individualistic, intransigent behavior can be suddenly transformed into a world of productive social agents.

The extreme transition motif that we observed in our primitive systems might also be at play in more mature social systems. Such motifs could drive modern social and political upheavals, ranging from the Arab Spring to rapid changes in public opinion (for example, the acceptance of same-sex marriage and marijuana in the United States) to the collapse of an entire social or political order. Real-world systems may experience the slow accumulation of seemingly innocuous agents that create heretofore unknown niches, making the entire system vulnerable to a single mutational spark. If so, within such motifs are ways to detect the early signatures of such transitions as well as a means by which to either promote or inhibit them.

12.1 On Emerging Social Behavior

The CAM provides a constructive proof of the origins of social behavior. Using it, we found sets of conditions that led to the emergence of social behavior and, thus, we have identified one possible path for a system to go from asocial to social. By design, the CAM brought together a minimal set of elements—simple, interacting, choice-making machines, modified by a limited set of evolutionary forces—driven by the imperative that such elements could be available in primitive systems, whether on Earth or elsewhere in the universe. In Part II we explored a wide variety of challenging environments, each designed to make the emergence of social behavior difficult.

Thus, the modeling embraced both the primitive and the harsh, giving us increased confidence in the usefulness of our constructive proof.

We found that for a system to become social we need ICE:

(i) *(I)nteraction*: agents need a sufficient amount of interaction to become social, with longer interactions often increasing the degree of sociality,

(ii) *(C)omputation*: agents need a sufficient amount of computational ability to become social, with increasing computational ability often increasing the degree of sociality, and

(iii) *(E)nvironment*: in those environments with the potential for social behavior, there are identifiable regions of payoff parameters that favor the emergence of social behavior.

Throughout the experiments, computationally capable agents interacting with one another for only one round typically resulted in the system quickly locking into asocial regimes. Without repeated interaction, even the most sophisticated agent is reduced to a simple, unresponsive machine that cannot condition its actions on the opponent's behavior. Once interactions moved to multiple rounds, agents began to embrace social behavior and, as the level of interaction increased even more, higher-order social behaviors could emerge.

Computational ability was also a critical determinant of asocial versus social systems. One-state machines have a severe computational constraint and are unable to respond directly to inputs. Worlds composed of only one-state machines were incapable of forming social behavior in the more demanding environments,[2] though these types of simple machines were often involved in maintaining social behavior once it had formed. However, two-state machines (playing repeatedly) were often sufficient to bring about social behavior. Thus, the introduction of even the crudest ability to sense and respond to the world can lead to a dramatic change in the system's potential for social behavior.

When machines had more states, making them more computationally capable, we often found that the system took on more elaborate social behaviors. For example, agents moved from "sharing" the social gains across long time scales in alternating epochs to sharing such gains across short time scales in alternating rounds of a given game.

---

[2] There were some scenarios where one-state machines generated productive social outcomes, for example, in a game of pure coordination.

The relationship we observed between the number of states and amount of interaction during a given game was also interesting. Occasionally, the addition of states could devolve social behavior. This may be due to the constraints imposed on smaller machines that force them to develop simple response patterns, such as mimicking the opponent's previous move, rather than pursuing the more elaborate and idiosyncratic patterns available to larger machines.

Finally, the particular payoff parameters that specify a given game—the "social physics" of the environment—influenced whether a system became social. Across the various games we explored, there were well-defined regions of payoff space that demarcated social from asocial outcomes.

Thus, social behavior needs interactive, computationally able agents, operating in an appropriate environment. These three ICE elements are interdependent. Even with an appropriate environment, either minimal interactions (one-round games) *or* minimal computational ability (one-state machines) results in asocial outcomes. As interactions *and* machine sizes increase, so did the system's social potential in terms of the environments that support social behavior. More computationally capable and interactive systems also supported more elaborate forms of social behavior, such as agents achieving short-term equity.

As noted above, there is an important relationship between machine size and repeated interactions. If a machine interacts only once, then after its first move (made without any prior information or input) the game ends. Thus, even the most sophisticated multi-state machine is equivalent to a one-state machine during a one-round game. This explains the observation across our experiments that systems with *either* one-state machines or one-round games behave similarly, typically failing to achieve productive social behavior. It is only with machines of more than one state playing games of more than one round that agents can begin to sense and respond to each other in meaningful ways.

Computational ability is constrained by the amount of interaction. For example, in a two-round game machines must decide on what action to take at the start of the game and what action to take in response to the other player's initial action. Such limited behavior implies, at most, eight possible computations (see table 12.1). For example, in a two-round game well-known strategies like Tit For Tat and Grim Trigger merge together, since they both start off by doing action 0 and then base their next action on the opponent's first move. Of course, if the interaction continued for a third round, computational differences between these two strategies might become apparent depending on the second move of the opponent.

The relationship between potential computations (given by machine size) and interactions (given by rounds) is shown in table 12.2. As we saw in Chapter 3, adding states to a machine dramatically increases the number of unique structures (column 2). Machines of different structures may perform the same computation, so the number of unique computations is given by the possible number of unique minimized machines (column 3). Finally, the actual computations that can be performed are constrained by the number of interactions (rounds played or inputs received).

Thus, the number of rounds generates a computational bottleneck that constrains the number of possible computations, regardless of the potential computations available to a machine. As seen in table 12.2, two-round games compress the number of possible computations to eight (assuming that the machines have at least two states). Three-round games allow the realization of

MACHINE PROTOTYPE	TWO-STATE MACHINE EQUIVALENTS	
Always 0	:0:0.00	All0
Always 1	:0:1.00	All1
0 Then 1	:0:0.11:1:1.00	(Alternate01)
	:0:0.11:1:1.01	(0-1DoOnceOn0)
	:0:0.11:1:1.10	(0-1DoOnceOn1)
	:0:0.11:1:1.11	(0ThenAll1)
1 Then 0	:0:1.11:1:0.00	(Alternate10)
	:0:1.11:1:0.01	(1-0DoOnceOn0)
	:0:1.11:1:0.10	(1-0DoOnceOn1)
	:0:1.11:1:0.11	(1ThenAll0)
0 Then	:0:0.01:1:1.01	0TFT(SIS0:0-00/11)
Observed Action	:0:0.01:1:1.10	0WSLS(FF0ifEven1s)
	:0:0.01:1:1.11	0GrimT(Trig0unless1)
	:0:0.01:1:1.00	(0DoOnceOn1)
0 Then Opposite	:0:0.10:1:1.00	(0DoOnceOn0)
Observed Action	:0:0.10:1:1.01	0Costanza(FF0ifEven0s)
	:0:0.10:1:1.10	(0SID0:0-01/10)
	:0:0.10:1:1.11	(Trig0unless0)
1 Then	:0:1.10:1:0.00	(1DoOnceOn0)
Observed Action	:0:1.10:1:0.01	1Costanza(FF1ifEven0s)
	:0:1.10:1:0.10	1TFT(SIS0:1-00/11)
	:0:1.10:1:0.11	1GrimT(Trig1unless0)
1 Then Opposite	:0:1.01:1:0.00	(1DoOnceOn1)
Observed Action	:0:1.01:1:0.01	(1SID0:1-01/10)
	:0:1.01:1:0.10	1WSLS(FF1ifEven1s)
	:0:1.01:1:0.11	(Trig1unless1)

Table 12.1. Machine compression in a two-round, binary-action game. In a two-round, binary-action game there are eight prototypical computations possible using Moore machines. The table lists these eight prototypes (first column) and their equivalent, computationally unique, two-state automata (second column, coded as per figure 5.1). Every machine within a given prototype produces the same initial two outputs (the second of which is conditional on the initial input). Machines in different prototypes differ in their initial or transitional output. The top four prototypes are unresponsive to the first-round input, while the bottom four prototypes all condition their second-round output on their first-round input.

STATES	UNIQUE MACHINES	UNIQUE MINIMIZED	ROUNDS						
			1	2	3	4	5	6	7
1	2	2	2	2	2	2	2	2	2
2	64	26	2	8	26	26	26	26	26
3	5,832	1,054	2	8	116	690	1,054	1,054	1,054
4	1,048,576	57,068	2	8	128	5,936	33,302	52,696	57,068

Table 12.2. Machine compression given states and rounds for binary-action machines. For machines of a given number of states (column one), the table lists the total number of such automata (column two), the total number of unique, minimized machines (column three), and the number of possible unique computations (remaining columns) given the number of rounds (inputs).

the full twenty-six computations available to two-state machines, while constraining three- and four-state machines to around one hundred computations each (a compression of 11% and 0.2% for the three- and four-state machines, respectively). As the number of rounds increases, eventually the full complement of computations becomes available to machines of a given size.

Increasing the number of rounds has two impacts on the system. The first, just discussed, is that more rounds allow more possible computations. The second, is that more rounds increase the shadow of the future. As rounds increase, so does the potential long-term benefit of acquiring productive interactions. For example, receiving an initial Sucker payment in the Prisoner's Dilemma may be worth the sacrifice if it allows mutual cooperation to be established for a long enough period of subsequent play. Relatedly, in the analysis of extreme transitions, as the number of rounds increases the system needs fewer neutral invaders to construct the niche required to spark a transition.

To improve our understanding of the impact of interactions on the emergence of social behavior, consider a coevolving world with two-state machines. The various experiments presented throughout the book have shown that two-state machines were incapable of establishing social behavior when playing for only one round, but four (or ten) rounds were sufficient for social behavior to emerge in some regions of the payoff spaces.[3]

To further refine our results, we conducted some experiments on two- and three-round games. For example, in a Prisoner's Dilemma (in a favorable part of the payoff space), mutual cooperation fails to arise in two-round games, but does emerge in three-round games. As we saw in Chapter 9, one possible transition from mutual defection to mutual cooperation is facilitated by the simultaneous emergence of Tit-For-Tat-like machines in both populations, and as the number of rounds increases, the number of machines required for such a transition decreases.[4] Three rounds were also required before mutual trade could be established in the Simple Trading model in Chapter 10. For the Battle of the Sexes, while one-round games resulted in coordination on the same pure equilibrium for the entire experiment, two rounds were sufficient to generate extreme transitions that allowed epochs to alternate between the two pure equilibria, resulting in long-run equity in the system.

~269~

Thus, there are at least some systems where two-state machines playing two-round games can produce social behavior. As noted earlier, in two-round games there are only eight possible computations. So, in these worlds a move from two to eight computations is sufficient to generate social behavior.

This eightfold path to sociality is shown in figure 12.1. At the top of the figure are the two possible one-state machines that are insufficient for sociality regardless of how much interaction occurs. (And, even larger-state machines are compressed to one-

---

[3] The number of rounds explored in the models was chosen *a priori* to reflect short, medium, and longer interactions.

[4] In the favorable part of the payoff space used here, two rounds require at least three mutant machines in each population, while three rounds require only two. Although the difference between these two scenarios seems trivial, there is a much lower likelihood of having three versus two of the appropriate mutants arising *simultaneously* in both populations.

state-like behavior if interactions are limited to one round.) The first increase in the complexity of the system occurs when machines of two or more states interact for two rounds. In such worlds, eight unique computations are possible and, in some environments, these eight computations are sufficient to initiate social behavior. These eight prototypes offer an interesting classification of the computations available to unconstrained, two-state machines (see table 12.1). For example, one of the prototypes captures machines like Tit For Tat, Grim Trigger, and Win Stay Lose Shift, all three of which have been identified as important strategies in the game theory literature.

Once the system has two-state machines playing for more than two rounds, the origins of social behavior are far more likely given the twenty-six available computations. Such worlds contain a virtual Burgess Shale of agent types that can promote the emergence and maintenance of social behavior.

Finally, as noted, the various (r)evolutions that allowed social behavior to arise were often tied to the emergence of self-reinforcing niches. Traditionally, niche construction occurs in the physical domain when, say, a beaver builds a dam that transforms a river basin. In the CAM, it is the transformation of the behavioral possibilities of the agents that creates new niches. Often, this transformation takes a simple behavior and makes it more complex, and thus vulnerable to exploitation. Once this happens, a sequence of self-reinforcing behavioral niches can open up, leading to a system-wide behavioral succession that results in a climax community of social behavior.

12.2 Conclusions

The exploration of the origins of social behavior is an interesting scientific maze. Even defining the basic notion of social behavior, a seemingly common and obvious phenomenon, is more difficult

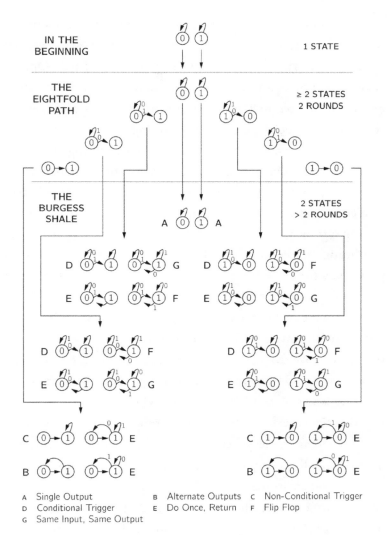

IN THE BEGINNING — 1 STATE

THE EIGHTFOLD PATH — ≥ 2 STATES, 2 ROUNDS

THE BURGESS SHALE — 2 STATES, > 2 ROUNDS

A Single Output
B Alternate Outputs
C Non-Conditional Trigger
D Conditional Trigger
E Do Once, Return
F Flip Flop
G Same Input, Same Output

Figure 12.1. The eight-fold path to social behavior. In the beginning, one-state machines are able to engage in a single action irrespective of input. Systems limited to such machines can acquire only the most simplistic types of social behavior. Machines of two or more states interacting for two rounds produce eight possible computations that can result in the emergence of some types of social behavior. Once two-state machines play games of more than two rounds, twenty-six computations arise that can support the emergence of more complex social behaviors. (Machines directly across from one another represent reflections, with the 0s and 1s flipped.)

than one might imagine. Based on a definition that embraces thoughtful interactions with the potential for mutual gain, social life may have arisen early in the history of life on Earth. Once it arose, it had profound consequences, ranging from the creation of the eukaryotes to the formation of city-states governed by constitutions. Social life is no narrow thing.

To order the creation of social life we strung together ideas from computer science, economics, evolutionary biology, game theory, and mathematics. This scientific amalgam resulted in an artificial world that produced a time machine driven by evolution honing primitive computational agents interacting with one another in simple, precisely defined environments. The model provided a substrate from which to explore the origins of social behavior in a way our minds could compass.

Such a model has many uses. It provides a constructive proof of the social universe. That is, it identifies a feasible path for a system to move from asocial to social. It also produces an easily observable world from which we can gain new insights into long-standing issues of social behavior, allowing us to create and test new theories via experiments on this artificial world. For example, we found that the leap between asocial and social systems can hinge on small changes in an agent's interactions, computational abilities, and environment.

Origins embrace the essentials, and such essentials often persist over time as the past is encapsulated in the present. For example, observations about the importance of, say, Tit For Tat in promoting the emergence of cooperation, provide insights into why that same strategy often governs the interactions of modern nation-states attempting to avoid nuclear destruction. Similarly, the transition motifs we identified may underlie the modern collapse or formation of various social and political norms and, at times, even entire societies.

The model also illustrates the power of (r)evolution—revolution by evolution. The underlying dynamics driving the model illustrate how the accumulation of incremental changes can silently poise a system in a state where a single spark can initiate a rapid and dramatic transformation. Such dynamics are capable of extreme transformations, including creating a bountiful social world out of a hopeless asocial one or upending a deeply entrenched social order. Such transformations are initially hard to detect as minor, random events conspire to allow the slow invasion of the system by an ostensibly innocuous agent that inadvertently forms a new and, at first, inconspicuous niche. Once fully formed, this niche contains a self-reinforcing portal that requires only a small spark to ignite a rapid, system-wide transformation. Gradual evolution can manifest rapid revolution, and such revolutions can produce the order in creation.

Our explorations found a path (perhaps even *the* path?) for the origins of social behavior. For social behavior to emerge we need computationally capable agents interacting in an appropriate environment. The demarcations among these requirements leading to social behavior can be quite specific, one- versus two-state machines, one versus two rounds of interaction, and payoff parameters crossing over narrow boundaries. Such seemingly small changes allow social behaviors tied to conflict, cooperation, coordination, and commerce, mediated by primitive forms of communication, to emerge by (r)evolution out of an asocial mire. Moreover, as agents become more computationally capable and interactive, the social phoenix can rise even further by embracing more sophisticated social behaviors such as equity.

The essence of *deus ex machina* is realized in our model: a hopeless asocial world gets rapidly transformed into a bountiful social one by a surprising mechanism. However, unlike the plays of old, the *deus* of this system is not a contrived means to move the story of life across a difficult plot point, but rather the natural result of emergent behavior arising from a system of coevolving (and quite literal) machines.

Once life forms, is social life inevitable?

Probably yes. 🖐

PART IV:
APPENDICES & BACK MATTER

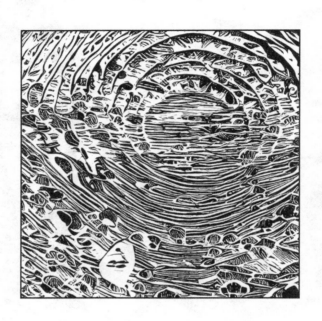

APPENDIX A:
WHEN DID SOCIAL BEHAVIOR ARISE
ON EARTH?

> *But I have long regretted that I truckled to public opinion & used Pentateuchal term of creation, by which I really meant "appeared" by some wholly unknown process.— It is mere rubbish thinking, at present, of origin of life; one might as well think of origin of matter.*

CHARLES DARWIN
Letter to Joseph Dalton Hooker (29 March, 1863)

Given the definition of social behavior derived in Chapter 1, when did it first arise on Earth?

The roots of social behavior likely run deep, as Robert Trivers notes in *Social Evolution* (1985, p. *vii*):

> *Everybody has a social life. All living creatures reproduce and reproduction is a social event, since at its bare minimum it involves the genetic and material construction of one individual by another. In turn, differences between individuals in the number of their surviving offspring (natural selection) is the driving force behind organic evolution. Life is intrinsically social and it evolves through a process of natural selection which is itself social. For these reasons social evolution refers not only to the evolution of social relationships between individuals but also to deeper themes of biological organization stretching from gene to community.*

Thus, Trivers would suggest that the emergence of social behavior coincides with the ability of a system to evolve. This is a generous view, suggesting that social behavior may have begun as soon as evolution took hold on this planet.

At what point in the history of life did organisms gain the ability to choose? We know that modern-day bacteria and other simple organisms are able to alter their behavior in response to molecular signals from the environment. In chemotaxis, bacteria such as *E. coli* move towards good things like food and away from bad things like toxins by altering the frequency at which they undergo random changes in their direction of movement. This behavior works via molecular receptors on the outside of the cell leading to cascades of internal molecular signals that alter the rotational direction of its flagellar motor resulting in the organism either tumbling or moving in a straight line. Thus, even without brains or neurons, simple organisms have the ability to make choices refined by evolution in response to their molecular environment. While chemotaxis itself may not qualify as a social behavior, slightly more advanced versions of such sensing and responding do.

Bacteria are capable of producing, receiving, and reacting to chemical signals from other bacteria (for a summary, see Waters and Bassler 2005). Depending on these signals, a bacterium can alter its behavior by expressing different genes.[1] Such quorum sensing meets our definition of social behavior since these signals allow interacting organisms to alter their behavior in

---

[1] Quorum sensing has arisen in various forms and species. For example, there is a marine bacterium (*Vibrio fischeri*) that, when concentrated, produces the wonderfully named enzyme luciferase to become bioluminescent. This bioluminescence is exploited by a Hawaiian squid that grows and concentrates the bacteria in a specialized organ located on its ventral side. The resulting light may mask the squid's shadow from below, allowing it to avoid predators. Other bacteria use quorum sensing for behaviors ranging from colonization to the coordinated release of toxins.

mutually beneficial ways. Quorum sensing has been observed in both prokaryotes and eukaryotes and there is evidence that these signaling mechanisms have a common evolutionary origin, suggesting that quorum sensing has been around for a long time.

The Earth formed around 4.5 billion years ago (Gya) (using estimates of the formation of solid bodies in our solar system) and the oceans began to form around 4.4 Gya. The earliest physical evidence of life on Earth, tied to putative fossils of microorganisms, varies from around 3.77 to 4.28 Gya based on the dating of sedimentary rocks from seafloor hydrothermal-vent-related precipitates in Canada (Dodd *et al.* 2017) to around 3.5 Gya given the dating of stromatolites formed by mat-building[2] prokaryotes in Australia (Schopf 2006). Thus, there is the possibility that social behavior on Earth has been around for 3.5 billion years or so.

The Great Oxygenation Event (around 2.45–2.32 Gya) created many new niches and paved the way for the emergence of eukaryotes that occurred around 1.8–1.2 Gya (Judson 2017). Eukaryotes were the result of various fusions between organisms, for example, an α-proteobacterium (which became the mitochondria that provides an efficient source of energy for the resulting cell) and an archaeon (a type of prokaryote) fused to form a ur-eukaryotic cell that eventually formed a branch of the eukaryotes. According to Margulis's endosymbiotic theory (Sagan 1967), the origin of the eukaryotes required the symbiotic joining of these two cell types, a relationship that requires social behavior.[3]

---

[2] Even the presence of such evidence is likely predicated on social behavior, since discovering such fossils requires large aggregations of microorganisms, perhaps indicative of social behaviors such as exchange.

[3] With time, the symbiont relegates dispensable functions to the host and becomes progressively more obligate (Sagan 1967). Thus, the initial social relationship responsible for the joining can become obscured.

Multicellularity, which arose in both the eukaryotes and prokaryotes, requires social behaviors like cell-to-cell communication and coordination. Multicellular organisms appeared early, and repeatedly, in the history of life, independently evolving at least twenty-five times (Grosberg and Strathmann 2007; Rokas 2008). The earliest evidence for multicellularity is tied to the previously mentioned microbial mats that arose around 3.5 Gya. Multicellular eukaryotes existed around 1 Gya (Knoll *et al.* 2006), with a major burst of diversification into large-sized eukaryotes occurring around 600–700 million years ago. Along with the social aspects of multicellularity itself, these larger organisms created new microbiomes that promoted socially based symbiotic relationships with various microorganisms (Douglas 2014).

Maynard Smith and Szathmáry (1997) identified the major evolutionary transitions that led from the origin of life to higher levels of social organization (see table A1). Their first three transitions focus on the underlying mechanisms required for evolution, namely the reproduction of molecules and the different chemical pathways that result in phenotypes. While some of these early transitions could involve social elements as per Trivers, even if we relegate them to just some evolutionary bookkeeping, the remaining five transitions are innately social. The transition from prokaryotes to eukaryotes and the move from asexual to sexual reproduction explicitly involve social behavior. The final three transitions in their hierarchy are also social, starting with the movement from single to multicellular organisms, followed by the formation of colonies from solitary individuals, and lastly the emergence of sociocultural evolution.[4]

---

[4] Their work and this book share other important themes, in particular the importance of complexity in systems and the application of transcendent models. Maynard Smith and Szathmáry were interested in the apparent

STAGE	TRANSITION
I. Replicating molecules	Populations of molecules in compartments
II. Independent replicators	Chromosomes
III. RNA as gene and enzyme	DNA + protein (genetic code)
IV. Prokaryotes	Eukaryotes
V. Asexual clones	Sexual populations
VI. Protists	Animals, plants, fungi (cell differentiation)
VII. Solitary individuals	Colonies (nonreproductive castes)
VIII. Primate societies	Human societies (language)

Table A1. Major transitions in the evolution of complexity. From Maynard Smith and Eörs Szathmáry (1997, p. 6), table 1.2.

The discussion above suggests that the origin of social behavior on Earth reaches back to the deep history of life on this planet. While this may be surprising to some— it is easy to conflate the need for cognition with social behavior—even a simple bacterium, without a neuron to be had, can implement behavioral repertoires and memories using molecular interactions that give it enough "thought" that it can interact in a social way.

Better living through chemistry indeed. ⚘

---

increase in the complexity of organisms over time: "Our thesis is that the increase [in complexity] has depended on a small number of major transitions in the way in which genetic information is transmitted between generations" (p. 3). They recognize that "complexity is hard to define or measure, but there is surely some sense in which elephants and oak tress are more complex than bacteria, and bacteria than the first replicating molecules" (p. 3). They also were driven by "our realization that a model one of us had developed to analyse the origin of compartments containing populations of molecules was formally and mathematically similar to a model that the other had developed to analyse the evolution of cooperative behavior in higher animals" (p. 7).

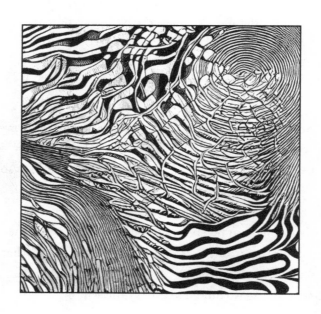

APPENDIX B:
SOCIAL SYMBIOGENESIS

Life did not take over the globe by combat, but by networking. Life forms multiplied and complexified by co-opting others, not just by killing them.

LYNN MARGULIS AND DORION SAGAN

Microcosmos (1997)

Social scientists often draw upon Darwin's theory of evolution when thinking about adaptive social systems. For the primitive origins of social behavior investigated here, Darwin's theory offers a wonderful means by which to drive our model. However, when thinking about higher social forms, such as organizations like governments and firms, more recent ideas from biology, in particular, ideas surrounding symbiogenesis, might provide a useful perspective into these more complex social structures.

Symbiogenesis in Biological Systems

Symbiogenesis (also known as endosymbiotic theory) is the idea that formerly free-living organisms can get tightly integrated into new free-living organisms in a symbiotic relationship (Mereschkowsky 1905, 1910; Sagan 1967). This integration can be so complete that the endosymbiont gives up some of its genetic autonomy, transfers most of its genes to the host cell's genome, and becomes an organelle of the host. Symbiogenesis was key to the formation of eukaryotic cells, as there is good evidence that mitochondria (energy-producing organelles) came from an α-proteobacterium and that chloroplasts (needed for photosynthesis) came from a cyanobacterium.

Symbiogenesis provides an interesting path for radical innovation in biology. In standard evolutionary theory, relatively small genetic changes provide the grist for the evolutionary mill—innovation by sparks. However, symbiogenesis embraces a more radical approach, whereby an entire cell's set of evolutionarily tested functions are integrated into a new entity—innovation by parts.

What might begin as one cell ingesting or being infected by another, can eventually result in a radically different, and much more fit, symbiotic organism.

When organisms combine, the endosymbiont often loses much of its genetic autonomy by transferring many of its genes to the host cell's nucleus, forming a genetic chimera. There are various theories about what promotes this loss of autonomy. For example, the newly combined organisms may be eliminating redundant genes or genes may be transferred outright (such horizontal gene transfer is common in bacteria). With time, the endosymbiont gives up much of its own genetic apparatus to the host and loses its ability to independently reproduce. The endosymbiont does retain some of its genetic structure, allowing it to avoid having to transfer unique resources across potentially hazardous intracellular distances, while maintaining an ability to quickly identify and respond to signals, as well as preventing any genetic misunderstandings brought about by subtle differences in the evolutionary paths of the organisms prior to their joining together.

Symbiogenesis in Social Systems

The notion that radical innovation can arise by the synthesis of independent entities has many potential applications in the social sciences. More complex social agents, such as institutions and cultures, can contain easily observable and transferable ideas and processes that make social systems ripe for the equivalent of horizontal gene transfer. Given the relative ease with which social ideas can be either appropriated outright or partially absorbed, it would not be too surprising to find evidence of social symbiogenesis.

There are many examples where social symbiogenesis might occur, including:

(i) firms can incorporate ideas from other firms, either via mergers or outright appropriation,

(ii) technological change can result from recombining existing technologies in new and productive ways (such behavior can be coded in patents that explicitly recognize the need to both include, and extend, prior art),

(iii) language families of the world, and local dialects, can embrace and modify prior languages,

(iv) laws and constitutions can incorporate elements from other legal institutions, such as the common law or the Magna Carta, and even the notion of legal precedent is fundamentally symbiogenetic,

(v) markets and auction institutions, such as the double auction, can absorb and adapt elements from other auction institutions, and

(vi) religions can incorporate elements from prior religions, for example, various Bible canons can both overlap and diverge from one another.

In each of the above social systems, and many more, symbiogenesis could play an important role.

Social symbiogenesis may provide a useful perspective on some types of complex social innovations. In biological systems, symbiogenesis has been involved in some of the most important and radical innovations of life on Earth. Given the ease of transferring ideas in social systems, akin to horizontal gene transfer in biology, social symbiogenesis might play an equally important role in innovations tied to complex social life. 🌱

APPENDIX C:
ON ANALYZING EVOLUTIONARY
SYSTEMS

The method of nature: who could ever analyze it?
That rushing stream will not stop to be observed. We
can never surprise nature in a corner; never find the
end of a thread; never tell where to set the first stone.

RALPH WALDO EMERSON
An Oration Delivered before the Society of the Adelphi,
Waterville College, Maine (August 11, 1841)

The focus of this research is on the complex adaptive systems formed by interacting, thoughtful agents that adapt their behavior using an evolutionary algorithm. Analyzing such systems can be challenging as the standard tool sets from the social sciences tend to be ill-suited for such a task.

Below we discuss both the computational approach used in the models here as well as some formal dynamic models developed for understanding adaptive systems. As in all modeling, trade-offs abound. The formal models require a vastly simplified adaptive system to produce precise, albeit limited, insights. The computational models create a much richer adaptive system with less precise predictions.

The two approaches are research complements. Nonetheless, given our limited understanding of complex adaptive systems we side with (Tukey 1962): "Far better an approximate answer to the right question, which is often vague, than an exact answer to the wrong question, which can always be made precise."

Analyzing Computational Models of Coevolving Machines

The analysis of computational models of coevolving machines is multifaceted. Such models create an easily observable system that provides grist for the scientific mill. To understand the behavior of the resulting system a variety of techniques from across the sciences can be deployed. Detailed observations of the system can provide a useful "natural" history that can lead to new insights. Also, these systems can be experimented upon at an unprecedented level of access and control. Finally, the standard tool bags of science, such as the application of various statistical techniques and analytic methods like mathematical modeling can be used.

Understanding in science often begins with the observation of a phenomenon, and computational models are easy to observe. Of course, knowing what to observe is key and, unlike the real world, when an interesting phenomenon arises in a computational model—often a prelude to a new discovery—the model can be reset and the phenomenon can be reproduced as often as needed. Observations can range from fairly general summaries of behavior across thousands of experiments to intensive case-studies where a single experiment is carefully analyzed. Such observations can be conducted at extremely fine levels of detail, for example, in the coevolutionary model every mutation, every selection event, every roll of the evolutionary dice is observable. Such intensive investigations provide a "constructive" proof of how a particular phenomenon came about, and such proofs can lead to more general hypotheses about the system's behavior.

Computational models are also amenable to experiments. These systems are easy to reset and rerun with alternative conditions, and thus they can serve as a nice experimental platform. Like any experiment, we want to generate insightful tests of useful hypotheses. Computational models even have the ability to run rather funky experiments, like introducing an agent evolved in one world into another world à la *Jurassic Park*.

It is easy to generate large amounts of data for statistical analyses using computational models. Given this ability to produce large sample sizes, statistically significant results are easy to acquire, so the focus needs to be on identifying scientifically significant results. Another issue in the statistical analysis of these systems is their potential for path dependence within a given experiment. For example, a system may lock into, say, one of two possible behaviors, so averaging outcomes over many such trials can obscure the system's actual nature. Another statistical issue is that the ability to add new data probes warrants caution, as access to new variables and observations can, if not carefully done, invalidate some commonly used statistical practices.

A Tale of Evolution and Transition

To get a sense of analyzing the Coevolving Automata Model (CAM), we consider a simplified version of one of the experiments in Chapter 8 based on the Battle of the Sexes shown in table C1. In this game, both players want to coordinate their outputs by sending the same symbol rather than different symbols. However, the two players differ on which of the two coordination points they prefer, with the row player wanting {0,0} and the column player wanting {1,1}. Thus, this game has agents both wanting to coordinate and having a conflict of interests.

This game has three Nash equilibria. The first two equilibria are the pure coordination points noted above where both agents send the same signal. There is also a mixed equilibrium where Row plays 0 with probability 5/8 and Column plays 0 with probability 3/8. In this mixed equilibrium, both players receive the same expected payoff regardless of what they choose as long as the other player mixes appropriately, and thus neither player can improve

COLUMN

PLAYER

		0	1
ROW	0	5, 3	0, 0
PLAYER	1	0, 0	3, 5

Table C1. Payoff matrix for a Battle of the Sexes. Both the row and column players must choose either 0 or 1. If they both output 0 the row player receives 5 and the column player receives 3, if they both output 1 the payoffs are reversed, and if they mis-coordinate and output different symbols they both receive 0. The structure of the game is such that the players are better off coordinating than not, but their preferred coordination points differ.

its expected payoff by deviating from the assigned mix, implying a Nash equilibrium.

To contain the discussion and ensure that the formal analyses presented later can be compared, we focus on a system composed of either one-state machines or one-round games, implying that agents can either always send 0 or always send 1.

As discussed in Chapter 8, in a one-state or one-round world the CAM converges to a single epoch where only one of the two possible pure coordination equilibria is focal across all generations. While the CAM concentrates play (about 80% of the time) on only one of the pure equilibria, players occasionally mis-coordinate. These mis-coordinations are asymmetric (even though the game payoffs are symmetric) with {0,1} arising about twice as often as {1,0}. These observed frequencies are inconsistent with the mixed strategy (though both suggest that mis-coordination favors {0,1}).[1]

---

[1] If agents use the mixed strategy, the outcome probabilities are 15/64 for {0,0}, 25/64 for {0,1}, 9/64 for {1,0}, and 15/64 for {1,1}. Therefore, {0,1} mis-coordination happens about 2.8 times as often as {1,0}.

As an aside, anomalies arising in computational models may be due to programming errors. Complicating this issue is that models of complex adaptive systems are, not surprisingly, inherently adaptive and seemingly anomalous behavior may actually be an emergent feature of the system rather than a coding error—"life finds a way." While most models tend to be brittle, as even small changes to their structure can lead to dramatic breakdowns, computational models of complex adaptive systems are less so given their ability to adapt, making tracking down errors more difficult. As in all models there is the potential for "debugging" bias, whereby the researcher spends effort debugging the model only when it is not meeting prior expectations.

In the simplified CAM studied below there are two populations, row and column, each with ten machines that can either always send 0 or 1. During each generation, each member of a population plays every member of the other population in the game defined in table C1. The system then evolves using tournament selection without any mutation.

Table C2 provides the details of a single run of this model. For example, in generation 2 there are eight row players that always send 0. These players are able to coordinate at {0,0} with the three column players that also send 0, but they fail to coordinate with the remaining seven column players. Thus, each receives a mean payoff of 1.5 $((5 \times 3 + 0 \times 7)/10)$ per game across the ten matches. The remaining two row players coordinate with seven of the column players at {1,1}, and thus they receive a mean payoff of 2.1 $((0 \times 3 + 3 \times 7)/10)$ per game. Given these payoffs, during tournament selection the proportion of Always 1 machines in the row population will tend to grow.

An interesting feature arises in the evolution of this simplified system. At the end of the first generation, the machines (in either population) that played for their preferred equilibrium received

GENERATION	ROW POPULATION		COLUMN POPULATION		PLAYS OF	
	ALWAYS 0	ALWAYS 1	ALWAYS 0	ALWAYS 1	{0,1}	{1,0}
1	6 (3.0*)	4 (1.2)	6 (1.8)	4 (2.0*)	24	24
2	8 (1.5)	2 (2.1*)	3 (2.4*)	7 (1.0)	56	6
3	6 (2.0*)	4 (1.8)	4 (1.8)	6 (2.0*)	36	16
4	8 (1.0)	2 (2.4*)	2 (2.4*)	8 (1.0)	64	4
5	4 (2.5*)	6 (1.5)	5 (1.2)	5 (3.0*)	20	30
6	6 (2.5*)	4 (1.5)	5 (1.8)	5 (2.0*)	30	20
7	9 (1.5)	1 (2.1*)	3 (2.7*)	7 (0.5)	63	3
8	9 (2.0*)	1 (1.8)	4 (2.7*)	6 (0.5)	54	4
9	10 (3.5)	0 (–)	7 (3.0*)	3 (0.0)	30	0
10	10 (4.5)	0 (–)	9 (3.0*)	1 (0.0)	10	0
11	10 (5.0)	0 (–)	10 (3.0)	0 (–)	0	0

Table C2. A sample run of the Battle of the Sexes using a simplified CAM. Two populations of ten automata each represent the Row and Column players in the Battle of the Sexes given by table C1. Automata are restricted to always sending either 0 or 1. The evolution proceeds using tournament selection. Data in the table indicate the number of that specific player type in the population and the mean payoff per game (in parentheses), which only depends on the composition of the other population. Given selection, player types with higher relative payoffs (indicated by *) in their own population are more likely to appear in the next generation, modulo small-sample stochastic effects. Once the number of a particular player type reaches 0, it goes extinct for the remainder of the game.

higher payoffs and their population proportions increased in the second generation. However, the resulting imbalance in types now favors machines that seek their less-preferred coordination point. In subsequent generations, selective forces alternate between the two types of players within any given population as the populations chase each other's changing proclivities. At generation 6 the column population has equal numbers of each type of agent, and this allows for a fortuitous set of selection events in the row population to boost the number of Always 0s enough so that the best response for the column population is to play Always 0 as well. In generation 8, the symmetry of the system is finally broken by the accumulated selection events and the die is cast for the system to converge on {0,0}. In generation 9, Always 1 in the row population becomes extinct and the entire system becomes locked into the pure equilibrium that favors the row population by generation 11.

The observed asymmetry in the mis-coordinated play results from each population trying to achieve its preferred coordination point. The row population wants {0,0} and the column population wants {1,1}. Thus, mismatched outputs are likely to involve a 0 from the row and a 1 from the column players, leading to a preponderance of {0,1} mis-coordinations. While the game is symmetric, the desires of the players are not.

To fully understand the behavior emerging from the CAM we may need a variety of tools and models. Above, we used a simplified version of the CAM to improve our understanding of the system. In the next few sections we introduce and apply some alternative models of evolutionary systems to the same simplified scenario. Each alternative provides new insights, conditional on differing sets of assumptions.

Modeling complex systems is always a challenge, as we want our models to be rich enough to capture the systems we seek to understand while still being simple enough to deliver new insights. In the modeling process it is all too easy to assume away the interesting parts of the system—as the Zen teacher Ts'ai Ken T'an noted, "water that is clear has no fish" (Zicheng 2007). If we are not careful our models can end up purifying the theoretical waters so much that the resulting ponds are devoid of the life that we care to understand, rather than embracing just enough complexity so that there is the hope of seeing, and understanding, some fish.

Mathematical Models of Evolution

There have been many attempts to formulate concise theoretical models of evolutionary processes. Each such model relies on a different set of simplifications and analytic techniques to gain some understanding of how adaptive systems behave. The three models we explore below are replicator dynamics, Moran processes, and a newer method tied to Markov chain Monte Carlo techniques.

REPLICATOR DYNAMICS

The best known dynamic approach to analyzing endogenous evolutionary systems is the replicator equation (Taylor and Jonker 1978). The key idea of the replicator equation is that changes in the proportion of a given type of agent in a population depend on its relative performance, with agent types with higher fitness than average increasing in the population. Of course, as the proportions of agent types change over time so does the fitness landscape, leading to the potential for interesting population dynamics. The continuous version of the replicator equation gives the change in the proportion of agent type i, $\dot{x}_i$, in the population as

$$\dot{x}_i = x_i(f_i(x) - \langle f(x) \rangle), \qquad (\text{C}1)$$

where x_i is the proportion of type i in the population, $f_i(x)$ is the fitness of type i given the existing population distribution across all types, x, and $\langle f(x) \rangle$ is the mean fitness in the population (that is, the weighted average fitness across all types). Since the proportions of types sum to one, the dynamics of this equation can be tracked on a simplex of dimension $n - 1$, where n is the number of distinct agent types in the population. Implicit in the replicator approach is that we have an infinite population of agents with perfect mixing.

To illustrate a replicator dynamic, consider the Battle of the Sexes explored in the previous section. Here we assume a single population with two possible types of agents, one that sends 0 and another that sends 1. Let x_i^t give the proportion of machines

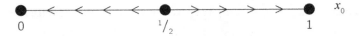

Figure C1. Phase diagram for a one-population replicator playing the Battle of the Sexes. The model assumes a single population of agents, each able to output either a 0 or a 1. The simplex gives the proportion of agents in the population that outputs a 0. The dynamic has stable equilibria at each endpoint and an unstable equilibrium at 1/2. The flow of the replicator dynamic is given by the arrows, which imply that the system will likely end up with a population of homogeneous agents.

~299~

at time t that send i (thus, $x_1^t = 1 - x_0^t$). The expected fitness of a machine that sends 0 at time t is $f_0^t = 5x_0^t$ since it receives a payoff of 5 when paired with itself (coordinating on {0,0}) and 0 otherwise. The resulting replicator equation is

$$\dot{x}_0 = x_0(5x_0 - [x_0(5x_0) + (1 - x_0)(5(1 - x_0))]), \qquad \text{(C2)}$$

implying that the system has steady states at $x_0 = 0, 1/2$, and 1. The phase diagram for this system is shown in figure C1. Of the three steady states, the two endpoints are stable equilibria and the midpoint is unstable, with the replicator dynamic always pulling the system toward the nearest endpoint. Thus, once one of the agent types constitutes more than half of the population, it continues to grow and takes over the entire population.

To better match the coevolutionary experiment explored in the previous section, we can implement a replicator-like equation on two interacting populations, both of which have agents that always output either 0 or 1. The fitness of an agent is determined by its performance against the composition of agents in the other population.

The phase diagram for this more complicated replicator is given in figure C2. Here, the four corner points are steady states, with the bottom-left (both populations composed of only agents that send 1) and top-right (both populations composed of only agents that send 0) being the two stable attractors. There is also an unstable interior steady state at $(0.625, 0.375)$ that is associated with the mixed strategy of the game. The dynamics around this point are interesting, as they mostly flow away from it, slowly at first and more rapidly the further away, though there are flows toward it along the diagonal from $(0,1)$ to $(1,0)$.

The replicator analysis complements our earlier findings, suggesting that the system will likely fixate on playing only one of the two pure equilibria, but in so doing there will be some mis-coordination that favors {0,1} since the system flows relatively slowly in the lower-right quadrant.

The phase diagrams emerging from the replicator dynamics are useful. Unfortunately, these diagrams become difficult to visualize and understand if the system has more than a couple of strategy types, and thus this technique becomes ill-suited for analyzing systems with rich collections of potential agent behaviors.[2] The replicator approach also assumes an infinite population with perfect mixing, allowing it to average out some of the small-sample dynamics that characterized the model we studied in the previous section. Ultimately, like any theory, if we are willing to accept its simplifications, replicator dynamics provides a useful view of basic evolutionary process.

MORAN PROCESS

Moran (1958) developed a random process to describe the evolution of a finite population of fixed size. In each time step a single agent arises from a birth process and replaces a randomly chosen agent, thus keeping the population size constant. Like the replicator equation, practical applications of the Moran model are

---

[2] There are alternative formulations of replicator dynamics that allow mutation that could partially surmount such issues.

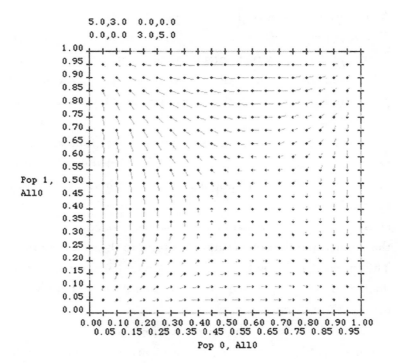

Figure C2. Phase diagram for a two-population replicator playing the Battle of the Sexes game. The model assumes two populations (with population 0 playing row and population 1 playing column) that play only against members of the other population. Each population contains agents that output either a 0 or a 1. Each axis gives the proportion of agents sending a 0 in the respective population (with the remaining proportion composed of agents sending a 1). The flow of the replicator dynamic is given by the interior arrows, in the direction away from the associated grid point. *Please refer to the Github repository (https://github.com/SantaFeInstitute/ExMachina) for full-sized, full-color versions of all images in this book.*

limited to a small space of agent types specified in advance, but such is the nature of many theoretical models.

To apply a Moran process to the CAM we follow an approach outlined by Zhang (2018) based on the work of Traulsen and Hauert (2009). Consider two populations, *A* and *B*, each of size

N. Let A have n_A possible agent types, $\{A_1, A_2, \ldots, A_{n_A}\}$, and B have n_B types, $\{B_1, B_2, \ldots, B_{n_B}\}$. Agents in one population receive payoffs when they interact with all of the agents in the other population. Thus, the fitness of an agent type in one population depends on the distribution of agent types in the other population.

The Moran process used here operates in the following way. On rare occasions, a mutation occurs with probability μ in one of the (randomly chosen) populations. This mutation replaces a randomly chosen member of that population with a randomly chosen agent type. Mutations are assumed to be rare enough that numerous selection events occur prior to the next mutation. This implies (see below) that selection always has enough time to operate so that a single agent type takes over the finite population prior to the next mutation.

Thus, the system is normally in a state where each of the two populations has fixated on a homogeneous agent type. On rare occasions, a single mutant emerges in one of the populations. Given subsequent selection events, that mutant either takes over its population or dies out (allowing the incumbent to reestablish itself). The long-term implications of this dynamic can be traced using standard mathematical methods.

The selection mechanism we will use is a version of tournament selection. It has three steps: 1) randomly pick two members of the current population with replacement, 2) make a copy of the one with higher fitness (or, if they have the same fitness, randomly pick one to copy), and 3) replace a randomly chosen member of the current population with the copy, thus keeping the population size constant. This mechanism biases selection by fitness (since better performing agents are more likely to be copied given the first two steps, and that copy replaces a randomly chosen agent). As shown below, when this selection mechanism is repeatedly applied to a finite population it results in a homogeneous population of agents.

Thus, the overall dynamics of the Moran system move it through the space of homogenous populations, with the system in one of $n_A \times n_B$ possible states determined by the homogenous agent type in each of the two populations: $\{A_i, B_j\}$. Occasionally, a single mutant invades one of the populations with the potential, driven by selection, to displace the incumbent and take over that population. If the mutant dies out, the system remains in its prior state. If it displaces the incumbent, the system moves to a new state with the invaded population now homogeneous in the mutant type.

Given that each population is normally composed of a single type of agent, the fitness of any agent is easily calculated since it only encounters a single agent type in the other population. This implies that the relative fitness between the mutant and incumbent—key to the selection dynamics—is constant as long as the other population remains fixed.

The analysis begins by deriving an equation that describes the likelihood that a single mutant entering a homogenous population of incumbents takes over via selection. Let $P(s, e)$ give the probability that the number of mutants in the population goes from s to e during the current selection step when facing the homogeneous incumbents. If the mutant is eliminated, it cannot come back so $P(0,0) = 1$. If it takes over the entire population, no further changes are possible so $P(N, N) = 1$. Since selection only replaces one agent per step, the number of mutants either stays the same or increases or decreases by one, so $P(s, e) = 0$ for $0 < s < N$ if $|s - e| > 1$.

The selection dynamic between the mutant and incumbent is shown in figure C3. The initial mutation starts the system in state $\{N - 1, 1\}$, with $N - 1$ incumbents and 1 mutant.

$$\{N,0\} \xrightarrow{} \{N-1,1\} \xrightarrow[P(2,1)]{P(1,2)} \{N-2,2\} \cdots$$
$$P(1,0)$$

$$\cdots \{2, N-2\} \xrightarrow[P(N-1,N-2)]{P(N-2,N-1)} \{1, N-1\} \xrightarrow{P(N-1,N)} \{0, N\}$$

Figure C3. The random walk induced by tournament selection with two types of agents. There are N agents in the population and each state of the system, $\{i, m\}$, gives the number of incumbents (i) and mutants (m). $P(s, e)$ gives the probability that during a selection step the mutant population goes from having s to e members. The initial mutation starts the system in state $\{N-1, 1\}$ and the left and right endpoints are absorbing with homogeneous populations of either all incumbents (left) or all mutants (right).

From this starting point the system takes a random walk driven by selection that, at each step, either keeps the distribution the same or shifts it by 1. The system moves from state to neighboring state with the given probabilities until it is absorbed by one of the endpoints, at which point the population becomes homogeneous in either the incumbent (left endpoint) or mutant (right endpoint).

Let $\phi(m)$ give the probability that a population with m mutants eventually ends up with N mutants (that is, the mutants take over the entire population). We know that $\phi(0) = 0$ and $\phi(N) = 1$, given the absorbing nature of the endpoints. When $0 < m < N$ the following equation applies:

$$\phi(m) = P(m, m-1)\phi(m-1) + P(m, m+1)\phi(m+1)$$
$$+ (1 - P(m, m-1) - P(m, m+1))\phi(m),$$

which can be rearranged as

$$P(m, m-1)(\phi(m) - \phi(m-1)) = P(m, m+1)(\phi(m+1) - \phi(m)).$$
$$(C3)$$

Let $\gamma_m = P(m, m-1)/P(m, m+1)$ give the ratio of the probabilities of either decreasing or increasing the number of mutants by one given m and let $y_m = \phi(m) - \phi(m - 1)$. Condensing the notation of equation C3 gives $y_{m+1} = \gamma_m y_m$. Using this last equation to recursively replace y_m on its right-hand side and noting that $y_1 = \phi(1) - \phi(0) = \phi(1)$, gives $y_{m+1} = \phi(1) \prod_{j=1}^{m} \gamma_j$, or

$$y_m = \phi(1) \prod_{j=1}^{m-1} \gamma_j. \tag{C4}$$

Note that $\sum_{k=1}^{N} y_k = \sum_{k=1}^{N} (\phi(k) - \phi(k-1)) = \phi(N) - \phi(0) = 1 - 0 = 1$, since the interior $\phi(k)$ terms in the summation cancel out, implying that $\sum_{k=1}^{N} y_k = 1$. Therefore

$$\sum_{k=1}^{N} y_k = y_1 + \sum_{k=2}^{N} y_k$$

$$= \phi(1) + \sum_{k=2}^{N} \phi(1) \prod_{j=1}^{k-1} \gamma_j$$

$$= \phi(1) + \sum_{k=1}^{N-1} \phi(1) \prod_{j=1}^{k} \gamma_j$$

$$= \phi(1) \left(1 + \sum_{k=1}^{N-1} \prod_{j=1}^{k} \gamma_j \right) = 1, \tag{C5}$$

where we incorporated the result from equation C4 in the second step and made a simple change of the indices in the third step. Solving equation C5 for $\phi(1)$ gives:

$$\phi(1) = \frac{1}{1 + \sum_{k=1}^{N-1} \prod_{j=1}^{k} \gamma_j}, \tag{C6}$$

which produces the needed probability that a single mutant will take over the population.

To find $\gamma_i = P(i, i-1)/P(i, i+1)$, recall that the selection mechanism has three steps: 1) randomly pick two members of the current population with replacement, 2) make a copy of the one with higher fitness, and 3) replace a randomly chosen member of the current population with that copy. If there are i mutants in the population, then the random draws in the first step have a $((N - i)/N)^2$, $2((N - i)/N)(i/N)$, and $(i/N)^2$ chance of either selecting two incumbents, an incumbent and a mutant, or two mutants, respectively. If two of the same type of agents are drawn then the copy will always be of that type. Thus, it is only in the case where an incumbent and a mutant are drawn that the fitness comparisons in the second step matter. Since the agents play against a fixed and homogeneous set of agents in the other population during a given sequence of selection events, the relative fitness between the incumbent and mutant never changes. Finally, in the third selection step there is an $(N-i)/N$ chance that an incumbent and an i/N chance that a mutant will be selected for replacement.

We can calculate γ_i by using the various probabilities discussed in the previous paragraph. For example, suppose that the mutant has a higher fitness than the incumbent. In this case, there is an $((N - i)/N)^2$ chance that an incumbent will be copied and an i/N chance that a mutant will be replaced by that copy, lowering the number of mutants by one. In the other two selection cases, which happen with probability $1 - ((N - i)/N)^2$, a mutant will always be copied and there is an $(N - i)/N$ chance that an incumbent will be replaced by a mutant, raising the number of mutants by one. Taking the ratio of the probabilities for these two events gives the value of γ_i when the mutant is fitter. The other two cases can be calculated in a similar spirit. Thus, we have:

$$\gamma_i = \frac{P(i, i-1)}{P(i, i+1)} = \begin{cases} \dfrac{N-i}{2N-i} & \text{if the mutant is more fit,} \\ 1 & \text{if the mutant is equally fit,} \\ \dfrac{N+i}{i} & \text{if the mutant is less fit.} \end{cases}$$

$$(C7)$$

Note that the value of γ_i depends only on the relative fitness of the mutant and incumbent, and this remains unchanged throughout a given sequence of selection.

By combining equations C6 and C7 we can calculate the probability that a single mutant takes over the population. In the case of a neutral mutation, where the mutant and incumbent have the same fitness, $\gamma_i = 1$ for all i and therefore $\phi(1) = 1/N$. In the case where the mutant is more fit than the incumbent, $\phi(1) \approx 1/2$. Finally, when the mutant is less fit than the incumbent, $\phi(1) \approx 0$. The two approximations improve as N increases. With a population of size 40, the values of $\phi(1)$ are 0.5125, 0.0250, and 0.0000, for the cases where the mutant's fitness is better than, the same as, and worse than the incumbent, respectively.

Given the above, we can now specify the system's transition matrix under the Moran process. With a probability of mutation of μ, the probability that the system, say, transitions from state $\{A_i, B_j\}$ to $\{A_k, B_j\}$ is given by $\mu\phi(1)$, where $\phi(1)$ is calculated using equation C6 (which requires knowing the relative fitness of the mutant type, A_k, to the incumbent type, A_i, when each plays type B_j). For any given row of the matrix, $\{A_i, B_j\}$ is assigned the residual transition probability from that row. Once the transition matrix is calculated, standard Markov techniques can be used to find the stationary distribution over the various states.

In the case of Battle of the Sexes, with agent types that always output either 0 or 1 (designated by the subscript), the Moran transition matrix with $N = 40$ and $\mu = 0.1$ is:

$$T = \begin{array}{c@{\quad}c} & \begin{array}{cccc} A_0, B_0 & A_0, B_1 & A_1, B_0 & A_1, B_1 \end{array} \\ \begin{array}{c} A_0, B_0 \\ A_0, B_1 \\ A_1, B_0 \\ A_1, B_1 \end{array} & \left(\begin{array}{cccc} 1.00000 & 0.00000 & 0.00000 & 0.00000 \\ 0.05125 & 0.89750 & 0.00000 & 0.05125 \\ 0.05125 & 0.00000 & 0.89750 & 0.05125 \\ 0.00000 & 0.00000 & 0.00000 & 1.00000 \end{array} \right) \end{array}.$$

Each element of the matrix gives the probability of the row state transitioning to the column state from a single mutation. This matrix has an unusual structure, as there are two absorbing states, namely $\{A_0, B_0\}$ and $\{A_1, B_1\}$. In both of these states, the two populations are coordinating on one of the two possible pure equilibria, so a mutant playing for the other pure equilibrium is always inferior to the incumbent. In any of the states where the two populations are mis-coordinating, if a mutation occurs (with probability μ, here equal to 0.1) it will always do better than the incumbents and take over with probability 0.5125. The transition matrix predicts that the system eventually finds itself in either $\{A_0, B_0\}$ or $\{A_1, B_1\}$. Under different games or agent types, Moran processes can lead to more interesting dynamics where the system moves across its various states characterized by a steady-state distribution.

The Moran process suggests that in the simplified Battle of the Sexes with two populations and two simple agent types, agents will coordinate on only one of the two pure equilibria. The replicator dynamic applied to the same system also recognized these two absorbing states (along with the potential for a mixed strategy). The replicator equation assumes a simple adaptive dynamic that allows for subtle mixes of agent types, while the Moran process assumes a dynamic much closer to the CAM with finite populations and similar mutation and selection mechanisms.

MARKOV CHAIN MONTE CARLO

The final approach we consider recognizes and exploits an isomorphism noted by Miller (2016) between Markov chain Monte Carlo (MCMC) methods and adaptive systems. MCMC algorithms were originally developed to generate, using a Markov chain, a sequence of samples from a state space that is tied to an underlying probability distribution. To do this, the MCMC only needs access to a measure that is proportional to the underlying distribution and not to the distribution itself. Thus, if $p(x)$ is the true distribution, the algorithm needs access to $f(x) = cp(x)$, where c is a (potentially unknown) constant. Not needing to know c makes it possible to sample from a distribution without knowing its normalization factor, allowing some important but previously intractable distributions (like high-dimensional Bayesian conditionals) to be sampled.

MCMC algorithms rely on two simple steps, and the iteration of these steps results in the algorithm's characteristic behavior. Of particular interest here is that adaptive systems can be driven by forces that have close analogs to the two iterative steps used in MCMC algorithms, thus it is as if adaptive systems are executing a MCMC algorithm. Given this connection, we can use results arising from MCMC methods to make useful predictions about the long-run dynamics of an adaptive system.

The original MCMC algorithm (Metropolis *et al.* 1953) was invented to analyze the likelihood that a system driven by some measure of interest (originally, the energy of a configuration of atoms) will be found in a particular state. This approach was generalized by Hastings (1970) and is now known as the

Metropolis–Hastings (MH) algorithm. The algorithm works by iterating a system across a state space, where any state of the system, x, has a measure, $f(x)$, that is proportional to an underlying probability distribution, $p(x)$. To start the algorithm a status quo state, x^s, is initially chosen at random (the starting point does not matter as the transition matrix will be ergodic).

The algorithm then iterates two steps. The first step proposes a new state of the system, x^p, using a *proposal distribution*, $q(x^p|x^s)$, and the status quo state (x^s). For MH it is convenient to have a symmetric proposal distribution: $q(x^i|x^j) = q(x^j|x^i)$. The second step uses an *acceptance criteria*, $a(x^p|x^s)$, to decide if the proposed state will become the new status quo. This criteria is driven by the values of $f(x)$ for both the status quo and proposed state, more precisely, the MH acceptance criteria replaces the current status quo with the proposed state with probability $\min\{1, f(x^p)/f(x^s)\}$. Thus, the proposed state always replaces the status quo if $f(x^p) > f(x^s)$ and, if not, it does so with probability $f(x^p)/f(x^s)$. Since $f(x)$ is proportional to the underlying distribution, $p(x)$, the acceptance criteria implicitly operates on the ratio $p(x^p)/p(x^s)$.

The output of the algorithm is a sequence of status quo states that, given the dependence of each element of this sequence on the previous one, forms a Markov chain.

The steps of the MH algorithm produce a transition matrix, t, that gives the probability of the system moving from one state to another. Given the algorithm, $t(x^p, x^s) = q(x^p|x^s)a(x^p|x^s) = q(x^p|x^s)\min\{1, f(x^p)/f(x^s)\}$, that is, the probability of going from state x^s to x^p is equal to the joint probability of proposing and accepting x^p given x^s.

The Markov chain induced by this transition matrix converges to the stationary distribution given by $p(x)$ under certain conditions. A sufficient condition for this stationary distribution is detailed balance: $p(x^i)t(x^j|x^i) = p(x^j)t(x^i|x^j)$, which, if it holds, eliminates any limit cycles from the system since a cycle requires an imbalance of the system moving between x^i and x^j. The stationary distribution is unique if the Markov process is ergodic, which requires that it is possible to eventually reach any state from any other state in a finite number of steps—that is, there must be some connected path between any two states in the transition matrix that involves only positive transition probabilities.

By a thoughtful choice of the proposal distribution and acceptance criteria, the MH algorithm ensures that the induced Markov chain converges to the unique stationary distribution given by $p(x)$. Rearranging the detailed balance requirement and substituting in for the transition matrix gives

$$\begin{aligned}
\frac{p(x^i)}{p(x^j)} &= \frac{t(x^i|x^j)}{t(x^j|x^i)} \\
&= \frac{q(x^i|x^j)\min\{1, f(x^i)/f(x^j)\}}{q(x^j|x^i)\min\{1, f(x^j)/f(x^i)\}} \\
&= \frac{q(x^i|x^j)}{q(x^j|x^i)}\frac{\min\{1, f(x^i)/f(x^j)\}}{\min\{1, f(x^j)/f(x^i)\}}.
\end{aligned} \qquad (C8)$$

The right-hand side of equation C8 can be simplified using two observations. First, given a symmetric proposal distribution $q(x^i|x^j) = q(x^j|x^i)$, we know $\frac{q(x^i|x^j)}{q(x^j|x^i)} = 1$. Second, the last term can be simplified since

$$\frac{\min\{1, f(x^i)/f(x^j)\}}{\min\{1, f(x^j)/f(x^i)\}} = \frac{f(x^j)}{f(x^i)},$$

whether $f(x^j)$ is greater than, equal to, or less than $f(x^i)$. Thus,

$$\frac{q(x^i|x^j)}{q(x^j|x^i)}\frac{\min\{1, f(x^i)/f(x^j)\}}{\min\{1, f(x^j)/f(x^i)\}} = 1\frac{f(x^i)}{f(x^j)}. \qquad (C9)$$

Combining equations C8 and C9, and given the proportionality of $f(\cdot)$ to $p(\cdot)$, we have

$$\frac{p(x^i)}{p(x^j)} = 1 \frac{f(x^i)}{f(x^j)} = \frac{cp(x^i)}{cp(x^j)} = \frac{p(x^i)}{p(x^j)},$$

ensuring detailed balance. Finally, ergodicity is easy to achieve by a judicious choice of $q(\cdot)$. Thus, given detailed balance and ergodicity, the Markov chain induced by the MH algorithm has a unique stationary state given by $p(x)$.

To summarize, by design the MH algorithm generates a Markov chain that provides a sequence of states, x^t, that is characterized by a stationary distribution given by the probability distribution $p(x)$, using simple iterative steps that only require relative information from a proportionate measure of $p(x)$. A key implication here is that the algorithm works without ever having to know the normalization factor for the underlying probability distribution.

While the algorithm operates using only simple comparisons of a measure proportionate to the underlying distribution, it manipulates the system at a much deeper level by generating samples as if they were drawn from $p(x)$. This behavior is akin to what occurs in a genetic algorithm that, while explicitly operating at the simple level of modifying entire structures using basic genetic operators, it implicitly implements a clever sampling process across a large set of schemata (see Chapter 4).

Evolutionary systems have analogs to the key parts of the MCMC algorithm. The MH algorithm creates a stream of samples by iterating two simple steps: proposing a new sample given the existing one and either accepting or rejecting it. Evolutionary systems rely on similar cycles of reproduction with variation and selection. A simplified model of evolution takes an existing structure, x^s, generates a variant of it, x^p, and allows one of these structures to survive depending on relative fitness.

This simplified view of evolution is similar to the MH algorithm. The proposal distribution from MH, $q(x^p, x^s)$, provides a new sample given an existing one. If we think of samples as actual structural forms, then the evolutionary equivalent to $q(x^p, x^s)$ is a set of genetic operators that takes one structure and creates a related structure. MH provides a lot of leeway for the design of $q(x^p, x^s)$, so a proposal distribution based on, say, a simple mutation operator that puts equal weight on all possible one-step mutants provides the needed ergodicity. Selection in evolution is tied to a structure's fitness, with fitter variants being more likely to survive. The MH acceptance criteria uses $\min\{1, f(x^p)/f(x^s)\}$, where $f(\cdot)$ is proportionate to the underlying probability distribution. If we reinterpret $f(x)$ as the fitness of structure x, then the MH acceptance criteria says that a new structure will survive if it is fitter than its parent, otherwise it will survive with a probability given by its fitness relative to its parent's fitness. Other selection mechanisms, as long as they result in the proper ratio, also work. For example, the chance of survival could be given by the fitness of the variant divided by the sum of the fitness of the variant and its parent.

Thus, our simple evolutionary system implicitly implements an MH algorithm. It takes a parent structure and creates a variant using genetic operators like mutation. It then tests that variant in the world, and using an MH-compatible acceptance criteria it either keeps the variant or returns to the parent. This process is iterated over time, and the resulting path through the space of structures (for example, organisms or strategies) gives us the evolutionary dynamics.

What new insights does this MCMC perspective provide on evolutionary dynamics?

Normally, the acceptance criteria in an MH algorithm is driven by a measure that is proportional to some underlying probability distribution and this, together with the magic inherent in the MH algorithm, allows the algorithm to generate a set of samples tied to the underlying distribution. Since our simplified evolutionary system implements an MH algorithm where the proportionate measure of probability is replaced by fitness, the resulting set of structures generated by the evolutionary system are samples drawn from the distribution of normalized fitness.[3]

That is, the above evolutionary system produces a sequence of structures drawn from $prob(x^i) = f(x^i)/\sum_{\forall j} f(x^j)$, where $f(x^i) > 0$ gives the fitness of structure x^i. Thus, while structures of higher fitness are more likely to be observed in the future, there is always a (lower) chance that a low-fitness structure arises in the sequence.

In the theoretical world of MCMC adaptive systems, agent structures are destined to rise and fall based on their relative fitness.

Though this is a powerful result, it imposes a very specific view of how evolution works. At any one time, there is a single agent that reproduces (with variation) a single child and either the parent or child survives based on the relative (exogenous) fitness of the two structures, and then the cycle continues anew.

While the above argument is framed as following the evolution of a single line of succession, we can reframe it as a population of agents, each member of which is following an evolutionary MCMC. In this view, many independent MCMCs are being pursued by the population, and as long as each member has run its chain a sufficient number of iterations to remove the influence of the

---

[3] Recall that the genius of the MH algorithm is that the normalization factor for the underlying probability distribution does not need to be explicitly calculated.

starting state, the aggregation over the current members of the population will be a set of samples from the underlying exogenous fitness distribution.

We can extend the MCMC approach developed above to the more complex coevolutionary world investigated earlier. We assume two populations, and instead of tracking a single structure we now track one from each population. Much like the Moran process, the simplification here is that the system follows a single agent type that, occasionally, faces a mutant. As in the Moran process, the state space of this system has $n_R \times n_C$ possible states, each of which is determined by a single row- and column-type agent: $\{R_i, C_j\}$.[4] Each of the two populations has an associated transition matrix, say, T_r and T_c respectively, with elements determined by an MH proposal and acceptance function.

The transition matrix for the whole system depends on the dynamic we impose. For example, one can alternate periods where one population is "frozen" while the other is allowed to adapt. This freeze-thaw dynamic results in a meta-transition matrix of $T = T_r^{m_r} T_c^{m_c}$, where m_r and m_c give the number of steps in the row and column thaw periods, respectively. An alternative dynamic is one where at each time step there is a random chance that one of the populations adapts. This chance dynamic implies a meta-transition matrix of $T = \alpha T_r + (1 - \alpha)T_c$, where α is the probability that the row population is chosen during the adaptive step.

To illustrate this coevolutionary MH approach, we return to the Battle of the Sexes using only Always 0 or Always 1 strategies. At each time step one population is randomly chosen to adapt, a mutant of the status quo strategy is created, and then the MH acceptance criteria selects either the

---

[4] Though here, the focus is on following a single agent, versus a population of homogeneous agents in the Moran process.

OUTCOME	FREQUENCY
$\langle 0,0 \rangle$	0.487
$\langle 0,1 \rangle$	0.016
$\langle 1,0 \rangle$	0.010
$\langle 1,1 \rangle$	0.487

Table C3. Battle of the Sexes using MCMC. Two populations of either Always 0 or Always 1 machines coevolve using the MH algorithm discussed in the text. The second column gives the frequency of the observed outcome given by the first column during 1,000,000,000 iterations of the algorithm. At each iteration, one of the populations is randomly chosen and the status quo structure is compared against a randomly selected structure from the same population. An MH acceptance criteria is then used to select the next status quo structure.

status quo or mutant based on their relative fitness versus the other population.[5] We iterate the system for 1,000,000,000 steps and track the frequency of each output at each step. Table C3 shows the coevolutionary walk using MCMC (the results are identical to finding the steady-state distribution of the meta-transition matrix). An important feature of this algorithm is that it provides a frequency distribution over the various outcomes. Here, most of the weight is on the two pure coordination points, though mis-coordination arises with asymmetric frequencies.

The MCMC approach provides a different picture compared with replicator dynamics or the Moran process. Both of those prior methods, while allowing for short-term dynamics, eventually enter into an absorbing state at one of the pure coordination equilibria, implying that the frequency of mis-coordination goes to 0. The MCMC, however, implies a steady state distribution that allows the system to flow among the various outcomes across the generations.

---

[5] To avoid having a fitness of 0, the payoffs in table C1 are all increased by 0.1.

The MCMC approach can be easily applied to systems with larger numbers of possible strategies. For example, running the previous MCMC on populations inhabited by all possible two-state machines (64 in all), gives the results shown in table C4. Given two-state machines, in a repeated game it is possible to have more elaborate limit cycles than before (interacting one-state machines can only have limit cycles of length one). Of the 64 possible limit cycles, the table shows the 14 that are most likely to arise (accounting for over 96.4% of the probability mass—none of the remaining 50 cycles had a likelihood over 0.2%). As before, the system still concentrates on machines that lead to pure coordination outcomes, though the likelihood of pure coordination is lower (74.2% of the plays, versus 97.4% in the one-state automata system shown in table C3). When the machines fail to achieve the pure-coordination points there is, as before, an asymmetry with the mis-coordination outcomes being biased toward {0,1}.

Comparing the Approaches

Replicator dynamics, Moran processes, and MCMC methods provide additional ways to gain insights into adaptive systems. These analytic approaches simplify adaptive systems in different ways, in hopes of distilling the evolutionary waters enough that relatively simple mathematical results can be generated. They each make different assumptions about how evolutionary dynamics unfold. For example, replicator dynamics assume the perfect mixing of infinite populations, Moran processes focus on finite populations with rapid fixation, and MCMC methods have a single structure wandering across the adaptive landscape (though a population of structures can be accommodated in this framework). The insights generated by these three techniques do not always align

CYCLE	MEAN PAYOFF	LIKELIHOOD
$\langle 1,1 \rangle$	3.00,5.00	0.371
$\langle 0,0 \rangle$	5.00,3.00	0.371
$\langle 0,1\ 0,0 \rangle$	2.50,1.50	0.026
$\langle 0,1\ 1,1 \rangle$	1.50,2.50	0.026
$\langle 1,1\ 0,1 \rangle$	1.50,2.50	0.025
$\langle 0,0\ 0,1 \rangle$	2.50,1.50	0.025
$\langle 1,1\ 1,0 \rangle$	1.50,2.50	0.019
$\langle 0,0\ 1,0 \rangle$	2.50,1.50	0.019
$\langle 1,0\ 1,1 \rangle$	1.50,2.50	0.019
$\langle 1,0\ 0,0 \rangle$	2.50,1.50	0.019
$\langle 0,0\ 1,1 \rangle$	4.00,4.00	0.013
$\langle 1,1\ 0,0 \rangle$	4.00,4.00	0.013
$\langle 0,1 \rangle$	0.00,0.00	0.012
$\langle 1,0 \rangle$	0.00,0.00	0.008

Table C4. Battle of the Sexes using MCMC with two-state machines. Two populations of all possible two-state machines coevolve using the MH algorithm discussed in the text. When structures from the two populations interact they play a repeated game and receive the mean, per-round payoff given by the associated limit cycle. The first column gives the limit cycle, the second column provides the mean payoffs for the two machines, and the third column gives the observed frequency of that cycle during 1,000,000,000 iterations of the algorithm. At each iteration, one of the populations is randomly chosen and its status quo machine is compared against a randomly selected two-state machine. An MH acceptance criteria is then used to select the next status quo machine. The table shows the 14 most likely cycles, accounting for 96.4% of the probability mass. None of the remaining 50 cycles had a likelihood above 0.002.

with one another, even in simple cases. For example, in the Battle of the Sexes with only two types of agents the models can predict divergent long-run behavior.

The advantage of these three analytic methods is that, if one is willing to accept a simplified notion of evolutionary dynamics, there is the possibility of obtaining precise analytic results. Unfortunately, adding just a bit of realism to the evolutionary system, such as having more than a handful of agent types, tends to overwhelm the formal analytics (for example, the number of states in the Moran process scale as the square of the number of types in each population, implying that the elements in the resulting transition matrix scale as the fourth power of the number of types).

Thus, to explore nontrivial systems using these methods one is relegated to solving these formal systems computationally. Given this, it may make more sense to explore the richer computational system directly rather than using a set of simplifications introduced to generate an analytic solution that is no longer tractable.

Computational models allow us to directly observe a coevolving system. Our understanding of such models can be improved by using a variety of analytic techniques, ranging from algorithms that recognize the onset and dissolution of epochs to mathematical ideas such as minimizing a machine or forming a meta-machine from two interacting automata. Whenever potentially important behaviors arise in the model, we have the ability to rerun the tape of time and watch the events unfold again while deploying new observational probes and analytic techniques as needed. We also have the ability to manipulate and experiment on these systems, treating our *in silico D. cognosco* agents as model organisms akin to Morgan's milk bottles filled with fruit flies.

Our model of coevolving automata produces a world that is rich in possibilities. This richness is both a benefit and (potentially) a curse. The benefit comes from not purifying the theoretical waters so much so that we kill off the very life we wish to explore. The (potential) curse is that while we have simplified the world as best we can, it still may be too complex to understand or generalize. Ultimately, the final judgment about the value of any model depends on whether we can use it to explore and analyze worlds that are rich enough to provide the insights necessary for understanding the more complex worlds we care about.

As we explore the origins of social behavior we remain open to whatever tools that might provide insight and understanding—seventeenth-century mathematics can complement twenty-first-century computation, deep case studies of a single event can augment sparse models of dynamic systems, and biology-like experiments can enhance intensive statistical analyses. Understanding complex social behavior is not in the purview of any one field or analytic technique, and progress will likely depend on both an open mind and an eclectic mix of analytic techniques.

APPENDIX D:
BINARY, ONE-STATE AUTOMATA

A tree that fills the arms' embrace is born from a downy shoot; A terrace nine layers high starts from a basketful of earth; An ascent of a hundred strides begins beneath one's foot.

LAO TZU

Tao Te Ching (1990)

Here, we explore the entire space of one-state automata with binary inputs and outputs. This space is quite limited, but it provides a simplified introduction to the two-state machines explored in Appendix E. Table D1 shows the entire ensemble of one-state, binary automata. Table D2 shows the single, one-step mutant of each machine in the ensemble. Table D3 shows the eventual cycle achieved when two of the machines from the ensemble interact with one another, where the output of one machine becomes the input of the other (and where the cycle codes are given in table D4). ❦

MACHINE_#	MACHINE	MINIMIZED_MACHINE	NAME
0	:0:0.00	:0:0.00	A110
1	:0:1.00	:0:1.00	A111

Table D1. Ensemble of one-state automata with binary inputs and outputs. Machines always start in state 0 and are coded as $:S_0:A_0.T_0^0 T_1^0$, where S_0 is state 0, A_0 is the output in state 0, and T_i^0 is the transition state from state 0 on input i. For example, machine 1, coded as :0:1.00, is a machine that outputs a 1 in state 0 and stays in that state regardless of the input. The third column gives the minimized, isomorphic machine—in the case of one-state, binary machines, the minimized machine is identical to the original machine. The last column gives a common name for the minimized behavior.

```
    01
0  :X
1  X:
```

Table D2. One-step mutation space of one-state automata with binary inputs and outputs. The labels on the left- and top-most borders specify the machine given by the codes in the first column of table D1. A one-step mutation in this space is a change in the machine's action (since transitions must always return to the single state), thus each machine has only one possible mutation. An X in the matrix indicates that the column machine is a one-step mutation of the row machine.

```
    01
0  ab
1  cd
```

Table D3. Cycle resulting from dyadic interactions of one-state automata with binary inputs and outputs. The labels on the left- and top-most borders specify the machine given by the codes in the first column of table D1. Each element of the matrix codes for the cycle that results when the row machine interacts with the column machine. There are four possible pairings of the machines. Cycle codes are given in table D4.

CYCLE_#	CYCLE_CODE	COUNT	OUTCOME
0	a	1	< 0,0 >
1	b	1	< 0,1 >
2	c	1	< 1,0 >
3	d	1	< 1,1 >

Table D4. Possible cycles from dyadic interactions of one-state automata with binary inputs and outputs. Each of the four possible machine pairings given in table D3 results in one of the four unique cycles given here (the codes given in the second column are used in table D3). The third column gives the number of times that the given cycle occurs out of the four possible pairings. The actual cycles are given in the fourth column. In each cycle, the outputs are ordered row,column. Thus, a cycle of $\langle 0,1 \rangle$ indicates that the two machines output 0,1 forever. In the case of one-state machines, all cycles begin immediately.

APPENDIX E:
BINARY, TWO-STATE AUTOMATA

For the great doesn't happen through impulse alone,
and is a succession of little things that are brought
together.

VINCENT VAN GOGH
Letter to Theo van Gogh (22 October 1882)

Here, we explore the entire space of two-state automata with binary inputs and outputs. Table E1 shows the entire ensemble of two-state, binary machines. Table E2 shows the six, one-step mutants of each machine in the ensemble. Table E3 shows the eventual cycle achieved when two of the machines from the ensemble interact with one another, where the output of one machine becomes the input of the other (and the cycle codes are given in table E4). ✦

EX MACHINA

MACHINE_#	MACHINE	MINIMIZED_#	MINIMIZED_MACHINE	NAME
0	:0:0.00:1:0.00	0	:0:0.00	All0
1	:0:0.00:1:0.01	0	:0:0.00	All0
2	:0:0.00:1:0.10	0	:0:0.00	All0
3	:0:0.00:1:0.11	0	:0:0.00	All0
4	:0:0.00:1:1.00	0	:0:0.00	All0
5	:0:0.00:1:1.01	0	:0:0.00	All0
6	:0:0.00:1:1.10	0	:0:0.00	All0
7	:0:0.00:1:1.11	0	:0:0.00	All0
8	:0:0.01:1:0.00	0	:0:0.00	All0
9	:0:0.01:1:0.01	0	:0:0.00	All0
10	:0:0.01:1:0.10	0	:0:0.00	All0
11	:0:0.01:1:0.11	0	:0:0.00	All0
12	:0:0.01:1:1.00	13	:0:0.01:1:1.00	(0DoOnceOn1)
13	:0:0.01:1:1.01	2	:0:0.01:1:1.01	0TFT(SIS0:0-00/11)
14	:0:0.01:1:1.10	3	:0:0.01:1:1.10	0WSLS(FF0ifEven1s)
15	:0:0.01:1:1.11	4	:0:0.01:1:1.11	0GrimT(TrigOunless1)
16	:0:0.10:1:0.00	0	:0:0.00	All0
17	:0:0.10:1:0.01	0	:0:0.00	All0
18	:0:0.10:1:0.10	0	:0:0.00	All0
19	:0:0.10:1:0.11	0	:0:0.00	All0
20	:0:0.10:1:1.00	5	:0:0.10:1:1.00	(0DoOnceOn0)
21	:0:0.10:1:1.01	6	:0:0.10:1:1.01	0Costanza(FF0ifEven0s)
22	:0:0.10:1:1.10	7	:0:0.10:1:1.10	(0SID0:0-01/10)
23	:0:0.10:1:1.11	8	:0:0.10:1:1.11	(TrigOunless0)
24	:0:0.11:1:0.00	0	:0:0.00	All0
25	:0:0.11:1:0.01	0	:0:0.00	All0
26	:0:0.11:1:0.10	0	:0:0.00	All0
27	:0:0.11:1:0.11	0	:0:0.00	All0
28	:0:0.11:1:1.00	9	:0:0.11:1:1.00	(Alternate01)
29	:0:0.11:1:1.01	10	:0:0.11:1:1.01	(0-1DoOnceOn0)
30	:0:0.11:1:1.10	11	:0:0.11:1:1.10	(0-1DoOnceOn1)
31	:0:0.11:1:1.11	12	:0:0.11:1:1.11	(0ThenAll1)
32	:0:1.00:1:0.00	1	:0:1.00	All1
33	:0:1.00:1:0.01	1	:0:1.00	All1
34	:0:1.00:1:0.10	1	:0:1.00	All1
35	:0:1.00:1:0.11	1	:0:1.00	All1
36	:0:1.00:1:1.00	1	:0:1.00	All1
37	:0:1.00:1:1.01	1	:0:1.00	All1
38	:0:1.00:1:1.10	1	:0:1.00	All1
39	:0:1.00:1:1.11	1	:0:1.00	All1
40	:0:1.01:1:0.00	14	:0:1.01:1:0.00	(1DoOnceOn1)

CONTINUED ON NEXT PAGE

MACHINE_#	MACHINE	MINIMIZED_#	MINIMIZED_MACHINE	NAME
41	:0:1.01:1:0.01	15	:0:1.01:1:0.01	(1SID0:1-01/10)
42	:0:1.01:1:0.10	16	:0:1.01:1:0.10	1WSLS(FF1ifEven1s)
43	:0:1.01:1:0.11	17	:0:1.01:1:0.11	(Trig1unless1)
44	:0:1.01:1:1.00	1	:0:1.00	All1
45	:0:1.01:1:1.01	1	:0:1.00	All1
46	:0:1.01:1:1.10	1	:0:1.00	All1
47	:0:1.01:1:1.11	1	:0:1.00	All1
48	:0:1.10:1:0.00	18	:0:1.10:1:0.00	(1DoOnceOn0)
49	:0:1.10:1:0.01	19	:0:1.10:1:0.01	1Costanza(FF1ifEven0s)
50	:0:1.10:1:0.10	20	:0:1.10:1:0.10	1TFT(SIS0:1-00/11)
51	:0:1.10:1:0.11	21	:0:1.10:1:0.11	1GrimT(Trig1unless0)
52	:0:1.10:1:1.00	1	:0:1.00	All1
53	:0:1.10:1:1.01	1	:0:1.00	All1
54	:0:1.10:1:1.10	1	:0:1.00	All1
55	:0:1.10:1:1.11	1	:0:1.00	All1
56	:0:1.11:1:0.00	22	:0:1.11:1:0.00	(Alternate10)
57	:0:1.11:1:0.01	23	:0:1.11:1:0.01	(1-0DoOnceOn0)
58	:0:1.11:1:0.10	24	:0:1.11:1:0.10	(1-0DoOnceOn1)
59	:0:1.11:1:0.11	25	:0:1.11:1:0.11	(1ThenAll0)
60	:0:1.11:1:1.00	1	:0:1.00	All1
61	:0:1.11:1:1.01	1	:0:1.00	All1
62	:0:1.11:1:1.10	1	:0:1.00	All1
63	:0:1.11:1:1.11	1	:0:1.00	All1

Table E1. Ensemble of two-state automata with binary inputs and outputs. Machines always start in state 0 and are coded as $:S_0:A_0.T_0^0 T_1^0:S_1:A_1.T_0^1 T_1^1$, where S_n is state number n, A_n is the output in state n, and T_i^n is the transition state from state n on input i. For example, machine 13, coded as :0:0.01:1:1.01, outputs a 0 in state 0, stays in state 0 if the input is a 0, and transitions to state 1 if the input is a 1. In state 1, it outputs a 1 and either transitions to state 0 if the input is a 0 or stays in state 1 if the input is a 1. The final columns provide information on the associated minimized, isomorphic machine, with the third column providing a code number (not tied to those in the first column), the fourth column showing the minimized structure, and the last column giving the common name if available and a more technical designation in parentheses.

```
        0........1........2........3........4........5........6...
 0  :XX:X::X:::::::X:::::::::::::X:::::::::::::::::::::::::::::::::
 1  X::X:X::::X:::::::X:::::::::::::X:::::::::::::::::::::::::::::::
 2  X::X::X:::X:::::::X:::::::::::::X:::::::::::::::::::::::::::::::
 3  :XX::::X:::X:::::::X:::::::::::::::X:::::::::::::::::::::::::::::
 4  X::::XX::::X:::::::X:::::::::::::::X:::::::::::::::::::::::::::::
 5  :X::X:X::X:::::::X:::::::::::::::X:::::::::::::::::::::::::::::::
 6  ::X:X:X:::X:::::::X:::::::::::::::X:::::::::::::::::::::::::::::
 7  ::X:XX:XX:::::::::X:::::::X:::::::::X:::::::::::::::::::::::::::
 8  X:::::::XX:X:::::::X:::::::::X:::::::::::::::::::::::::::::::::::
 9  :X::::::X::X:X:::::::::::::::::X:::::::::::::::::::::::::::::::::
10  ::X:::::X::X::X:::::::::::::::::X:::::::::::::::::::::::::::::::
11  :::X::::XX:::X:::::::::::::::::::X::::::::::::::::::::::::::::::
12  ::::X::X::XX:::::::::::::::X:::::::::X::::::::::::::::::::::::::
13  ::::X::X::X::X:::::::::::::::X:::::::::X:::::::::::::::::::::::
14  :::::X::X:X:X:::::::::::::::::X:::::::::X::::::::::::::::::::::
15  ::::::X::X:XX:::::::::::::::::::X:::::::::X:::::::::::::::::::
16  X::::::::::XX:X::::::::::::::::::::X:::::::::::::::::::::::::::
17  :X::::::::::X::X::X::::::::::::::::X::::::::::::::::::::::::::::
18  ::X::::::::::X::X::X::X::::::::::::::X::::::::::::::::::::::::::
19  :::X:::::::::XX:::X:::X::::::::::::::X:::::::::::::::::::::::::
20  ::::X:::::::::X:::XX:::::X:::::::::::::X:::::::::::::::::::::::
21  :::::X:::::::::X::X::X::::X::::::::::::::X:::::::::::::::::::::
22  ::::::X:::::::::X::X::X::::::::::::::::::X::::::::::::::::::::::
23  :::::::X:::::::::X::XX:::::::X:::::::::::::X:::::::::::::::::::
24  ::::::::X:::::::::X:::::XX:X:::::::::::::::X::::::::::::::::::::
25  :::::::::X::::::::X:::::X::X:X:X::::::::::::X:::::::::::::::::::
26  ::::::::::X::::::::X:::::X:::X:X:X::::::::::::X:::::::::::::::::
27  :::::::::::X:::::::X:::::XX:::X::::::::::::::::X::::::::::::::::
28  ::::::::::::X:::::::X:::::X::X::XX::::::::::::::X:::::::::::::::
29  :::::::::::::X:::::::X:::X::X::X::X::::::::::::::X:::::::::::::
30  ::::::::::::::X:::::::X:::X::X::X:X:::::::::::::::X:::::::::::
31  :::::::::::::::X:::::::X:::X::X:XX:::::::::::::::::X::::::::::X
32  X:::::::::::::::::::::::::::::::::XX:X::X:::::::::::::::::::::
33  :X:::::::::::::::::::::::::::X::X:X::X::X::::::::::::::::::::::
34  ::X::::::::::::::::::::::::::X::X::X::X::X:::::::::::::::::::::
35  :::X::::::::::::::::::::::::XX::::X::X::X::::::X::::::::::::::::
36  ::::X::::::::::::::::::::::::X:::XX::::X::::X:::::::::::::::::::
37  :::::X:::::::::::::::::::::::X::X::X:::X::::::X:::::::::::::::::
38  ::::::X:::::::::::::::::::::X:X:X::X:::X::::::X::::::::::::::::
39  :::::::X:::::::::::::::::::::X:XX:::::X::::::::X::::::::::::::::
40  ::::::::X:::::::::::::::::::::::X:::::XX:X::::::X::::::::::::::
41  :::::::::X:::::::::::::::::::X::X::X:X:X::::::::X:::::::::::::
42  ::::::::::X:::::::::::::::::::X:X:X::X::::::::::X::::::::::::::
43  :::::::::::X:::::::::::::::::X:::XX:::X::::::::::X:::::::::::::
44  ::::::::::::X:::::::::::::::::X::X::XX::::::::::::X::::::::::::
45  :::::::::::::X:::::::::::::::::X::X::X::X:::::::::X::::::::::::
46  ::::::::::::::X:::::::::::::::::X::X:X:X::::::::::::X:::::::::::
47  :::::::::::::::X:::::::::::::::::X::X::X::::::::::::X:::::::::X
48  ::::::::::::::::X:::::::::::::::X:::::XX:X:::::::::::::::::::::
49  :::::::::::::::::X:::::::::::::::::X:::X::X:X::X::::::::::::::::
50  ::::::::::::::::::X:::::::::::::::X:::X::X::X::X::::::::::::::
51  :::::::::::::::::::X:::::::::::::::X:::XX:::X::X::::::::::::::
52  ::::::::::::::::::::X:::::::::::::::X:::X:::XX::::X:::::::::::
53  :::::::::::::::::::::X:::::::::::::::X:::X::X::X::X:::::::::::
54  ::::::::::::::::::::::X:::::::::::::::X:::X::X::X::::X::::::::
55  :::::::::::::::::::::::X:::::::::::::::X::XX:::::::X::::::::X
56  ::::::::::::::::::::::::X:::::::::::::X::::X:::X::::XX:X::::::
57  :::::::::::::::::::::::::X:::::::::::::X:::X::X::::X::X:X::::
58  ::::::::::::::::::::::::::X:::::::::::::X::X::X::::X::X::X:::
59  :::::::::::::::::::::::::::X:::::::::::::X::X::X::::X:::XX:::X
60  ::::::::::::::::::::::::::::X::::::::::::::X::X::X::::X::::XX:
61  :::::::::::::::::::::::::::::X:::::::::::::X::::X::::X::X:X::X
62  ::::::::::::::::::::::::::::::X:::::::::::::X:::::X::X:::X:X:X
63  :::::::::::::::::::::::::::::::X:::::::::::::X::::X::::X::X:XX:
```

Table E2. One-step mutation space of two-state automata with binary inputs and outputs. The labels on the left- and top-most borders specify the machine given by the codes in the first column of table E1. A one-step mutation in this space is a change of either a state's action or one of its transitions, and thus each machine has six possible one-step mutations. An X in the matrix indicates that the column machine is a one-step mutation of the row machine.

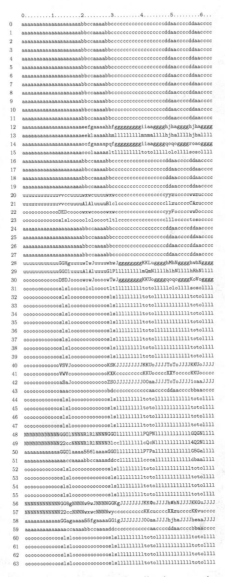

Table E3. Cycle resulting from dyadic interactions of two-state automata with binary inputs and outputs. The labels on the left- and top-most borders specify the machine given by the codes in the first column of table E1. Each element of the matrix codes for the cycle that results when the row machine interacts with the column machine. To simplify the presentation, we consider only the cycle resulting from the interaction and ignore any outputs that occur prior to the start of the cycle. There are 4,096 possible pairings of the machines. Cycle codes are given in table E4.

CYCLE_#	CYCLE_CODE	COUNT	OUTCOME	CYCLE_#	CYCLE_CODE	COUNT	OUTCOME
0	a	782	< 0,0 >	32	G	26	< 1,0 0,1 >
1	b	90	< 0,0 0,1 >	33	H	1	< 0,0 1,0 0,1 1,1 >
2	c	782	< 0,1 >	34	I	1	< 0,0 1,1 0,1 1,0 >
3	d	90	< 0,1 0,0 >	35	J	90	< 1,1 0,1 >
4	e	5	< 0,0 0,1 1,0 >	36	K	26	< 1,1 0,0 >
5	f	5	< 0,0 0,1 1,1 >	37	L	1	< 0,1 1,1 0,0 1,0 >
6	g	90	< 0,1 1,1 >	38	M	1	< 0,1 1,0 0,0 1,1 >
7	h	26	< 0,1 1,0 >	39	N	90	< 1,0 0,0 >
8	i	5	< 0,1 1,1 0,0 >	40	O	5	< 1,0 0,1 1,1 >
9	j	5	< 0,1 1,0 0,0 >	41	P	5	< 1,1 1,0 0,1 >
10	k	1	< 0,0 0,1 1,1 1,0 >	42	Q	5	< 1,1 1,0 0,0 >
11	l	782	< 1,1 >	43	R	5	< 1,0 0,0 1,1 >
12	m	5	< 0,1 1,1 1,0 >	44	S	5	< 1,0 1,1 0,1 >
13	n	1	< 0,1 1,1 1,0 0,0 >	45	T	5	< 1,1 0,1 1,0 >
14	o	782	< 1,0 >	46	U	5	< 1,1 0,0 1,0 >
15	p	1	< 0,0 0,1 1,0 1,1 >	47	V	5	< 1,0 1,1 0,0 >
16	q	5	< 0,1 1,0 1,1 >	48	W	1	< 1,0 1,1 0,1 0,0 >
17	r	1	< 0,1 1,0 1,1 0,0 >	49	X	5	< 1,1 0,1 0,0 >
18	s	90	< 1,0 1,1 >	50	Y	1	< 1,1 0,1 0,0 1,0 >
19	t	90	< 1,1 1,0 >	51	Z	1	< 1,0 1,1 0,0 0,1 >
20	u	90	< 0,0 1,0 >	52	0	5	< 1,1 0,0 0,1 >
21	v	5	< 0,0 1,0 0,1 >	53	1	1	< 1,1 0,0 0,1 1,0 >
22	w	26	< 0,0 1,1 >	54	2	5	< 1,0 0,1 0,0 >
23	x	5	< 0,0 1,1 0,1 >	55	3	1	< 1,0 0,1 0,0 1,1 >
24	y	5	< 0,1 0,0 1,1 >	56	4	1	< 1,1 1,0 0,1 0,0 >
25	z	5	< 0,1 0,0 1,0 >	57	5	5	< 1,0 0,0 0,1 >
26	A	5	< 0,0 1,1 1,0 >	58	6	1	< 1,0 0,0 0,1 1,1 >
27	B	1	< 0,0 1,1 1,0 0,1 >	59	7	1	< 1,1 1,0 0,0 0,1 >
28	C	1	< 0,1 0,0 1,1 1,0 >	60	8	1	< 1,0 0,1 1,1 0,0 >
29	D	5	< 0,0 1,0 1,1 >	61	9	1	< 1,0 0,0 1,1 0,1 >
30	E	1	< 0,0 1,0 1,1 0,1 >	62	@	1	< 1,1 0,0 1,0 0,1 >
31	F	1	< 0,1 0,0 1,0 1,1 >	63	#	1	< 1,1 0,1 1,0 0,0 >

Table E4. Possible cycles from dyadic interactions of two-state automata with binary inputs and outputs. Each of the 4,096 possible machine pairings given in table E3 results in one of the sixty-four unique cycles given here (the codes given in the second column are used in table E3). The third column gives the number of times that the given cycle occurs out of the 4,096 possible pairings. The actual cycles are given in the fourth column. In each cycle, the outputs are ordered row,column. Thus, a cycle of ⟨1,0 1,1 0,1⟩ indicates that the two machines first output 1,0, then 1,1, and then 0,1, at which point the cycle begins anew starting at 1,0. Note that, depending on the pair of interacting machines, some of these cycles are proceeded by noncyclic outputs.

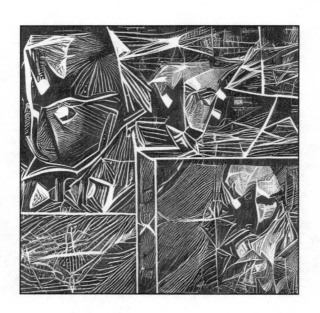

APPENDIX F:
TESTING EVOLVING AUTOMATA

*I think that in the discussion of natural problems
we ought to begin not with the Scriptures, but with
experiments, and demonstrations.*

GALILEO GALILEI

The Authority of Scripture in Philosophical Controversies

(1614)

Here, we consider three simple experiments to explore the basis
of the Coevolving Automata Model. All three experiments
evolve a single population of automata to see if the machines
can learn to solve some useful computational tasks. The first
experiment tests whether an automaton can learn to take a
preformed input string and produce a target output string.
This experiment provides a very basic test of whether automata
can learn to respond in useful ways to inputs. The second
experiment extends the first, by having the automata attempt to
identify particular patterns within a set of input strings. Such
pattern matching is fundamental to perceiving and reacting
to more complex environments. The final experiment creates
an environment that extends the previous pattern-matching
problem by adding coevolution to the set of patterns that must
be solved by the machines, providing a useful test of the impact
of coevolution on the adapting automata.

Can Evolving Automata Produce a Target Output?

Suppose we have a particular behavior that we want to induce
in an automaton, that is, we have a predefined input stream

and want the automaton to respond by producing a predefined output stream. We consider binary problems of size 1 to 20. To create a problem of size n we randomly draw two binary strings: an input sequence of length $n - 1$ and an output sequence of length n.[1] Given these two sequences, the automaton's task is to produce the required output sequence given the associated input sequence.

We begin with a population of forty randomly generated automata and a randomly drawn problem of length n that remains fixed throughout the evolutionary process. During each generation, each automaton in the population is tested on the problem and receives a payoff given by the proportion of its output stream that matches the targeted output stream. Based on these payoffs a new population is created using the tournament selection and mutation procedures discussed in Chapter 5, and the generation concludes. This process is iterated for 100 generations and the mean performance of the final generation of automata is used as a measure of success.

Table F1 summarizes the results of this experiment across problems of sizes 1 to 20 using automata from 1 to 10 states long. Each condition was run for 1,000 separate evolutionary trials and the data in the table are the mean performance of the automata in the 100th generation of each trial. Given a binary output sequence, the base-rate solution always outputs the majority bit in the desired output stream. Thus, a base-rate machine can always match at least half of the bits, if not more (given the potential variance from the small-sample draws that define a problem's output sequence). The second column of the table provides the expected base-rate performance over all possible sample draws.

---

[1] Since a machine begins with an initial output from its starting state prior to any input, only $n - 1$ inputs are needed to produce n outputs.

PROBLEM	EXPECTED	AUTOMATON SIZE									
SIZE (*n*)	BASE RATE	1	2	3	4	5	6	7	8	9	10
1	1.00	0.91	0.96	0.97	0.98	0.98	0.99	0.99	0.99	0.99	0.99
2	0.75	0.71	0.95	0.96	0.97	0.98	0.98	0.98	0.99	0.99	0.99
3	0.75	0.70	0.89	0.96	0.97	0.97	0.98	0.98	0.98	0.99	0.99
4	0.69	0.66	0.85	0.95	0.96	0.97	0.98	0.98	0.98	0.98	0.98
5	0.69	0.65	0.83	0.93	0.95	0.96	0.97	0.98	0.98	0.98	0.98
6	0.66	0.62	0.80	0.90	0.94	0.96	0.96	0.97	0.97	0.98	0.98
7	0.66	0.63	0.78	0.88	0.92	0.94	0.95	0.96	0.97	0.97	0.97
8	0.64	0.61	0.76	0.86	0.91	0.93	0.94	0.95	0.96	0.96	0.96
9	0.64	0.61	0.75	0.84	0.89	0.91	0.93	0.94	0.95	0.96	0.96
10	0.62	0.60	0.73	0.83	0.88	0.90	0.92	0.93	0.94	0.94	0.95
11	0.62	0.60	0.72	0.82	0.86	0.89	0.91	0.92	0.93	0.93	0.94
12	0.61	0.59	0.72	0.80	0.85	0.88	0.90	0.91	0.92	0.93	0.93
13	0.61	0.59	0.71	0.79	0.84	0.86	0.88	0.90	0.91	0.92	0.92
14	0.60	0.59	0.70	0.78	0.83	0.86	0.88	0.89	0.90	0.91	0.91
15	0.60	0.59	0.69	0.77	0.82	0.85	0.87	0.89	0.90	0.90	0.91
16	0.60	0.58	0.68	0.76	0.81	0.84	0.86	0.88	0.88	0.89	0.90
17	0.60	0.58	0.68	0.76	0.80	0.83	0.85	0.86	0.88	0.88	0.89
18	0.59	0.58	0.67	0.75	0.79	0.82	0.84	0.86	0.87	0.88	0.89
19	0.59	0.58	0.67	0.74	0.79	0.81	0.83	0.85	0.87	0.87	0.88
20	0.59	0.57	0.66	0.73	0.78	0.81	0.83	0.85	0.86	0.87	0.87

Table F1. Evolving automata to reproduce a desired output stream given an input stream. In each trial a single binary input and output stream of problem size *n* was randomly generated. Initially, a population of forty automata of fixed machine size was randomly generated and subjected to tournament selection and a mutation rate of 0.33 for 100 generations. Each automaton received a fitness given by the proportion of the target output stream it was able to reproduce given the input stream. The second column gives the expected performance of an automaton that always outputs the majority symbol in the target output stream, averaged over all possible output streams. Columns 3–12 give the mean performance of the automata in the population after 100 generations of evolution, averaged across 1,000 separate evolutionary trials for each condition.

The initial population in this system receives a mean fitness of about 0.50 regardless of automaton size. Since the automata in this population are randomly generated, they randomly guess each output and thus do worse than the base rate. The mean performance of the final generation is above the expected base rate as long as the problems are larger than size one and the automata have more than one state. With problems of size one the populations never achieve the expect base-rate performance (though larger-sized automata get close). A single-state automaton with the appropriate output will perform at the base rate, so the inefficiency observed here is due to mutation. Recall that modified machines are subject to a single mutation regardless of the machine's size. Mutation applied to a one-state machine, even in a highly evolved population, changes its output symbol and forces the machine to do the opposite of the optimal, base-rate behavior. As machines get larger, mutations are less disruptive, so near-base-rate performance is easier to achieve.

For problems of size two or more the evolved machines always do better than the base rate as long as they have more than one state. One-state machines can, at best, achieve the base rate performance modulo mutation disruptions. Adding even one additional state to the machines provides a noticeable boost above base-rate performance. Thus, larger automata are able to exploit the underlying structural regularities that arise in a problem's input and output streams.

As the machines get larger, evolved performance nears 1.0, with some diminution in overall performance across all sizes of automata as problem size increases. In theory, a problem of size n can be perfectly solved by an automaton of size n by associating each state of the automaton with the desired output and having the machine transition from state to state completely ignoring the input stream.

While the system has the potential to evolve such structures, they are difficult to maintain as they tend to be brittle given the potential impact of mutations. Here, the more likely path to evolutionary success exploits underlying regularities that arise in the (initially randomly generated) strings, as evidenced by the leap in performance we observe when we move from one- to two-state machines, as well as the relatively small decline in performance when problem sizes begin to exceed machine sizes.

Thus, we find that evolving automata using a genetic algorithm works well on problems where we want to generate a target output stream associated with a given input stream. We find that even the introduction of a small amount of conditional behavior, that is, using automata of more than one state, has a dramatic impact on performance even when the problem size exceeds the machine size. The system was able to evolve relatively large machines that achieved (often slight) improvements in performance. Overall, the system generated novel and productive machines that exploited the underlying, and potentially subtle, patterns contained within a problem. For example, machines of size four or five were able to find enough patterns in even randomly generated sequences of twenty bits to perform well above the expected base rate.

Can Evolving Automata Perceive Their Environment?

A second test of our ability to evolve useful automata is a "perception" task. Here, the evolving automata must identify whether a given input string has a particular pattern. The automaton is given the input string and the machine's final output is used to classify that string. Potential patterns could include, say, whether the input string has a majority of 1s, an even number of 0s, a 1 in the third position, an occurrence of the sequence of

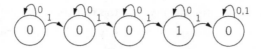

Figure F1. An automaton able to identify an input stream with exactly three 1s. This automaton's final output is 1 if there are exactly three 1s in its binary input string, otherwise it outputs a 0.

'0101' somewhere in the string, and so on.[2] Such problems are at the heart of sorting the world into various equivalence classes, an important ability for the survival of sensing organisms. Here, we use this pattern-finding task as an additional test of our ability to evolve automata.[3]

In this experiment we evolve machines that attempt to identify whether there are exactly three 1s in a given binary string. An automaton needs at least five states to flawlessly identify this pattern. The machine shown in figure F1 stays in its start state as long as no 1s have been observed. The next three states of the machine count the number of 1s that have been observed thus far. If the machine reaches the fourth state, exactly three 1s have been seen. The fifth state is needed to deal with input strings that have more than three 1s, in which case this fifth absorbing state is reached indicating a sure violation of the pattern regardless of additional input. The pattern of exactly three 1s is observed if and only if the machine ends up in its fourth state on the last input, allowing it to output a 1 versus a 0.

Evolving automata often find unique, unanticipated solutions to problems. For example, a four-state machine similar to the one

---

[2]Not all patterns are amenable to being solved by a finite automata. For example, a pattern that identifies whether there is an equal number of 0s and 1s in a string of *any* length cannot be solved by finite machines.

[3]It would be easy to harness this general idea for exploring a variety of interesting models—ranging from how an agent wants to respond to the individual actions of another *group* of agents to creating a network of layered automata that can build upon each other's pattern recognition abilities to perform a higher-level classification of complex patterns.

in figure F1, except with the transition from the fourth state returning to the starting state instead of the fifth state, could recognize
strings with exactly three 1's as long as the strings were shorter than
seven bits long, and even for longer strings it does relatively well as
it outputs a 1 for strings with exactly $3 + 4i$ 1s (for nonnegative
integer values of i).

For this experiment we evolve a population of forty automata
of fixed size. At the start of each trial an in-sample set of 240 binary
input strings is randomly generated with random uniform lengths
between three and ten bits long—this in-sample set remains fixed
during each generation of a trial. Each machine in the population
is tested against the 240 in-sample strings and the machine's
final output is used to classify the string, with a 1 indicating the
presence of the pattern of exactly three 1s and a 0 its absence. A
machine's fitness is given by the proportion of the in-sample input
strings it correctly classifies. The automata are evolved using the
same tournament selection and mutation operator as before.

The results of this pattern-matching experiment are given in
Table F2. The data in columns 2–5 give the mean performance
across 1,000 separate evolutionary trials of either the entire population (Pop.) or the best[4] (Best) automaton. The performance measures reported in the table use the automata's out-of-sample performance on a set of 1,000 randomly created problems. The sixth
column (Min.) gives the mean minimized size of the best in-sample
automaton in the population. The final three columns give the proportion, across all 1,000 trials, where the best automaton perfectly
solved the out-of-sample problem set.

At the start of the evolution the automata are generated
randomly so, on average, half the machines output a 1 and half a 0.
However, the base rate of seeing exactly three 1s in our randomly
generated input streams is around 22%, so an automaton that

---

[4]Based on in-sample performance.

AUTO	GENERATION 1		GENERATION 500			BEST IS PERFECT GENERATION		
SIZE	Pop.	Best	Pop.	Best	Min.	250	500	1,000
1	0.50	0.78	0.73	0.78	1.0	0.00	0.00	0.00
2	0.50	0.78	0.74	0.77	1.5	0.00	0.00	0.00
3	0.50	0.78	0.76	0.79	2.6	0.00	0.00	0.00
4	0.50	0.78	0.80	0.83	3.4	0.00	0.00	0.00
5	0.50	0.78	0.85	0.89	4.2	0.15	0.31	0.47
6	0.50	0.78	0.88	0.91	4.7	0.22	0.39	0.54
7	0.50	0.77	0.90	0.92	5.0	0.24	0.41	0.61
8	0.50	0.77	0.91	0.94	5.3	0.28	0.49	0.63
9	0.50	0.76	0.92	0.94	5.4	0.29	0.46	0.63
10	0.50	0.76	0.92	0.94	5.7	0.26	0.46	0.59

Table F2. Evolving automata to solve the perception problem of exactly three 1s in the input stream. In a given trial, 240 random binary input strings, of random uniform length between three and ten bits long, were generated. These input strings remained fixed throughout the subsequent generations of evolution. A population of forty automata of fixed size was randomly generated and subjected to tournament selection and a mutation rate of 0.33. Each automaton received a fitness given by the proportion of the 240 in-sample strings it was able to correctly classify as having exactly three 1s anywhere in the string. The reported performance measure is the mean proportion correct across every member of the population (Pop.) and the best member (Best) against an out-of-sample test set with 1,000 randomly generated problems. (The best performing automaton in the population was determined based on its performance on the 240 in-sample strings.) The sixth column (Min.) gives the mean minimized size of the best machines in generation 500. The final three columns give the proportion across all trials where the best automaton in that generation perfectly solved the 1,000 out-of-sample problems. The data are based on means over 1,000 separate evolutionary trials.

always outputs a 0 gets 78% of the test problems correct, while the mean performance of the entire population is 50% (since half of the machines get the base rate and half get one minus that rate).

We see a slight performance improvement of the best machines over the base rate after 500 generations of evolution for machines with more than a few states. This improvement is higher when the machines have at least four states. While five states are needed to perfectly identify the pattern, four-state machines do relatively well. With five states or more, 31–49% of the top machines achieve a perfect score on the out-of-sample test set after 500 generations of evolution. As these larger machines undergo further evolution, the proportion of perfect best machines increases (see the last three columns of table F2).

As the number of states increases beyond six, the number of perfect best machines begins to plateau at slightly over 60%. This plateau is not surprising as the problem can be solved using only five states and this is roughly the number of minimized states used by the best machines. Machines with more than five states show a slight increase in the number of perfect best machines versus those with only five. The extra slack in these larger machines may make it easier for evolution to converge on more effective machines. The use of larger automata doesn't appear to hurt performance too much, which is reassuring as larger machines have the potential to make evolution more difficult given the increased number of components and possible machines. Recall that the mutation operator used here makes a single mutation per machine regardless of the number of states, so the larger-sized machines have a lower effective mutation rate per state along with an increased potential for mutations to land on inaccessible states.

The two experiments above demonstrate the effectiveness of evolving automata to solve novel problems. The two problems are quite different from one another and they serve as interesting proofs of concept for this approach. Of course, the set of potential problems is huge and there is no guarantee that evolving automata will always find good solutions to any possible problem. Nonetheless, the results above, along with those from previous work, provide good evidence that evolving automata using a genetic algorithm is an effective way to discover good solutions to the types of problems that involve effectively responding to a series of discrete inputs.

Can Coevolution Improve Automata?

A key feature of the systems that we study involves coevolution, where fitness is endogenous and depends on other agents that are also evolving. To explore such environments we add coevolution to the previous perception problem. Again, the automata in the population receive a fitness measure tied to their ability to detect when a given binary input string has exactly three 1s. In the previous experiment, the forty automata were evolved against a fixed set of 240 randomly created in-sample problems. For the coevolutionary system considered here we will simultaneously evolve the set of in-sample problems. The fitness measure of a *problem* is given by the number of the forty automata that fail to correctly classify that problem. Like the population of automata, the population of in-sample problems is reproduced by using tournament selection and a mutation rate of 0.33. However, when a problem is mutated it is replaced with a randomly generated problem.

Table F3 gives the results for this coevolutionary system. Based on the mean performance of either the entire population or best automaton in the population, the coevolutionary system does worse than the non-coevolutionary system during the first 500 generations. However, coevolution is able to produce more top machines that can perfectly solve the out-of-sample test

					BEST IS PERFECT		
AUTO	GENERATION 1		GENERATION 500			GENERATION		
SIZE	*Pop.*	*Best*	*Pop.*	*Best*	*Min.*	250	500	1,000
1	0.50	0.78	0.58	0.56	1.0	0.00	0.00	0.00
2	0.50	0.78	0.64	0.67	1.5	0.00	0.00	0.00
3	0.50	0.78	0.66	0.67	1.8	0.00	0.00	0.00
4	0.50	0.78	0.71	0.74	2.6	0.00	0.00	0.00
5	0.50	0.78	0.80	0.84	3.8	0.14	0.38	0.71
6	0.50	0.78	0.84	0.88	4.3	0.22	0.52	0.82
7	0.50	0.77	0.85	0.87	4.5	0.23	0.50	0.82
8	0.50	0.77	0.85	0.87	4.9	0.19	0.51	0.86
9	0.50	0.76	0.85	0.86	5.2	0.18	0.49	0.79
10	0.50	0.76	0.83	0.85	5.5	0.16	0.42	0.77

Table F3. Coevolving automata to solve a perception problem of recognizing exactly three 1s in the input stream. Conditions are identical to those in the non-coevolutionary environment (see table F2) with the exception that the 240 in-sample problems are coevolved. At each generation of the algorithm, each problem receives a payoff given by the number of automata that misclassify it. The population of 240 problems uses the same selection and mutation parameters as the evolving automata, though when a mutation occurs the problem is replaced with a new, randomly generated problem. The identification of the "Best" machine is tied to the fitness received when facing the final set of 240 coevolving problems, versus the 1,000-problem out-of-sample test set used for the performance measures in the table. Column definitions are identical to those used in the previous table.

than the non-coevolved system—with only a slight increase after 500 generations and a more dramatic 33% increase after 1,000 generations (moving from around 60% to 80%).

One seemingly odd result under coevolution is that the best evolved automata do worse than base-rate performance for machines smaller than five states. For example, with two-state automata the best machines from the 500th generation have an average performance of 67%, even though the base-rate performance is around 78%. We also find that the best random machines in the first generation outperform the best evolved machines with smaller-sized automata.

These apparent anomalies are an artifact of coevolution. Recall that the fitness used in selecting the best machine is tied to its performance against the 240 coevolved in-sample problems, while the measures shown in the table are against an out-of-sample test set. If we evolve, say, one-state automata without coevolution, a machine will get the highest fitness by playing the base rate (here, always outputting 0). However, in a world of coevolving problems, problems that embody the base-rate answer will be solved more often than those with the non-base-rate answer, so coevolutionary forces will create sets of in-sample problems that deviate from the base rate, namely sets where the pattern occurs roughly half the time.[5] In such a coevolutionary world, either variant of a one-state machine might emerge as "best" based on in-sample performance, even though only one of these variants performs well against the out-of-sample problems. As automata have access to more states, their additional processing ability allows the machines to exploit some of the inherent structure in the problems, resulting in coevolutionary pressure that promotes problems that befuddle less-than-optimal machines while encouraging the evolution of better-adapted automata.

One benefit of coevolution is that the machines avoid overfitting the fixed set of in-sample problems. Perhaps coevolution is just producing machines that are less likely to overfit these problems?

To test this hypothesis we compare automata evolving against a fixed set of in-sample problems (as in the initial non-coevolutionary experiment in table F2), a set of in-sample problems that gets randomized every generation (but not optimized by coevolution), and finally a set of coevolving problems. The results of these three scenarios are summarized

---

[5] The mean scores of each problem, not shown in the table, are consistent with this explanation.

AUTO	GENERATION 250			GENERATION 500			GENERATION 1,000		
SIZE	F	R	C	F	R	C	F	R	C
1	0.00	0.00	0.00	0.00	0.00	0.00	0.00	0.00	0.00
2	0.00	0.00	0.00	0.00	0.00	0.00	0.00	0.00	0.00
3	0.00	0.00	0.00	0.00	0.00	0.00	0.00	0.00	0.00
4	0.00	0.00	0.00	0.00	0.00	0.00	0.00	0.00	0.00
5	0.15	0.13	0.14	0.31	0.29	0.38	0.47	0.55	0.71
6	0.22	0.20	0.22	0.39	0.40	0.52	0.54	0.68	0.82
7	0.24	0.28	0.23	0.41	0.50	0.50	0.61	0.75	0.82
8	0.28	0.30	0.19	0.49	0.53	0.51	0.63	0.74	0.86
9	0.29	0.34	0.18	0.46	0.57	0.49	0.63	0.77	0.79
10	0.26	0.33	0.16	0.46	0.57	0.42	0.59	0.77	0.77

Table F4. Performance of evolving automata using fixed, random, and coevolving in-sample problems. Proportion of 1,000 trials where the highest-fitness (based on the last in-sample problem set) machine in the population had a perfect score on the 1,000 out-of-sample problem set. The 240 in-sample problems were either fixed across all generations (F), randomly generated at the start of each generation (R), or coevolved (C).

in table F4, which reproduces the data from the previous two experiments (columns labeled F and C) and adds an additional condition (R) where the in-sample problem set is randomly redrawn every generation. The values in the table give the proportion of the highest-fitness machines that perfectly classify the out-of-sample test set. As the number of generations increases, the coevolution of the problem set produces better performing machines than either randomized or fixed problem sets, especially for intermediate-sized machines. Thus, while forcing the machines to adapt to a more unpredictable set of problems does improve performance, having problems coevolve improves performance even more given a sufficient number of generations and intermediate-sized machines.

Two additional variants of coevolution were also tried. The first variant used coevolving problem sets where each set received the average fitness of the group. The results of this variant were similar to the coevolution results reported above. The second variant created mutants one-step away from the parent problem by either flipping a bit or making the string either one bit shorter or longer (in the latter case, the additional bit was randomly chosen). This latter system resulted in diminished performance, likely due to the one-step mutant lacking reasonable connections to its parent.

Finally, the above experiments show that the genetic algorithm is very efficient in its search. There are over 312,000,000 possible five-state machines (see table 3.1). The number of automata explored in one trial of the experiments is, at most,[6] 20,000 in 500 generations and 40,000 in 1,000 generations. Thus, the genetic algorithm is exploring less than 0.0064% of the possible machines over 500 generations (or 0.0128% over 1,000 generations), yet it often discovers an ideal machine—a machine that would arise by chance[7] with probability 7.7×10^{-8}. ↰

---

[6]Since only 33% of the machines receive mutations, and some of these mutations revisit prior machines, at least two thirds of the machines in a new generation have previously existed. Thus, in experiments with exogenous payoffs, the actual number of unique machines explored is less than one third of the stated values.

[7]There are twenty-four five-state machines equivalent to the one shown in figure F1 since we can reorder the four states after the start state in twenty-four different ways. Thus, the proportion of ideal machines in the five-state ensemble is $24/3.12 \times 10^{-8}$.

APPENDIX G:
CONSTRAINED TRADE WITH
ASYMMETRIC COMPLEMENTS

The propensity to truck, barter and exchange one thing
for another is common to all men, and to be found in
no other race of animals.

ADAM SMITH

The Wealth of Nations (1776)

In the Edgeworth experiments in Chapter 10 the two goods were perfect complements, implying that one-to-one exchanges would give each agent a complementary pair of goods. Such exchange ratios can be thought of as a price—the amount of one good that has to be given up for the other. What happens to this system when prices are less trivial?

To explore this question we use the identical Coevolving Automata Model as in Chapter 10 in an environment that requires unequal amounts of the two goods to form the payoff-providing complementary set. We assume that agents gain one unit of payoff by acquiring *two* units of α and one unit of β. To accommodate this new design, we modify the initial endowments so that twenty αs are given to each A agent at the start of the game, keeping the total number of possible complementary sets of goods in the system at ten. We also double the maximum number of rounds so that either agent could, potentially, acquire all of the goods in the system. The automata have the same construction and actions as before, thus only a single good (of either type) can be exchanged in any given round, even though the price needed for efficient and equitable trade is now two for one.

Social outcomes require that agents realize at least some of the potential gains to trade. Such gains occur when at least one of the agents sends its goods to the other. A more socially interesting outcome entails both efficiency and equity, whereby the agents trade two α goods for one β good.

Figure G1 shows the Edgeworth box resulting from a single experiment with 5,000 generations of coevolution using three-state machines playing a ten-round game. The initial endowment places the system in the bottom-right corner, with one population of agents having twenty units of the x-axis (α) good and the other having ten units of the y-axis (β) good. The agents get one unit of payoff for every bundle of goods composed of two units of α and one unit of β, implying that the contract curve for this system is the diagonal line going from the bottom-left to top-right corners of the box. The figure plots the density of the final allocation of goods across all games over the last 4,000 generations of the experiment.

As can be seen in figure G1, the modal final allocation ends up on the contract curve, but the two agents received different final payoffs, with one having seven completed bundles (composed of fourteen α and seven β goods) and the other having three completed bundles. The coevolution achieves such outcomes by evolving machines that often take on elaborate sequences, for example, meta-play of 1,1 1,0 1,1 1,1 $\langle 0,0 \rangle$ in a ten-round game has the player with twenty goods sending six of them to the other player in return for seven goods. This outcome is consistent with the agents maintaining one for one trade behavior up to the point where the agent who holds the α good maximizes its payoff. Of course, if the machines could converge on meta-play of, say, $\langle 0,1$ $0,0 \rangle$, they could achieve both efficiency and equity with each agent holding five complementary sets of goods.

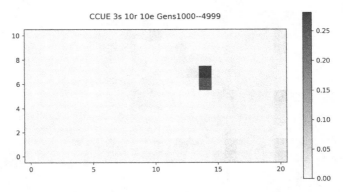

Figure G1. Edgeworth box of three-state coevolving machines trading with unequal endowments and asymmetric complements. The two agents had endowments that initially placed them in the lower-right corner of the Edgeworth box, with one agent having twenty units of the x- and none of the y-axis good, and the other agent having no units of the x- and ten units of the y-axis good. Agents received one unit of payoff for every bundle of goods composed of two units of the x- and one unit of the y-axis good. Two populations of agents coevolved for 5,000 generations playing ten-round repeated games, and the figure displays the density of the final allocations at the end of the repeated game averaged over the last 4,000 generations of the coevolution. The contract curve connects the lower-left and upper-right corners of the diagram.

Figures G2 and G3 show parameter sweeps for the asymmetric Edgeworth system. These sweeps differ from the ones in Chapter 10 in that the number of rounds goes from two to twenty in increments of two. The overall results are similar to what we saw in the symmetric Edgeworth experiments, though with more noise in the final outcomes and less equity—the final allocations tend to favor the agents with the endowments of twenty units of the good that is needed twice in every bundle. Similar to the previous systems, more states and rounds tend to encourage more efficiency and too many rounds can cause the system to break down with smaller-sized machines. While not achieving equity, the system does have regimes that allow the emergence of productive social outcomes. 𝔶

~354~

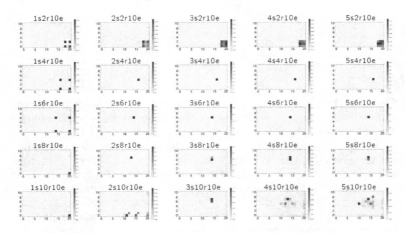

Figure G2. Parameter sweep of Edgeworth trade with unequal endowments and asymmetric complements (1/2). For each configuration of automaton states and repeated rounds, the associated system underwent evolution for 5,000 generations, starting from the lower-right point in the Edgeworth box where one agent had twenty units of α and none of β and the other player had ten units of β and none of α. To create a complementary set of goods required two units of α and one unit of β. The number of automaton states and repeated rounds is given in each subplot's title: states go from one (left-most column) to five (right-most column) and rounds go from two (top row) to ten (bottom row) in increments of two. Each subplot shows the Edgeworth box of the outcomes observed at the end of the repeated game over the last 4,000 generations of the experiment. (Note that the density scale can vary across the diagrams.) *Please refer to the Github repository (https://github.com/SantaFeInstitute/ExMachina) for full-sized, full-color versions of all images in this book.*

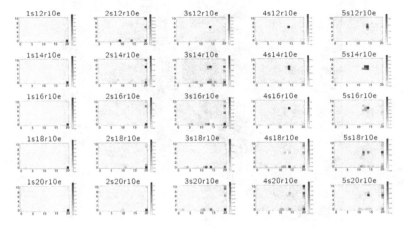

Figure G3. Parameter sweep of Edgeworth trade with unequal endowments and asymmetric complements (2/2). The conditions and interpretation are identical to figure G2, with the exception that the number of rounds goes from twelve (top row) to twenty (bottom row) in increments of two.

BIBLIOGRAPHY

Abbey, E. 1975. *The Monkey Wrench Gang.* New York, NY: Rosetta Books.

Alexander, R. D. 1974. "The Evolution of Social Behavior." *Annual Revue of Ecological Systems* 5 (1): 325–383. https://doi.org/10.1146/annurev. es.05.110174.001545.

Anderson, P. W. 1972. "More is Different." *Science* 177 (4047): 393–396. https://doi.org/10.1126/science.177.4047.393.

Andreoni, J., and J. H. Miller. 1995. "Auctions with Artificial Adaptive Agents." *Journal of Games and Economic Behavior* 10 (1): 39–64. https://doi.org/10.1006/game.1995.1024.

Axelrod, R. 1984. *The Evolution of Cooperation.* New York, NY: Basic Books.

Banisch, S. 2016. *Markov Chain Aggregation for Agent-Based Models.* Cham, Switzerland: Springer.

Berry, M. V., N. Brunner, S. Popescu, and P. Shukla. 2011. "Can Apparent Superluminal Neutrino Speeds be Explained as a Quantum Weak Measurement?" *Journal of Physics A: Mathematical and Theoretical* 44 (49): 492001. https://doi.org/10.1088/1751-8113/44/49/492001.

Boulding, K. E. 1978a. *Ecodynamics: A New Theory of Societal Evolution.* Beverly Hills, CA: Sage Publications.

———. 1978b. *Stable Peace.* Austin, TX: University of Texas Press.

Brooks, A. S., J. E. Yellen, R. Potts, A. K. Behrensmeyer, A. L. Deino, D. E. Leslie, S. H. Ambrose, *et al.* 2018. "Long-Distance Stone Transport and Pigment Use in the Earliest Middle Stone Age." *Science* 360 (6384): 90–94. https://doi.org/10.1126/science.aao2646.

Brown, G. W. 1951. "Iterative Solutions of Games by Fictitious Play." In *Activity Analysis of Production and Allocation,* edited by T. C. Koopmans, 374–376. New York, NY: Wiley.

Bush, R., and F. Mosteller. 1955. *Stochastic Models for Learning.* New York, NY: Wiley.

Camerer, C., and T.-H. Ho. 1999. "Experience-Weighted Attraction Learning in Normal Form Games." *Econometrica* 67 (4): 827–874. https://doi.org/10.1111/1468-0262.00054.

Campbell, J. 1990. *The Hero's Journey.* Novato, CA: New World Library.

Coase, R. H. 1937. "The Nature of the Firm." *Economica* 4 (16): 386–405. https://doi.org/10.1111/j.1468-0335.1937.tb00002.x.

Cox, B., and J. Forshaw. 2010. *Why Does E = mc²? (And Why Should We Care?)* Cambridge, MA: Da Capo Press.

Dante Alighieri. 1867 (2017). *The Divine Comedy: Inferno, Purgatory, Paradise, 1265–1321.* Translated by H. W. Longfellow. Mineola, NY: Dover Publications.

Darwin, C. 1859. *On the Origin of Species.* London: Murray.

———. 1863. *Letter to J. D. Hooker.* Darwin Correspondence Project, "Letter no. 4065," https://www.darwinproject.ac.uk/letter/?docId= letters/DCP-LETT-4065.xml. Accessed: October 19, 2022.

Diamond, J. 2005. *Collapse: How Societies Choose to Fail or Succeed.* New York, NY: Viking.

Dodd, M. S., D. Papineau, T. Grenne, J. F. Slack, M. Rittner, F. Pirajno, J. O'Neil, and C. T. S. Little. 2017. "Evidence for Early Life in Earth's Oldest Hydrothermal Vent Precipitates." *Nature* 543 (7643): 60–64. https://doi.org/10.1038/nature21377.

Douglas, A. E. 2014. "Symbiosis as a General Principle in Eukaryotic Evolution." *Cold Spring Harbor Perspectives in Biology* 6 (2): a016113. https://doi.org/10.1101/cshperspect.a016113.

Edgeworth, F. Y. 1881. *Mathematical Psychics: An Essay on the Application of Mathematics to the Moral Sciences.* London, UK: C. Kegan Paul & Co.

Emerson, R. W. 1841. *The Method of Nature.* An Oration Delivered before the Society of the Adelphi, Waterville College, Maine, August 11, 1841.

Epstein, J. M. 2006. *Generative Social Science: Studies in Agent-Based Computational Modeling.* Princeton, NJ: Princeton University Press.

Erev, I., and A. Roth. 1998. "Predicting How People Play Games: Reinforcement Learning in Experimental Games with Unique, Mixed Strategy Equilibria." *American Economic Review* 88 (4): 848–881.

Friedman, M. 1953. *Essays in Positive Economics.* Chicago, IL: University of Chicago Press.

Fudenberg, D., and D. K. Levine. 1998. *The Theory of Learning in Games.* Cambridge, MA: MIT Press.

Goldschmidt, R. B. 1940. *The Material Basis of Evolution.* New Haven, CT: Yale University Press.

Golman, R., D. Hagmann, and J. H. Miller. 2015. "Polya's Bees: A Model of Decentralized Decision-Making." *Science Advances* 1 (8): e1500253. https://doi.org/10.1126/sciadv.1500253.

Gould, S. J. 1989. *Wonderful Life: The Burgess Shale and the Nature of History.* New York, NY: W. W. Norton.

———. 1993. "This View of Life: A Special Fondness for Beetles." *Natural History* 102 (1): 4–12.

Grosberg, R. K., and R. R. Strathmann. 2007. "The Evolution of Multicellularity: A Minor Major Transition?" *Annual Review of Ecology, Evolution, and Systematics* 38:621–654. https://doi.org/10.1146/annurev.ecolsys.36.102403.114735.

Harrison, M. A. 1965. *Introduction to Switching and Automata Theory.* New York, NY: McGraw-Hill.

Hastings, W. K. 1970. "Monte Carlo Sampling Methods Using Markov Chains and Their Applications." *Biometrika* 57 (1): 97–109. https://doi.org/10.1093/biomet/57.1.97.

Hillis, W. D. 1990. "Co-Evolving Parasites Improve Simulated Evolution as an Optimization Procedure." *Physica D* 42:228–234. https://doi.org/10.1016/0167-2789(90)90076-2.

Hobbes, T. [1651]1982. *Leviathan.* London, UK: Penguin Classics.

Holland, J. H. 1962. "Outline for a Logical Theory of Adaptive Systems." *Journal of the ACM* 9 (3): 297–314. https://doi.org/10.1145/321127.321128.

———. 1975. *Adaptation in Natural and Artificial Systems.* Ann Arbor, MI: University of Michigan Press.

Holland, J. H., and J. H. Miller. 1991. "Artificial Adaptive Agents in Economic Theory." *American Economic Review* 81 (2): 365–370.

Hopcroft, J. E., R. Motwani, and J. D. Ullman. 2006. *Introduction to Automata Theory, Languages, and Computation.* 3rd ed. London, UK: Pearson.

Huttegger, S. M., and K. J. S. Zollman. 2013. "Methodology in Biological Game Theory." *The British Journal for the Philosophy of Science* 64 (3): 637–658. https://doi.org/10.1093/bjps/axs035.

Jevons, W. S. 1875. *Money and the Mechanism of Exchange.* London, UK: Henry S. King & Company.

Judson, O. P. 2017. "The Energy Expansions of Evolution." *Nature Ecology & Evolution* 1:0138. https://doi.org/10.1038/s41559-017-0138.

Kallus, Y., J. H. Miller, and E. Libby. 2017. "Paradoxes in Leaky Microbial Trade." *Nature Communications* 8:1361. https://doi.org/10.1038/s41467-017-01628-8.

Kimura, M. 1968. "Evolutionary Rate at the Molecular Level." *Nature* 217:624–626. https://doi.org/10.1038/217624a0.

Knoll, A. H., E. J. Javaux, D. A. Hewitt, and P. Cohen. 2006. "Eukaryotic Organisms in Proterozoic Oceans." *Philosophical Transactions of the Royal Society B* 361 (1470): 1023–1038. https://doi.org/10.1098/rstb.2006.1843.

Lewis, C. S. 2015. *Mere Christianity.* 1952 repr. New York, NY: Harper Collins.

Margulis, L., and D. Sagan. 1997. *Microcosmos: Four Billion Years of Evolution from Our Microbial Ancestors.* Berkeley, CA: University of California Press.

Maynard Smith, J. 1974. "The Theory of Games and the Evolution of Animal Conflicts." *Journal of Theoretical Biology* 47 (1): 209–221. https://doi.org/10.1016/0022-5193(74)90110-6.

———. 1982. *Evolution and the Theory of Games.* Cambridge, UK: Cambridge University Press.

Maynard Smith, J., and G. R. Price. 1973. "The Logic of Animal Conflict." *Nature* 246:15–18. https://doi.org/10.1038/246015a0.

Maynard Smith, J., and E. Szathmáry. 1997. *The Major Transitions in Evolution.* New York, NY: Oxford University Press.

McBeath, M. K., D. M. Shaffer, and M. K. Kaiser. 1995. "How Baseball Outfielders Determine Where to Run to Catch Fly Balls." *Science* 268 (5210): 569–573. https://doi.org/10.1126/science.7725104.

McCarthy, C. 1985. *Blood Meridian Or The Evening Redness in the West.* New York, NY: Random House.

Mereschkowsky, K. 1905. "Über Natur und Ursprung der Chromatophoren im Pflanzenreiche [On the nature and origin of chromatophores in the plant kingdom]." *Biologisches Centralblatt* 25 (18): 593–604.

———. 1910. "Theorie der zwei Plasmaarten als Grundlage der Symbiogenesis, einer neuen Lehre von der Entstehung der Organismen" [Theory of two types of plasma as the basis of symbiogenesis, a new study of the origin of organisms]." *Biologisches Centralblatt,* 30: 278–288, 289–303, 321–347, 353–367.

Metropolis, N., A. W. Rosenbluth, M. N. Rosenbluth, A. H. Teller, and E. Teller. 1953. "Equation of State Calculations by Fast Computing Machines." *Journal of Chemical Physics* 21 (6): 1087–1091. https://doi.org/10.1063/1.1699114.

Miller, J. H. 1988. "The Evolution of Automata in the Repeated Prisoner's Dilemma." In *Two Essays on the Economics of Imperfect Information,* 49–97. PhD Diss., University of Michigan.

———. 1996. "The Coevolution of Automata in the Repeated Prisoner's Dilemma." *Journal of Economic Behavior and Organization* 29 (1): 87–112. https://doi.org/10.1016/0167-2681(95)00052-6.

———. 1998. "Active Nonlinear Tests (ANTs) of Complex Simulation Models." *Management Science* 44 (6): 820–830. https://doi.org/10.1287/mnsc.44.6.820.

———. 2016. *A Crude Look at the Whole.* New York, NY: Basic Books.

Miller, J. H., C. Butts, and D. Rode. 2002. "Communication and Cooperation." *Journal of Economic Behavior and Organization* 47 (2): 179–195. https://doi.org/10.1016/S0167-2681(01)00159-7.

Miller, J. H., and S. Moser. 2004. "Communication and Coordination." *Complexity* 9 (5): 31–40. https://doi.org/10.1002/cplx.20034.

Miller, J. H., and S. E. Page. 2007. *Complex Adaptive Systems: An Introduction to Computational Models of Social Life*. Princeton, NJ: Princeton University Press.

Miller, S. L., and H. C. Urey. 1959. "Organic Compound Synthesis on the Primitive Earth." *Science* 130 (3370): 245–251. https://doi.org/10.1126/science.130.3370.245.

Moran, P. A. P. 1958. "Random Processes in Genetics." *Mathematical Proceedings of the Cambridge Philosophical Society* 54 (1): 60–71. https://doi.org/10.1017/S0305004100033193.

Nash, J. 1950a. "Equilibrium Points in N-Person Games." *Proceedings of the National Academy of Sciences* 36 (1): 48–49. https://doi.org/10.1073/pnas.36.1.48.

———. 1950b. "Non-Cooperative Games." PhD diss., Princeton University.

———. 1951. "Non-Cooperative Games." *The Annals of Mathematics* 54 (2): 286–295.

Nowak, M., and K. Sigmund. 1993. "A Strategy of Win–Stay, Lose–Shift that Outperforms Tit-For-Tat in the Prisoner's Dilemma Game." *Nature* 364 (6432): 56–58. https://doi.org/10.1038/364056a0.

Okasha, S. 2018. *Agents and Goals in Evolution*. Oxford, UK: Oxford University Press.

Pirsig, R. 1974. *Zen and the Art of Motorcycle Maintenance: An Inquiry into Values*. New York, NY: William Morrow.

Pynchon, T. 1973 [2012]. *Gravity's Rainbow*. New York, NY: Penguin Books.

Ricardo, D. 1817. *On the Principles of Political Economy and Taxation*. London, UK: John Murray.

Rokas, A. 2008. "The Origins of Multicellularity and the Early History of the Genetic Toolkit for Animal Development." *Annual Review of Genetics* 42:235–251. https://doi.org/10.1146/annurev.genet.42.110807.091513.

Roth, A. E., and I. Erev. 1995. "Learning in Extensive-Form Games: Experimental Data and Simple Dynamic Models in the Intermediate Term." *Games and Economic Behavior* 8 (1): 164–212. https://doi.org/10.1016/S0899-8256(05)80020-X.

Rousseau, J.-J. [1755]2018. *A Discourse upon the Origin and the Foundation of the Inequality among Mankind.* Frankfurt am Main, Germany: Outlook Verlag.

Sagan, L. 1967. "On the Origin of Mitosing Cells." *Journal of Theoretical Biology* 14 (3): 225–274. https://doi.org/10.1016/0022-5193(67)90079-3.

Schopf, J. W. 2006. "Fossil Evidence of Archaean Life." *Philosophical Transactions of the Royal Society B* 361 (1470): 869–885. https://doi.org/10.1098/rstb.2006.1834.

Smith, A. [1776]1977. *An Inquiry into the Nature and Causes of the Wealth of Nations.* Edited by E. Cannan. Chicago, IL: University of Chicago Press.

Tasoff, J., M. T. Mee, and H. H. Wang. 2015. "An Economic Framework of Microbial Trade." *PLoS One* 10 (7): e0132907. https://doi.org/10.1371/journal.pone.0132907.

Taylor, P. D., and L. B. Jonker. 1978. "Evolutionarily Stable Strategies and Game Dynamics." *Mathematical Biosciences* 40 (1--2): 145–156. https://doi.org/10.1016/0025-5564(78)90077-9.

Tennyson, A. 1851. *In Memoriam.* 4th ed. London, UK: Edward Moxon, Dover Street.

Traulsen, A., and C. Hauert. 2009. "Stochastic Evolutionary Game Dynamics." In *Reviews of Nonlinear Dynamics and Complexity vol. II,* edited by H. G. Schuster, 25–63.

Trivers, R. 1985. *Social Evolution.* Menlo Park, CA: Benjamin/Cummings.

Tsu, Lao. 1990. *Tao Te Ching: The Classic Book of Integrity and The Way.* Translated by Victor H. Mair. London, UK: Random House.

Tucker, A. W. 1950. "A Two-Person Dilemma." *Stanford University,* www.rasmusen.org/x/images/pd.jpg.

Tukey, J. W. 1962. "The Future of Data Analysis." *The Annals of Mathematical Statistics* 33 (1): 1–67. https://doi.org/10.1214/aoms/1177704711.

Turing, A. M. 1937. "On Computable Numbers, With an Application to the *Entscheidungsproblem*." Correction ibid., (1938) s2-43 (1): 544–546. [Note: The paper was received on May 28, 1936, and read to the Society on November 12, 1936.] *Proceedings of the London Mathematical Society* s2-42 (1): 230–265. https://doi.org/10.1112/plms/s2-42.1.230.

Ulam, S. M. 1991. *Adventures of a Mathematician*. Berkeley, CA: University of California Press.

van Gogh, Vincent. 1882. *Letter to Theo van Gogh, October 22*. https://vangoghletters.org/vg/letters/let274/letter.html. Accessed: October 26, 2022.

von Neumann, J., and O. Morgenstern. 1944. *Theory of Games and Economic Behavior*. Princeton, NJ: Princeton University Press.

Wadhams, G. H., and J. P. Armitage. 2004. "Making Sense of it All: Bacterial Chemotaxis." *Nature Reviews Molecular Cell Biology* 5 (12): 1024–1037. https://doi.org/10.1038/nrm1524.

Wagner, A. 2015. *Arrival of the Fittest: How Nature Innovates*. New York, NY: Current.

Waters, C. M., and B. L. Bassler. 2005. "Quorum Sensing: Cell-to-Cell Communication in Bacteria." *Annual Review of Cell and Developmental Biology* 21:319–346. https://doi.org/10.1146/annurev.cellbio.21.012704.131001.

Weaver, W. 1958. "A Quarter Century in the Natural Sciences. II Science and Complexity." In *The Rockefeller Foundation Annual Report*, 7–15. New York, NY: Rockefeller Foundation.

Weber, M. 1978. *Economy and Society: An Outline of Interpretive Sociology*. Edited by G. Roth and C. Wittich. Berkeley and Los Angeles, CA: University of California Press.

Williamson, O. E. 1981. "The Economics of Organization: The Transaction Cost Approach." *American Journal of Sociology* 87 (3): 548–577. https://doi.org/10.1086/227496.

Wilson, E. O. 2000. *Sociobiology: The New Synthesis.* Cambridge, MA: Harvard University Press.

Zhang, H. 2018. "Errors Can Increase Cooperation in Finite Populations." *Games and Economic Behavior* 107:203–219. https : / / doi . org / 10 . 1016/j.geb.2017.10.023.

Zicheng, H. 2007. *Vegetable Roots Discourse: Wisdom from Ming China on Life and Living.* Translated by Aitken, R. Berkeley, CA: Counterpoint.

INDEX

☿

THE IMAGES IN THIS VOLUME

The artwork in this volume was created with DiffusionBee, an AI image-generating program that uses Stable Diffusion to output pictures based on text prompts or images. Each chapter frontispiece was created using language from the text as a prompt (listed here below each image).

Stable Diffusion is released under the CreativeML OpenRAIL M license.

Table of Contents
prisoner's dilemma, woodcut

Acknowledgments
thoughtful equilibrium, woodcut

Prologue
*social behavior is inevitable,
detailed woodcut*

Chapter 1
*long epochs focused on pure
equilibria, woodcut*

Part I
*the approach, a path forward,
woodcut*

Chapter 2
social games, woodcut

Chapter 3
*finite automata,
detailed woodcut*

Chapter 4
*genetic algorithms,
detailed woodcut*

Chapter 5
*model of coevolving automata,
detailed woodcut*

Part 2
*social origins, detailed
woodcut*

Chapter 6
*coevolving automata model,
woodcut*

Chapter 7
*human social conflict,
woodcut*

Chapter 8
cooperation, detailed woodcut

Chapter 9
social conflict, woodcut

Chapter 10
*commerce, detailed
woodcut*

Chapter 11
*human communication,
detailed woodcut*

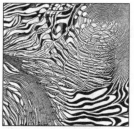

Chapter 12
ex machina, detailed woodcut

Appendix A
*when did social behavior arise on
earth, detailed woodcut*

Appendix B
*social symbiogenesis
detailed woodcut*

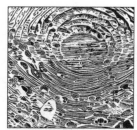

Appendix C
*on analyzing evolutionary systems,
detailed woodcut*

Appendix D
complexity matrix, woodcut

Appendix E
agent, earth, evolution, woodcut

Appendix F
*agent, algorithm, evolution,
woodcut*

Appendix G
*representation of trade with
asymmetric complements,
detailed woodcut, modernist*

Bibliography
agent, algorithm, evolution, woodcut

Index
complexity matrix, woodcut

Cover
*model of coevolving automata,
detailed woodcut, modernist*

Chapter End Pages
*prisoner's dilemma, game,
etching*

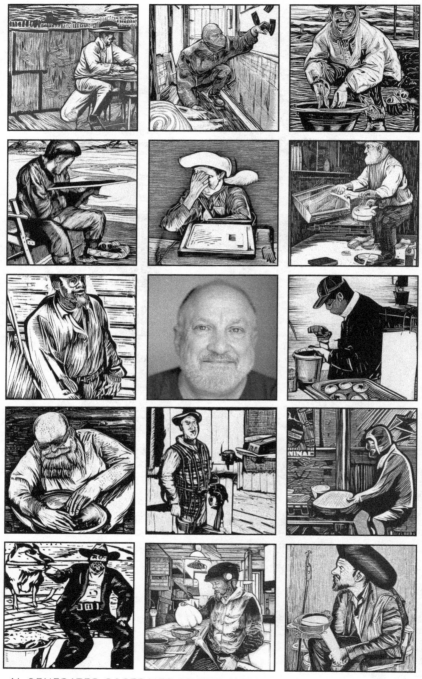

AI-GENERATED PORTRAITS OF THE AUTHOR (USING LINES FROM
HIS BIO AS PROMPTS), PLUS ONE ACTUAL PHOTO OF HIM

THE AUTHOR

JOHN H. MILLER received a B.A. in economics and B.S. in finance from the University of Colorado in 1982, a M.A. and Ph.D. in economics from the University of Michigan in 1988, where he worked with Ted Bergstrom and Hal Varian. In 1988 he joined the Santa Fe Institute as their first postdoctoral fellow. He started as an assistant professor in the Department of Social and Decision Sciences at Carnegie Mellon University in 1990, becoming an associate professor in 1995, and professor in 2000. He headed the Department of Social and Decision Sciences at Carnegie Mellon from 2002–2014 (and the Information Systems program from 1998–2001). He has been continually involved with the Santa Fe Institute since 1988, holding numerous appointments, and is currently on the external faculty and serves as chair of the Institute's Science Steering Committee (along with *ex officio* appointments to its Science Board and Board of Trustees). His scientific interests surround complex adaptive social systems, behavioral economics, adaptive algorithms, and computational modeling. He has published articles on these topics in various literatures, including anthropology, complex systems, decision science, economics, law, management, medicine, physics, political science, as well as general science journals. He has written a number of books, including *A Crude Look at the Whole* (Basic Books) and *Complex Adaptive Social Systems* (with Scott Page, Princeton University Press). He was born and raised in Denver, Colorado, the fourth generation of a family of cattle ranchers.

Prompts used for all images on the opposite page: *John H. Miller, man, complex systems, Coloradan, economist, money guy, Michigander, Santa Fe Institute, social science, decision science, Carnegie Mellon University professor, cattle rancher, drone flyer, turkey fryer, woodcut, grayscale, in the style of Rockwell Kent*

THE SANTA FE INSTITUTE PRESS

The SFI Press endeavors to communicate the best of complexity science and to capture a sense of the diversity, range, breadth, excitement, and ambition of research at the Santa Fe Institute. To provide a distillation of work at the frontiers of complex-systems science across a range of influential and nascent topics. *To change the way we think.*

SEMINAR SERIES
New findings emerging from the Institute's ongoing working groups and research projects, for an audience of interdisciplinary scholars and practitioners.

ARCHIVE SERIES
Fresh editions of classic texts from the complexity canon, spanning the Institute's four decades of advancing the field.

COMPASS SERIES
Provoking, exploratory volumes aiming to build complexity literacy in the humanities, industry, and the curious public.

SCHOLARS SERIES
Affordable and accessible textbooks and monographs disseminating the latest findings in the complex systems science world.

— ALSO FROM SFI PRESS —

Complexity Economics:
Proceedings of the Santa Fe Institute's 2019 Fall Symposium
W. Brian Arthur, Eric D. Beinhocker & Allison Stanger, eds.

Worlds Hidden in Plain Sight:
The Evolving Idea of Complexity at the Santa Fe Institute, 1984–2019
David C. Krakauer, ed.

The Energetics of Computing in Life and Machines
Chris Kempes, David H. Wolpert, Peter F. Stadler & Joshua A. Grochow, eds.

For additional titles, inquiries, or news about the Press, visit us at
WWW.SFIPRESS.ORG

ABOUT THE SANTA FE INSTITUTE

The Santa Fe Institute is the world headquarters for complexity science, operated as an independent, nonprofit research and education center located in Santa Fe, New Mexico. Our researchers endeavor to understand and unify the underlying, shared patterns in complex physical, biological, social, cultural, technological, and even possible astrobiological worlds. Our global research network of scholars spans borders, departments, and disciplines, bringing together curious minds steeped in rigorous logical, mathematical, and computational reasoning. As we reveal the unseen mechanisms and processes that shape these evolving worlds, we seek to use this understanding to promote the well-being of humankind and of life on Earth.

COLOPHON

The body copy for this book was set in EB Garamond, a typeface designed by Georg Duffner after the Ebenolff-Berner type specimen of 1592. Headings are in Kurier, created by Janusz M. Nowacki, based on typefaces by the Polish typographer Małgorzata Budyta. For footnotes and captions, we have used CMU Bright, a sans serif variant of Computer Modern, created by Donald Knuth for use in TeX, the typesetting program he developed in 1978. Additional type is set in Cochin, a typeface based on the engravings of Nicolas Cochin, for whom the typeface is named

The SFI Press complexity glyphs used throughout this book were designed by Brian Crandall Williams.

COMPLEXITY
GLYPHS

ZERO

ONE

TWO

THREE

FOUR

FIVE

SIX

SEVEN

EIGHT

NINE

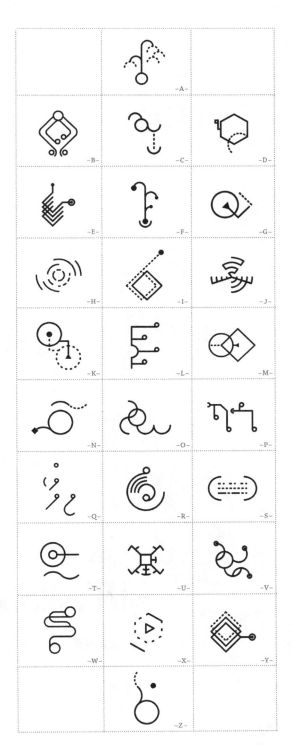

-A-

-B-

-C-

-D-

-E-

-F-

-G-

-H-

-I-

-J-

-K-

-L-

-M-

-N-

-O-

-P-

-Q-

-R-

-S-

-T-

-U-

-V-

-W-

-X-

-Y-

-Z-

SCHOLARS SERIES

CPSIA information can be obtained
at www.ICGtesting.com
Printed in the USA
LVHW090907240723
753027LV00094B/299/J